Annual Editions:
Business Ethics, 27/e

Eric Teoro

http://create.mheducation.com

ISBN-10: 1259664066   ISBN-13: 9781259664069

Contents

Detailed Table of Contents

UNIT 4: Ethical Issues and Dilemmas in the Workplace

Preface

In publishing ANNUAL EDITIONS we acknowledge and appreciate the important role played by the magazines, newspapers, Internet resources, and journals of the public press in providing current, first-rate educational information across a broad spectrum of interest areas. Many of the articles selected for inclusion in Annual Editions are appropriate and of significant value for students, researchers, policy makers, managers, and professionals seeking accurate, current material to help bridge the gap between principles and theories and the real world. These articles, however, become more useful for study when those of lasting value are carefully collected, organized, indexed, and reproduced in a low-cost format, which provides easy and permanent access when the material is needed. That is the role played by ANNUAL EDITIONS.

Welcome to the 27th edition of *Annual Editions: Business Ethics*. Since its inaugural issue, *Annual Editions: Business Ethics* has provided students and practitioners up-to-date articles to serve as a basis for analysis and discussion of business related ethical issues, theories, and practices. This edition continues that legacy with a collection of articles covering a wide-array of business ethics topics.

Ethics touch every facet of organizational life. Marketing managers and their staffs face ethical decisions regarding consumer research, privacy, product development, pricing, distribution, and advertising. Financial and accounting managers face challenges related to insider trading, risky financial products, money laundering, and "creative" accounting practices. Human resource and staff managers are confronted with decisions concerning lay-offs, outsourcing, diversity and inclusion, employee safety, employee privacy, sexual harassment, and other forms of hostile environments. Executives in multinational companies must deal with varying cultures and ethical systems, which can produce inconsistent, and at times contradictory, ethically acceptable business practices.

In the midst of these ongoing ethical concerns, businesses today face additional ethical challenges as societal expectations regarding the nature of business changes. What role should businesses play in addressing societal problems? Note that this moves beyond a question of could to one that has moral imperatives. Do businesses have a responsibility to help solve discrimination, poverty, lack of education, and lack of access to basic life necessities, or should executives focus on profit maximization while maintaining basic cultural norms? Do pharmaceutical companies have a responsibility to provide inexpensive or free drugs to individuals who do not have the means to pay the current market price? How should businesses interact with the environment? Is it sufficient for them to not cause harm, or do they have a responsibility to improve the environment given their resources? How do managers balance individual and organizational rights and responsibilities? Who defines these rights and responsibilities? Questions like these become more complex for public companies in which executives and boards have fiduciary responsibilities to stockholders.

Add to all of this the ethical issues and dilemmas surrounding the use of technology, such as privacy, smart "autonomous" machines and systems, and the replacement of human workers, the contemporary business ethics setting can be a very confusing and challenging environment.

Accompanying the articles in this edition are resources to help students, practitioners, and researchers to interact with the material more fully. Associated with each article are questions to generate discussion and analysis, and links to additional websites for further investigation.

It is our goal to continually improve *Annual Editions: Business Ethics*. We heartily welcome your comments, opinions, and recommendations as we strive to develop a text that will encourage and equip readers to uphold the highest standard of ethical business behavior.

Eric Teoro
Editor

Editor

Eric Teoro is the Director of the Business Administration Program at Lincoln Christian University. He teaches several ethics courses including business ethics and leadership ethics. Eric's research interests are the cultivation of an ethical character, virtue ethics, business ethics, philosophy of business, and organizational trust. He has conducted business training in Ghana and China, and serves as a board member for the Greater Ashburn Community Development Corporation and as the Education Officer for Aim to Work, not-for-profits serving one of Chicago's Southside neighborhoods. Prior to teaching, Eric worked in manufacturing and served in the United States Air Force.

Unit 1

UNIT

Prepared by: Eric Teoro, *Lincoln Christian University*

Ethical Behavior in the Workplace

Ethics can be defined as a body of moral principles or rules that govern behavior. It can also be defined as the area of study that examines ideas about moral principles. Business ethics considers the moral conduct of individuals within organizations, as well as the conduct of organizations as a whole. It must be remembered, though, that individuals establish the behavioral norms and cultures of organizations; so as one discusses business ethics at the corporate level, one is never far from discussing ethics at the individual level.

Values are beliefs about what is important in life, what one should hold in regard. Like ethics proper, values guide behavior. Individuals and cultures can disagree regarding which principles are ethically good and normative, about which values should be upheld and passed onto future generations. Ethics is different from law. Not every ethical standard has been codified in law, and history teaches us that not every law was grounded in ethics. Ethics and values seek to do good, not out of legal compliance, but out of an inherent sense of moral responsibility, out of a belief that associated behaviors are simply the right things to do.

The nine articles in this unit focus on individual ethics, with an emphasis on personal behavior. The essays provide guidance regarding ethical decision-making, introduce ethical challenges individuals face on a personal level, and offer suggestions on how to manage those challenges. They provide examples of individual misconduct, and the cost to the individuals, their families, their victims, and their organizations for such misconduct. Working through these nine articles will provide managers, employees, and students the opportunity to examine their personal values, recognize judgment traps and biases, consider emotional and psychological factors when confronted with ethical choices, and develop ethical tools they can apply in their personal and professional lives. The unit concludes with an article that poses the following question. When you look in the mirror, what kind of person do you want to see? The author describes an aspect of the managerial philosophy of Peter Drucker who believed that "management always deals with the nature of Man and (as all of us with any practical experience have learned), with Good and Evil as well."

Article

Prepared by: Eric Teoro, *Lincoln Christian University*

Sick about Unethical Business

It's crucial to teach students that bad business practices have a human cost, not just a financial one, say Rider University's Mark Promislo and Temple's Robert Giacalone.

MARK D. PROMISLO AND ROBERT A. GIACALONE

Learning Outcomes

After reading this article, you will be able to:

- Describe ways in which unethical behavior diminishes human wellbeing.

- Articulate benefits of emphasizing individual wellbeing.

When we were discussing the notorious Ford Pinto case with a recent undergraduate ethics class, we asked whether Ford should have proactively fixed the problems with its Pinto that exploded upon light impact—and if so, why? Immediately a student raised her hand and said, "If it didn't take care of this issue, Ford would take a hit to its reputation and lose credibility." Another student chimed in, "Investors would sell their stock, weakening the company's ability to raise capital and pay dividends." Yet another voiced his opinion that "Ford would have trouble maintaining a loyal customer base in the future."

These types of responses were echoed by many other students in the class. Only much later in the discussion did a student raise her hand to say that knowingly selling a dangerous car was wrong because it killed and injured people.

So we raised the stakes by showing the 2003 PBS *Frontline* documentary "A Dangerous Business," which examines the actions of McWane Corporation, a manufacturer of cast iron pipes. The company had a shocking record of negligence concerning employee safety. The filmmakers showed one horrific case after another, including instances of workers who were dismembered and even killed on the job due to unsafe working conditions at McWane's plants. Employees also were subjected to inhumane treatment. For example, some reported that they were refused bathroom breaks and resorted to urinating in their pants.

This time, reactions from the class were markedly different. One student, who never had shown any emotion previously, became visibly upset upon seeing the graphic photographs of a worker who was crushed to death at the factory. With tears on her face she cried, "Companies cannot let that happen to people!" The documentary was effective because it demonstrated clearly that when companies or individuals act unethically, people can be harmed.

Why don't students generally see this connection? In part, because few examples of unethical behavior are as extreme as those in the McWane case; after all, most workers don't die as a result of unethical acts. But another reason is that this is how students are taught to think in business school. Across most curricula, students learn to consider the financial implications of unethical acts, such as the risk of fines, penalties, lawsuits, and damaged reputations. Their professors show how these actions negatively affect organizational outcomes, such as profitability. But little time is spent teaching students that unethical behavior can actually harm employees in tangible, nonmonetary ways.

We believe it's critical for business students to recognize that many types of unethical behavior in the workplace damage people both physically and psychologically. In effect, people get sick because of immoral actions. As educators, we have the responsibility, and the ability, to help students better understand this phenomenon.

Bad Behavior at Work

Unethical behavior in the workplace may consist of something as minor as an employee stealing a few pens to something as major as an executive making immoral decisions that directly result in the deaths of workers. In between these extremes lie dozens of unethical behaviors that diminish people's well-being. Two unethical actions, workplace bullying and workplace discrimination, provide representative examples.

Workplace bullying consists of threatening or humiliating behavior; it can be initiated by supervisors and/or coworkers. Bullying can include harmful actions such as isolating employees, belittling them publicly, intimidating them physically, and abusing them verbally. Not surprisingly, victims of bullying suffer from depression, anxiety, stress, and insomnia. In extreme cases, victims sometimes even take their own lives. For example, Kevin Morrissey, a former managing editor of the literary journal *The Virginia Quarterly,* committed suicide after alleged bullying by his boss.

It's become easier to teach students about the devastating effects of bullying because television and Internet sites have brought prominence to the problem of bullying in schools. Celebrities have worked to promote awareness of the issue, and many of our students have had some experience with it during their years in school—either as bullies, victims, or witnesses to bad behavior. Business professors can use all of these sources to make the connections palpable simply by saying, "Hey, look at what bullying does to kids in school. Wouldn't we expect to see these effects in the workplace as well?"

Workplace discrimination can be blatant, such as when a manager states that he will not hire a woman for a job. It can also be more subtle—for example, when a manager overlooks a worker's superior performance because of his ethnicity. Whatever the form, discrimination can lead to serious psychological, behavioral, and physical problems such as alcohol abuse, anxiety, cardiovascular risks, and sleep disorders.

Yet even when students sympathize with victims of discrimination, they often make comments such as "That's really too bad. The company is losing a good employee." These kinds of responses illustrate, again, that many students do not fully appreciate the human costs of unethical acts.

To help students understand the negative effects of mistreatment in the workplace, teachers can use a prominent case of alleged discrimination. For instance, we've shown the documentary "The High Cost of Low Price," in which Walmart workers claim they were denied promotions due to their gender or race.

In classroom discussions afterward, we encouraged students to put themselves in those workers' shoes. Then we asked them to write down all the feelings and effects they might experience in a similar situation. Responses included comments such as "That's a tough spot. I would probably have trouble sleeping if that happened to me" and "I would be so angry if I got turned down because I'm a woman. Then I'd probably get really depressed. I might have to quit my job." These reactions convinced us that students were now thinking about the human costs of unethical workplace behavior.

Who's Being Hurt?

When discussing unethical workplace acts, professors and researchers often single out the direct victims as the sole injured parties. While clearly it is vital to recognize the victims, studies have shown that immoral behavior also can lead to harmful effects for others: people who witness it, such as coworkers; people who are indirectly affected, such as family and friends; and even the perpetrators themselves. It is essential that students appreciate the full range of individuals who suffer due to unethical workplace behavior. In our classrooms, we establish that range by putting the spotlight on two types of participants: witnesses or "associated persons," and those who commit unethical workplace actions.

People who either witness an unethical act or are associated with someone involved in the act can be affected due to their empathy for the victim. For example, an employee might be devastated to see his close friend bullied at work. A husband who knows that his wife is the target of sexual harassment can suffer from anxiety. The child of an abused worker may experience stress because she sees her father return home upset every day. Sometimes coworkers who witness immoral acts not only are traumatized, but they also wonder, "Am I next?"

Making these characters the focus of a lesson can lead to rich discussions in the classroom. We encourage students to describe times they witnessed unethical behavior or were associated with it in some way. We ask questions such as, "Did you ever notice another student cheating on an exam? How did it make you feel?" or "Have you ever seen someone you care about being mistreated? Did you start to feel their pain?" We note that witnessing such behavior introduces another stressful element: People start to wonder at what point they should step in and actively stop or report the action.

Studying the perpetrators is equally valuable, as studies suggest that unethical behavior can have a deleterious impact on the people who engage in it. Workers who commit immoral acts can experience severe shame, guilt, and stress, which can have adverse effects on them emotionally and physically. Whether these people are getting their just desserts for their wrongdoing is not the issue; at times, workers are pressured to do things that go against their own morals. Further, their diminished well-being can have a negative impact on their coworkers, subordinates, managers, and families, as well as the organization itself.

One way to bring this point home is to present guest speakers who have committed unethical acts at work. They can be tremendously effective as they convey the heavy price they paid for their behavior.

For one of our classes, we brought in Walt Pavlo, a former MCI employee who was convicted of wire fraud and money laundering. He spoke passionately about the guilt he still feels and the repercussions of his behavior, both for himself and many others.

In class discussions the next day, one student commented, "Wow, the guy still can't get a job. That would make me think very carefully before I did something wrong at work." Another observed, "Even if it helped my career, I just could never do something that went against my conscience. Plus, I think about how ashamed his family must feel."

Once we've highlighted the types of people who are affected by bad behavior, we use role-playing exercises to help students experience what it feels like to be a victim, a perpetrator, a witness, or an associated person. We believe this helps them develop an even deeper understanding of the full effects of unethical workplace behavior. One exercise we have used involves a fictional case of sexual harassment in which a male boss informs a female subordinate that she will never be promoted unless she goes out on a "date" with him.

Participating in this role-playing exercise has produced a wide variety of responses that show that students are starting to understand the harmful effects of bad behavior. A student playing the witness said that seeing the woman being harassed "turned my stomach," while a perpetrator admitted that he "felt awful having to say those words, and I would have a hard time living with myself." A victim recounted that she felt "dirty and disgusting," and an associated person said that feeling empathy for the victim "triggered some of my own painful memories of harassment." Indeed, what we see is that the simple act of role-playing helps students connect viscerally to the experiences of everyone involved in an unethical situation.

Types of Damage

Students should learn that while some kinds of unethical behavior at work can have an immediate impact on well-being—such as accidents or physical violence—the consequences of other behaviors might not be so immediate or direct. As a result, their long-term effects—stress, trauma, and poor health behaviors—are often ignored.

Stress arises when people cannot cope with the unethical behavior they have engaged in, been victimized by, or witnessed. Often this stress is tied to negative emotions, such as anger and shame, that are linked to mental and physical problems.

Employees experience trauma when an immoral action that they've witnessed, engaged in, or been victimized by challenges their beliefs about how the world operates. For example, Scott Jones, a former employee at the luxury San Diego hotel The Lodge at Torrey Pines, was repeatedly harassed for being gay; he was so traumatized he had to leave the company for health reasons. Some people cope with their distress by taking up unhealthy behaviors such as smoking, drinking, and eating poorly. For instance, one study related the case of a female psychiatric resident who started abusing alcohol after she was bullied by a coworker and a supervisor.

To get students to "connect the dots" between unethical behaviors and consequences, professors once again can turn

to discussion, guest speakers, and role-playing. In our courses, for instance, we ask students to explore the ways that being a victim of sexual harassment can lead to stress, trauma, and poor health behaviors. We also integrate examples from outside the business world—and outside the ethics classroom—by including doctors, psychologists, and social workers who offer firsthand accounts of how their patients have been damaged because of unethical acts at work. In fact, these individuals have been among our most effective guest speakers.

Finally, we've encouraged professors from other business disciplines to discuss the effects of unethical behavior at work. Organizational behavior professors cover issues such as abusive supervision; human resources professors highlight gender-based inequities in compensation; and marketing professors link moral principles to controversial behaviors such as advertising unhealthy foods to children. Within these discipline specific contexts, students acquire an even better understanding of why it is critical for them to behave ethically at work.

The Payoff

Why should an ethics class take an approach that emphasizes individual well-being? After all, some might say, we're teaching business, not medicine. Nevertheless, we believe this perspective offers four advantages:

It enables students to view ethics in very personal terms. They learn about the human costs of unethical decisions, which will prompt them to consider their actions more carefully if they encounter bad behavior in the workplace—as they probably will. When they do, they will immediately understand the personal impact of such behavior. They'll realize the damage isn't done to some amorphous bottom line, but to their own well-being—and that of their coworkers, friends, and family members.

It motivates students to behave ethically for reasons that go beyond moral codes. Certainly, we would like students to behave ethically because it is the right thing to do. But the truth is that some people engage in ethical behavior primarily to prevent the loss of money or reputation. If such students know that they and those around them can be harmed by bad behavior, they have another incentive to act morally.

It corresponds to topics taught in other business disciplines that focus on well-being. Work stress, for example, has long been an area of interest in management research, and more recently neuroscience has found its way into both marketing and management studies. Thus, making individual well-being a centerpiece of business ethics education enables faculty to incorporate cutting-edge research into their teaching.

It opens up new avenues for schools seeking financial support for scholarship. The focus on well-being creates possibilities that extend far beyond traditional social science research. For example, organizations like the U.S. National

Institutes of Health and the National Institute of Mental Health may be receptive to business management research that ordinarily would fall outside their domains. It's equally important to note that a focus on well-being is interdisciplinary; it enables business faculty to collaborate with their counterparts in psychology, public health, and medicine to develop interesting and innovative methods to ameliorate the damage of unethical behavior.

While making the connection between ethics and well-being can be a fruitful endeavor for business schools, understanding that connection is an essential skill for business students on their way to becoming global leaders. As students begin to see that unethical behavior can make them sick, or make others sick, new motives for ethical and socially responsible behavior will emerge. And perhaps in the future, when professors ask why Ford should have fixed its Pinto, more students will say, "Because human lives were at stake."

Critical Thinking

1. Why should business professionals be concerned with the human cost of unethical behavior?

2. How can you develop the habit of recognizing and considering the human cost of unethical behavior?

3. Describe an experience you, or someone you know, had with unethical behavior in the workplace. Identify associated costs to human well-being.

Internet References

Center for Christian Business Ethics Today
http://www.cfcbe.com/when-a-company-break-the-rules-the-reality-and-consequences-of-unethical-business-practices/

CNN Money
http://money.cnn.com/2015/09/17/news/companies/gm-recall-ignition-switch/

Greater Good: The Science of a Meaningful Life
http://greatergood.berkeley.edu/article/item/five_lessons_in_human_goodness_from_the_hunger_games

National Center for Biotechnology Information
http://www.ncbi.nlm.nih.gov/pmc/articles/PMC1071411/

TriNet Blog
http://www.trinet.com/blog/2014/08/04/are-your-people-ignoring-others-unethical-behavior/

MARK D. PROMISLO is an assistant professor in the department of management at Rider University's College of Business Administration in Lawrenceville, New Jersey. Robert A. Giacalone is a professor in the department of human resource management at Temple University's Fox School of Business in Philadelphia, Pennsylvania.

Promislo, Mark & Giacalone, Robert, "Sick About Unethical Business," *BizEd*, January 1, 2013. Copyright © 2013 by the Association to Advance Collegiate Schools of Business. This article is reprinted in full from the January 1, 2013 issue of *BizEd* with permission of the publisher, AACSB International-the Association to Advance Collegiate Schools of Business.

Article

Prepared by: Eric Teoro, *Lincoln Christian University*

Ethics Training Is Missing the Mark: Here's Why

S. L. YOUNG

Learning Outcomes

After reading this article, you will be able to:

- Recognize that ethics training and ethical decision-making need to incorporate emotional, psychological, and moral considerations.

- Recognize that ethical decision-making impacts individuals' emotional, psychological, and moral health.

Ethics is a topic that's often discussed by parents, schools, organizations, and employers. These discussions usually teach individuals about the importance of being ethical: what does it mean; why is it important; what are the costs of unethical activities? This subject matter must be taught; however, the toughest parts of being ethical are almost never discussed. That is . . . what are the emotional, physiological, and moral challenges that individuals who don't want to be complicit to unethical behavior experience?

Before exploring the affects of wanting to be ethical, the reason that ethics is important must be reviewed.

Ethics are behavioral standards that individuals, organizations, and societies apply and generally adhere to as acceptable. Without ethical standards, there can be numerous variables used to determine if something is right or wrong, good or bad. Notwithstanding these random variables, there are always individual considerations based on experiential learning; however, an individual's ethical standards are normally defined and developed by family, religious beliefs, friends, and societal practices. These standards provide common operating practices that are used to define the limits of acceptable behavior.

Generally, individuals know whether something is right or wrong. Although, there are times that ethical decisions will require additional consideration, input, or sometimes assistance to make the appropriate choice. The challenge—many times— is whenever a decision is within an unclear range or the biggest test is making a decision about whether to get involved to resolve a known ethical issue. During these times, individuals can experience an internal battle while attempting to make an ethical decision.

The internal impacts of making tough ethical choices can impact individuals:

- Emotionally—a feeling someone has related to a particular situation, event, or consideration;
- Physiologically—a body's reaction to making a tough decision, which could be stress, anxiety, sweat, depression, etc.;
- Morally—a challenge to an individual's belief system weighed against the things an individual believes to be true—but may be altered while making a tough decision.

These internal impacts are seldom (if ever) discussed during ethics training. This omission is unfortunate because an ability to process these intangible elements are important factors while individuals determine whether to be ethical during certain moments.

In a time that winning at almost any cost is more pervasive, there must be an increased focus given to educating individuals about the significance of internal processing in ethical decision making—beyond the mental processing. Otherwise, a larger number of individuals are more likely to bend the limits of standards, rules, policies, or laws to receive an unfair or personal advantage.

After the allegations of ball deflation by the New England Patriots prior to Super Bowl XLIX, my nephew and I discussed the potential ethical issues. During our conversation, my nephew made a couple of points to support his argument: 1) the deflation was found in the first half, but didn't impact the game's outcome and 2) everyone cheats at some point. What?!?!

The rationale used in his positioning is troubling for several reasons:

- First, a determination of whether something is ethical should never be decided based on an outcome, but instead by an evaluation of a consideration, situation, or an event;
- Second, a choice to be unethical cannot be validated based on attempting to justify the behavior by rationalizing the actions or activities of another;
- Third, individuals must be accountable and responsible for their actions—including complicit acceptance of wrongdoings by allowing known unethical behavior to continue unchallenged.

There is a cost to individuals, organizations, and societies if unethical activities aren't resolved in a timely manner. However, there are also costs to individuals' emotional, physiological, and moral health while making a choice whether to get involved with the prevention of unethical behavior.

Decisions individuals make cannot be necessarily managed by external factors; although, if ethical training helps individuals to understand and prepare for the internal factors that might be experienced while dealing with ethical dilemmas, then more individuals will be better prepared to handle the internal impacts that can be experienced while attempting to behave ethically.

Critical Thinking

1. Describe how ethical decision-making impacts the decision maker's emotional, psychological, and moral health.

2. What concrete steps can individuals take to incorporate emotional and psychological considerations into ethical decision-making?

3. What concrete steps can individuals take to incorporate emotional and psychological considerations into ethical training?

Internet References

A Guide to Ethics (St. Olaf College)
   http://pages.stolaf.edu/ein/themes/emotions-and-reason/

Practical Ethics (University of Oxford)
   http://blog.practicalethics.ox.ac.uk/2013/12/happiness-meaning-and-well-being/

Psychology Today
   https://www.psychologytoday.com/blog/hot-thought/201006/ethical-thinking-should-be-rational-and-emotional

Virtue Ethics Info Centre
   http://virtueethicsinfocentre.blogspot.com/2008/02/morality-and-emotions.html

Article

Prepared by: Eric Teoro, *Lincoln Christian University*

Everyday Ethics: Tougher Than You Think

STEVE GOLDBERG AND BRUCE BETTINGHAUS

Learning Outcomes

After reading this article, you will be able to:

- Describe various judgment traps and biases.
- Describe how to overcome judgment and decision-making traps and biases.

Management accountants' ethics training is often reduced to a list of rules to follow when making decisions. But recent research in the quickly developing area of behavioral ethics reveals an unsettling fact: The list approach isn't enough. That's because it overlooks innate biases that affect our business decisions in surprising ways. What can behavioral ethics research teach us about making less-biased decisions?

What Do People Actually Do?

Traditional ethics focus on what people should do. But the burgeoning field of behavioral ethics explores what people actually do.

That's a big difference, and it came about because the old approach didn't work well. Ann Tenbrunsel, professor of business ethics at the University of Notre Dame, asserts that ". . . efforts designed to improve ethical behavior in the workplace continue to over promise and under deliver." (See http://bit.ly/1cXD5R7.)

Those efforts fail partly because we all have unconscious ethical blind spots. In "Stumbling Into Bad Behavior" in the April 21, 2011, issue of *The New York Times,* Max H. Bazerman and Tenbrunsel wrote that ". . . we have found that much unethical conduct that goes on, whether in social life or

work life, happens because people are unconsciously fooling themselves." (See http://nyti.ms/1EGRRlV.)

Management accountants are becoming more aware of the bias problem. In 2012, the Committee of Sponsoring Organizations of the Treadway Commission (COSO) published a report by KPMG LLP, Steven M. Glover, and Douglas F. Prawitt, "Enhancing Board Oversight: Avoiding Judgment Traps and Biases" (see http://bit.ly/1bS5zdy). And a 2011 KPMG monograph, *Elevating Professional Judgment in Auditing and Accounting: The KPMG Professional Judgment Framework,* also dealt with accounting judgment issues (see http://bit.ly/1e3eJpd).

Both documents show that the accounting profession realizes that flawed decisions result from not following a sound judgment process. Management accountants also need to know that group decisions that aren't structured and conducted properly can make judgment traps and biases worse.

Why Do Biases Thrive in Accounting?

Accountants can have the best ethical intentions and believe they are meeting their responsibilities with competence and integrity. But there are known cognitive biases that can make them fall short. Unfortunately, corporate accounting and auditing are particularly prone to self-serving biases.

In their December 9, 2002, online article for Harvard Business School, "Most Accountants Aren't Crooks-Why Good Audits Go Bad," Bazerman, George Loewenstein, and Don A. Moore identified three structural aspects of accounting that create opportunity for self-serving biases (see http://hbs.me/1JKzNdW). First, biases thrive when there is *ambiguity.* Although some accounting decisions aren't ambiguous, many require considerable judgment—such as classifying an item as expense vs. capital, deciding when to recognize revenue, or estimating allowance for doubtful accounts.

Second, accountants have self-serving reasons to go along with their bosses' or clients' preferences. Psychologists refer to this as *attachment*. It's well documented that self-interest unconsciously biases decisions.

Third, as Bazerman and his colleagues note, research affirms that judgments become even more biased when people endorse others' similarly biased judgments. Psychologists call this condition *approval*. It especially can apply to external auditors, internal auditors, and financial analysts gathering evidence and expressing agreement or disagreement about proposed financial statements, budgets, or forecasts.

Our Bias-Boosting Nature. Bazerman, Loewenstein, and Moore also describe three tendencies of human nature that amplify unconscious decision bias. The first one, *familiarity*, means we are more willing to harm strangers than those with whom we have an ongoing relationship. The second, *discounting*, means that we weight immediate decision consequences more heavily than future consequences. The third tendency, *escalation*, means that we are more apt to ignore wrongdoing if it starts small and gradually escalates. This last tendency can provoke unconscious bias to evolve into conscious corruption or fraud-often despite our best intentions.

Regulators sometimes acknowledge this fact. In their article, Bazerman and his colleagues quoted then Securities & Exchange Commission (SEC) Chief Accountant Charles Niemeier, who said: "People who never intend to do something wrong end up finding themselves in situations where they are almost forced to continue to commit fraud once they have started doing this. Otherwise, it will be revealed that they had used improper accounting in the earlier periods."

Our Two Reasoning Systems. Unfortunately, judgment traps and biases have a greater effect on the decisions of competent, well-intentioned people than we realize. That's because researchers have found that we actually have two different reasoning systems in the brain, and sometimes we use the wrong one. Pioneering psychologists Keith E. Stanovich and Richard F. West named these reasoning processes "System 1" and "System 2" in their October 2000 article, "Individual differences in reasoning: Implications for the rationality debate," in *Behavioral and Brain Sciences*.

System 1 is automatic, mostly unconscious, fast, intuitive, and context sensitive. It's social in nature and is an evolutionary adaptation like our fight-or-flight instinct. System 2 is analytical, rational, based on rules, slow, not social in nature, works to achieve our goals, and is consistent with our beliefs.

System 1 reasoning comes into play when we make quick routine decisions like watching for traffic when crossing the street or moving away from signs of danger. Going through the day, it would be extremely time-consuming to apply analytical thinking to the hundreds of routine decisions we must make—such as what route to take to work, when to apply the brakes, when to use a turn signal, or when we should drink water.

We use System 2 thinking best for making thoughtful business decisions—such as choosing a raw materials supplier or what to accrue for obsolete inventory. But the more experience a decision maker has, the more he or she tends to rely on System 1 thinking. The judgment trap is that managers may rely on System 1 thinking in situations where System 2 would be more appropriate.

Five Key Judgment Steps

Talent and experience are key components of effective judgment. But consistently following a proper judgment process enhances judgment skills for both new and experienced accountants.

According to the COSO report and KPMG monograph mentioned earlier, key elements of a good judgment process include having the right mind-set; employing consultation, knowledge, and professional standards; being aware of influences and biases; and making use of reflection and coaching.

What does a good, professional judgment process look like? The five key steps are listed in "COSO's Professional Judgment Process."

COSO's Professional Judgment Process

1. Define the problem and identify fundamental objectives,
2. Consider alternatives,
3. Gather and evaluate information,
4. Reach a conclusion, and
5. Articulate and document your rationale.

For higher-quality decisions, don't cut short steps 1 and 2 of the decision process. Make sure you carefully identify the objective and consider all alternatives and diverging views. Encourage the expression of different opinions.

Source: Adapted from KPMG LLP, Steven M. Glover, and Douglas F. Prawitt, "Enhancing Board Oversight: Avoiding Judgment Traps and Biases," Committee of Sponsoring Organizations of the Treadway Commission (COSO), March 2012, http://bit.ly/1bS5zdy.

Notice that the first step is to define the problem and identify fundamental objectives. Don't assume everyone knows what they are and that you can skip the first step! Not properly defining the problem leads to a judgment trap called *solving the wrong problem* and wasting time. If you don't define the problem accurately, you could be influenced by a judgment trigger rather than a clearly defined decision objective. That's what happens when we underinvest in defining the fundamental issue.

Although the judgment process seems simple and intuitive, in the real world we encounter pressures, time constraints, limited resources, judgment traps, and self-interest biases.

Avoiding Judgment Traps and Biases

It takes hard work to avoid judgment traps and biases. For a list of the most prominent ones and how to handle them, see Table 1. Unintentional biases arise from using mental shortcuts, which are the results of System 1 thinking. Although these shortcuts are efficient and effective in some situations, they often result in predictable bias. When you cross the street in the United States, you automatically look to the left for oncoming traffic. This is an efficient and effective automatic response. But if you cross the street in the United Kingdom, where they drive on the opposite side of the road, this automatic response could lead to damaging consequences. Once you understand the implications of a shortcut, you can take measures to mitigate its impact. But you should be aware that mitigation is difficult and often has only a limited effect. City planners in London paint directions on the streets and take other measures to remind tourists to look to the right as well as the left when crossing the street.

To make quality ethical decisions, it's important for you to have an appropriate mind-set: an inquiring mind that analyzes objectives, information, and alternatives to reach a conclusion. But you must do all that objectively, critically, creatively, and somewhat skeptically.

Now let's follow a hypothetical CFO throughout her workday to show how hidden judgment triggers and biases affect her ethical decisions and what she can do about it.

A CFO's Pitfalls

Julie Smith is the CFO of a midsize manufacturing company. It's Friday, and many things are happening at once. Today is the end of the company's second quarter, she is finishing the last round of her staff evaluations, and she has to give Human

Table 1 How to Handle Common Judgment Traps and Biases

Judgment Trap of Bias	Mitigation Technique
Rush to solve: the tendency to want to solve a problem immediately by making a quick judgment	Follow a sound judgment process. Particularly emphasize steps 1 and 2 of COSO's Professional Judgment Process: defining the problem and considering alternatives. Ask "what" and "why" questions.
Groupthink: the tendency to suppress divergent views	Emphasize the problem definition and identifying alternatives (COSO steps 1 and 2). Ask "what" and "why" questions.
Solving the wrong problem	Emphasize COSO step 1, defining the problem and identifying fundamental objectives
Confirmation tendency: looking for or interpreting evidence to support a preference	Make the opposing case. Seek disconfirming or conflicting evidence.
Anchoring: a preference for not moving far from an initial numerical value	Introduce alternative independent numerical values based on historical precedent, past experience, industry data, or other sources. Seek evaluation from an alternative source or over a longer period of time.
Overconfidence: the tendency for confidence to grow more rapidly than competence as we become more experienced	Question experts' or advisors' estimates and underlying assumptions. Test key assumptions.
Judgment triggers and framing: the tendency to look at a problem from a limited perspective	Consider alternative frames or perspectives.
Availability: the tendency to only consider easily accessible information and ignore other relevant information	Define the problem and objectives (COSO step 1). Consider all identifiable alternatives (COSO step 2). Ask what would be most relevant.

Resources (HR) her final decision on the new hire for the controller's office. Instead of looking forward to a relaxing weekend, she's worried about tomorrow's emergency board meeting to approve the acquisition of the company's main raw materials supplier. In addition, her children's spring school break starts next week. Her whole family plans to get up early on Sunday and fly to Florida for a vacation.

Julie is a CMA® (Certified Management Accountant) and a member of IMA® (Institute of Management Accountants). She diligently tries to follow the *IMA Statement of Ethical Professional Practice* (see http://bit.ly/IMAStatement). But even if Julie were aware of all of her decision biases, behavioral research shows that it's difficult or impossible to eliminate them! Like most executives, Julie has little formal training in psychology, in how to make good judgments, or in how to spot human tendencies that threaten good judgment. Her bachelor's and master's degrees in accounting focused on technical knowledge needed to pass the CMA and CPA (Certified Public Accountant) exams. And her MBA focused only on managing change and strategic planning.

Julie has several important decisions to make before leaving on her vacation. This artificial deadline could lead to the judgment trap called *rush to solve* (see Table 1). Because she is rushed, Julie might not adequately consider all the job candidates and their qualifications before making a hiring decision. If she knows the previous salary of a job applicant, Julie's salary offer may be affected by a bias trap called *anchoring*—a preference to stay close to an initially named numerical value. Knowing the candidate's salary before the candidate earns an MBA may cause Julie's offer to fall short of what the candidate is really worth now.

The emergency board meeting presents other problems. Julie, the CEO, and the board chair are all urging the acquisition of their raw materials supplier for a price of $600 million. But business decisions made in a group setting like the board meeting can be biased because participants often suppress divergent views. In this case, no one wants to disagree with Julie and the CEO. The board doesn't encourage people to voice different opinions, which results in shallow thinking.

Also, the board may mistakenly believe that an early consensus is a sign of strength. It may not spend enough time defining the problem, clarifying issues and objectives, or considering alternative actions.

To see how Julie should have handled the acquisition issue using the COSO Professional Judgment Process to reduce decision-making bias, see Figure 1.

Don't Limit Perspectives

At the emergency board meeting, Julie presented the potential acquisition as a "slam dunk" move with low risk. But she didn't present any alternative viewpoints. That's a red flag!

Julie needs to understand the concept of *frames*—mental structures or perspectives used to determine the importance of information. Imagine you're in a house where each window gives you a different view. By considering all the windows—the frames—you get a better understanding of where the house is situated. Julie considered only one frame—that the acquisition was a "slam dunk." Better decision makers are aware when they are dangerously limiting the number of frames.

The board made this problem worse by not defining its objectives carefully. Is the objective securing a long-term source of raw materials? If so, did the board consider other actions—such as a long-term supply contract, purchasing alternative suppliers, or purchasing less than 100 percent of the current supplier? The board's narrow framing of the issue creates a *judgment trigger*. Executives pounce on one action but not necessarily the best one. As the KPMG monograph notes, studies show that we become more confident as we become more experienced and successful. But our confidence actually increases more rapidly than our competence. If board members realized this, they might be more skeptical of the "slam dunk" recommendation.

I've Made Up My Mind

We all know people who say, "Don't bother me with the facts. I've already made up my mind." This attitude illustrates our unconscious *confirmation tendency*. We tend to look for evidence confirming our viewpoint instead of being evenhanded. If board members are pressured into accepting Julie's viewpoint, their research may turn up supporting data only.

And the fact that Julie has already suggested it will cost $600 million to acquire the supplier makes the board vulnerable to the *anchoring* judgment trap—our tendency to not move far from an initially named numerical value. So even if buying the supplier is a good idea, Julie has biased the board to spend about $600 million on it.

But what if Julie didn't name a figure and assigns someone to investigate the supplier? The researcher finds that the supplier has been profitable for the past 10 years but that some older, difficult-to-find information hints at major unsolved problems. In that case, a judgment trap called *availability* might trip up both the researcher and the board because there's a tendency for decision makers to consider information that's easier to retrieve as being more relevant to a decision than less accessible information. Auditors can fall prey to this trap also. An auditor may follow an approach used in previous years or on a recent engagement even if other approaches may be more effective. Our "desires" heavily influence the way we interpret information.

In addition to considering alternatives, the way the board examines them can bias a decision. The board should consider

Decision Process	→	→	→	→	→
COSO Professional Judgment Steps	**Step 1: Define Problem and Objective**	**Step 2: Consider Alternatives**	**Step 3: Gather/Evaluate Information**	**Step 4: Reach Conclusion**	**Step 5: Document Rationale**
INITIAL ISSUE: Should Julie's company purchase its main raw materials supplier for $600 million?	**INITIAL PROBLEM DEFINITION:** whether or not to acquire supplier **REVISED FRAMING:** securing long-term source of materials	• Purchasing supplier • Long-term supply contract • Purchasing alternative suppliers • Purchasing less than 100% of supplier	• Primary analysis by CFO and CEO	• Board decision	
Typical traps and biases	• Solving the wrong problem • Judgment triggers • Narrow framing • Incomplete problem definition	• Judgment triggers • Narrow framing	• Confirmation tendency • Overconfidence • Availability • Anchoring • Rush to solve	• Groupthink • Rush to solve	
Mitigation techniques	• Be aware of framing, judgment traps, and biases • Define the objective clearly • Ask "what" and "why" questions	• Be aware of judgment traps and biases • Consider alternative frames	• Be aware of judgment traps and biases • Question acquisition cost figure—seek alternative estimates • Question underlying assumptions • Seek out the most relevant information • Make the opposing case and seek support	• Be aware of judgment traps and biases • Encourage diverse views • Follow a sound judgment process	• Be aware of judgment traps and biases. • Document each step. • Avoid conflicts of interest. • Include discarded alternatives.

Figure 1   How to Reduce Decision-Making Bias   Julie Smith, the hypothetical CFO of a midsize manufacturing company, was urging the board of directors to rush into acquiring the company's main raw materials supplier. Let's look at the way she should have handled the issue. Each step in the formal COSO decision-making process is shown below, along with judgment traps and biases that would come up and techniques to mitigate them. Note that the biases, judgment traps, and mitigation techniques apply at multiple steps in the decision process. We have minimized repetition for this example.

multiple options at the same time rather than one option at a time. If options are considered consecutively, there's a tendency to approve a suboptimal option and then not give equal consideration to other options, according to Kathrine L. Milkman, Dolly Chugh, and Max H. Bazerman in "How Can Decision Making Be Improved?" in *Perspectives on Psychological Science.*

Julie and the board also should consider all stakeholders' points of view. As Julie documents her conclusion, she should assess whether it makes sense and whether the underlying information supports it.

Thus Julie and the management team are facing judgment traps and unconscious biases in a variety of areas. But the biggest problem is that they aren't even aware of them.

Resources: Improving Your Ethical Judgment

Dan Ariely, *The (Honest) Truth About Dishonesty: How We Lie to Everyone Especially Ourselves,* **Harper Collins, New York, N.Y., 2013.**
Using original experiments and research, the author explains how and why we lie.

Max H. Bazerman and Ann E. Tenbrunsel, *Blind Spots: Why We Fail to Do What's Right and What to Do about It,* **Princeton University Press, Princeton, N.J., 2013.**
Learn about the ways we overestimate our ability to do what is right, acting unethically despite our best intentions.

Max H. Bazerman, George Loewenstein, and Don A. Moore, "Why Good Accountants Do Bad Audits," *Harvard Business Review,* **November 2002, http://bit.ly/1K87CsM.**
The authors argue that eliminating or lessening unconscious bias will require fundamental changes in the way accounting firms and their clients operate.

Francesca Gino, *Sidetracked: Why Our Decisions Get Derailed, and How We Can Stick to the Plan,* **Harvard Business Review Press, Boston, Mass., 2013.**
The author reveals how simple, irrelevant factors can have profound consequences on our decisions and behavior.

Daniel Kahneman, *Thinking, Fast and Slow,* **Farrar, Straus and Giroux, New York, N.Y., 2011.**
A major *New York Times* best seller, this book offers deep insights about our judgments and reactions.

Reducing Bias

The good news is that everyone can start reducing bias with four simple steps:

- Follow a sound judgment process,
- Be aware of judgment traps and biases,
- Reduce conflicts of interest, and
- Try to recognize situations causing vulnerability to bias.

Then you have to follow up and continue to work at it. Behavioral research consistently demonstrates that being aware of judgment biases is only a first step in reducing their effects. Even with awareness, it's very difficult to overcome biases. And other things can bias our decisions, such as anger, tiredness, stress, and how many issues we handle at the same time.

But working on this will pay big dividends. By following a sound judgment process, you can replace knee-jerk reactions with formal analysis. That's the way to make your everyday ethics excel and protect yourself, your company, and all its stakeholders.

Critical Thinking

1. Describe judgment traps and biases that you struggle with. What concrete steps can you take to overcome them?

2. Describe a situation and its associated judgment biases and traps. Work through the 5-step decision-making process, describing how one can overcome the biases and traps.

Internet References

Ethics Unwrapped
http://ethicsunwrapped.utexas.edu/video/self-serving-bias
Frontiers in Systems Neuroscience
http://journal.frontiersin.org/article/10.3389/fnsys.2014.00195/full
Mind Tools
https://www.mindtools.com/pages/article/avoiding-psychological-bias.htm

STEVE GOLDBERG, CPA, PhD, is a full professor of accounting at the School of Accounting, Seidman College of Business at Grand Valley State University in Grand Rapids, Mich. He teaches and does research in international accounting and ethics and has taught auditing, financial accounting, and managerial accounting. **BRUCE BETTINGHAUS, PhD,** is an associate professor of accounting at the School of Accounting, Seidman College of Business at Grand Valley State University. He teaches and does research in accounting ethics, financial reporting theory, and managerial accounting.

Goldberg, Steve & Bettinghaus, Bruce, "Everyday Ethics: Tougher than You Think," *Strategic Finance*, June 1, 2015. Copyright © 2015 by the Institute of Management Accountants. Used with permission.

Article   Prepared by: Eric Teoro, *Lincoln Christian University*

Acting Ethically Is Not Always Easy—Some Tough Questions for Estate Planners

RONALD DUSKA

Learning Outcomes

After reading this article, you will be able to:

- Recognize the inherent complexity in many ethical situations.

- Understand the role that goodness, fairness, and commitment play in ethical decision-making in complex ethical situations.

- Understand the role that the cardinal virtues—prudence, fortitude, justice, and temperance—play in carrying out the demands of an ethical decision.

There is much insistence that financial advisors act ethically, and on first glance, acting ethically seems fairly simple. "Do the right thing." "Do good and avoid evil." "Do unto others as you would have them do unto you." "Don't lie!" "Don't cheat!" "If you're a financial planner, treat your client like you would want to be treated." "Look out for your client's best interest." So, in many cases, acting ethically is simple. Still, it is not always simple. There are times you need to evaluate and act in more complicated situations. Consider the following cases.

- As an outside expert brought in to do some aspect of planning, should you tell the client that you are sure his accountant is giving him faulty advice?

- Should you split commissions with a lawyer on all insurance policies you sell to clients he has referred to you? Is that legally or ethically acceptable?

- Should you inform a wife, who is your client, that her husband, who is also a client, has asked you to put aside part of their estate for a woman with whom he has been having a long-term affair? To whom do you owe allegiance? How much confidentiality is required? To whom?

- If you are not sure about a certain investment area with a new client prospect, is it acceptable to give him advice anyway, knowing you will check it out later, because you do not want to appear less than knowledgeable about the area? Is this just wrong, self-serving behavior?

- Should you inform the children of an elderly client, who is acting irrationally and seems to exhibit signs of dementia, that he has greatly reduced their inheritance? The children are also your clients. Did you break confidentiality here? Is it fair to the elderly client? Is not telling fair to the children?

- Should you lower fees for services for new clients without a corresponding rate decrease for existing clients? What does fairness call for in this instance?

- Is it acceptable to set up a charitable remainder trust for the benefit of your client, and sell it to a charity for 5 percent of the funding amount as a finder's fee? Does this violate any rules? Does this violate conflict of interest principles?

- Should you expedite the transactions for a middle-aged client, with minimal investment experience, who insists on investing a significant portion of his total assets in high-risk funds? Should you be complicit in doing what you know may be detrimental to the interests of your client?

- Should you advise your clients to leave all their money under the control of their daughter, Mary, with the understanding that Mary will be under a moral obligation to make sure their son, John, who suffers mental retardation, is taken care of? In that way, John will not lose his government benefits. Is this a deceptive and problematic use of government funding?

- Is it appropriate to encourage a client to set up a charitable remainder trust in the name of a charity with which you have an arrangement that allows you to remain trustee of the assets? Is this permissible behavior according to your code of ethics as an estate planner? Does it involve a conflict of interest?

The complicated issues above involve whistleblowing, conflicts of obligations, confidentiality requirements, conflicts of interest, fairness issues, compliance issues, and gaming the system for the sake of the client or yourself. In many of these situations we are just not sure what's the right thing to do. It is not always easy to know what's right or do what's right.

There are, of course, as we said, times when it is clear what you should or should not do. It is clearly unethical to promote a product that is not suitable for your client just to meet your sales quotas or gain a bonus. Still, aren't there times you have to do something bad to achieve some good? Wouldn't you steal a loaf of bread like Jean Valjean in *Les Miserables* to help your sister's desperately hungry family? Stealing is bad but isn't it justified in this case? Wouldn't you lie to a Nazi to save Anne Frank? Lying is bad, but isn't it called for in this case? Those are classic examples of moral dilemmas. We may have our own less dramatic issues in our own lives. Would you give a friend who is desperately in need of some financing inside information on a stock? Sharing inside information is illegal, but wouldn't you at least think about doing it for a friend in desperate need? You are torn between loyalty to a friend and fidelity to the law. Would you report a friend whom you know is pushing questionable products to his clients? These are ethical situations where there seem to be reasons for acting in a certain way and also reasons for not acting in that way. How is one to resolve such dilemmas?

Determining what to do involves finding the right reasons for any proposed behavior. I want to suggest three broad areas of reasoning that should be considered in determining how to act ethically: goodness, fairness, and commitment. The first reason justifying an action is that it produces something good. We all aim at doing at least what we see as good. So we ask, "What good will come of acting this way or that?" Different people value different things and what seems good and desirable for one may not seem so to another, but there are also broad areas of agreement that some things like pain and suffering are not

good. A corollary of that, of course, is that we should not harm, and a reason for not doing something is that it will do harm.

A second reason for doing something is that fairness demands it. Fairness is usually defined as giving everyone their due—what they are entitled to. What is due everyone may not be that easy to determine, but we have criteria such as merit, need, and equality, which we can apply in different situations. If we have given a discount to one client, is it fair not to give it to another in a similar situation? Logical consistency requires that things that are the same be treated the same.

A third reason for doing something is that you have promised to do it. You are ethically required to keep your promises. However, promises sometimes conflict. What do you do then? What happens if keeping your promise causes great harm to someone else? What should we do in those situations where there are good reasons for performing an action and good reasons for not? For example, what should one do when meeting one's commitments will lead to harm for the client? In response to the opening scenarios, we can say that in many cases there are good reasons for acting in one way and good reasons for not acting that way. My suggestion is that we should probably follow the course of action with the preponderance of good reasons on its side.

To repeat, in dealing with complex issues we need to probe three different sets of questions. Is what I am doing going to produce good? Is what I am doing fair to all parties involved? Is what I am doing required by promises or commitments that I have made? But asking them will not always resolve the issue. The most one can say is that ethical decision making is not a science. It is an art. It takes an artist to resolve some of the issues raised. Some answers to the scenarios above are "yes" and some are "no." Some, however, might be yes and no. If we have good reasons for doing one thing and good reasons for doing the opposite, we are on what the ancient ethicists called "the horns of a dilemma." You are gored one way or another. The best approach is to be proactive and try to avoid facing dilemmas. One of the best pieces of advice I have received in responding to those kinds of issues is to make sure they don't come up. Be proactive. Set up situations where the temptations are minimized and the conflicts cannot occur. For example, be clear about how much confidentiality you will keep when dealing with a husband and wife, or a client and his children. Still, there may just be times when you can't find a path between the horns. In that case you are, as they say, "damned if you do and damned if you don't." The most one can say is there is no "right" answer. There are just good reasons to act this way and good reasons not to act this way. Do the best you can.

Not knowing what to do is not the only obstacle to acting ethically. Even if we know what's right, that doesn't mean we will always do it. There is a second factor which makes acting ethically difficult: being willing to do the right thing. Human beings are subject to temptations that entice them to act in an unacceptable unethical manner. Think of times you have been tempted to cheat, or take advantage of someone for your own gain. Sometimes we simply want to follow our passions and desires and do what we feel like doing rather than what we know we should do. If there were no temptations like wanting to make a sale to get a bonus or commission, or setting up a trust to benefit you, living an ethical life would be easy. If there were no such things as perverse incentives, being ethical would be easy. But temptations exist and we are not angels. There is a devilish side to us. It may not be a large side of us, but there are at least times when we do things that benefit us at the expense of others—things we shouldn't have done and that we regret. Guilt, a formidable part of the human condition, indicates when we think we have done wrong.

We are all inclined to act in our own interest. Adam Smith pointed that out, and it's what makes business tick. Is acting in our own interest wrong? No. However, being selfish is wrong. Despite what Ayn Rand claims in her book, *The Virtue of Selfishness*, selfishness is not a virtue. Your mother got it right when she told you, "Don't be selfish." The difference between self-interest and selfishness is this: Selfishness is the pursuit of self-interest at the expense of someone else. When one is acting in one's own interest, self-interested behavior is good. We need to love ourselves, otherwise the maxim prompting us to love our neighbor as ourselves would be meaningless. However, to look out for our interests at the expense of our neighbor is problematic. At any rate, one difficulty in being ethical and doing the right thing is getting beyond our own interests and becoming other-regarding. Most human beings will look out for their interests first and oftentimes act on unbridled passions. It is not always easy to do what's right. We need strength of character to overcome that. That is why companies need to be careful to look at what behavior they are incentivizing.

Ancient and medieval philosophers indicated that the ethical person had several virtues: the practical wisdom to evaluate options, a sense of fairness to evaluate who deserved what, the courage and strength to do the right thing, and the self-control to avoid giving in to destructive passions. These were dubbed "the cardinal virtues," the hinges on which all other virtues rested. They named them prudence, justice, temperance, and fortitude. Having them allows one to know what's right and gives one the strength and willpower to do what's right. It is not always easy to act ethically, but given some practical wisdom and willpower we can probably achieve it most of the time.

Critical Thinking

1. Describe an ethical dilemma you faced in which the right course was unclear. How could the various courses have been justified?

2. In the above dilemma, which course would be most supported by goodness, fairness, and commitment? Why?

3. In addition to the cardinal virtues, what character traits or virtues would help someone discern the most ethically supported course of action when facing ethical dilemmas? Why?

Internet References

InfoWorld
   http://www.infoworld.com/article/2607452/application-development/12-ethical-dilemmas-gnawing-at-developers-today.html

Markkula Center for Applied Ethics
   http://www.scu.edu/ethics/practicing/decision/framework.html

Steps of the Ethical Decision-Making Process (University of Kansas)
   https://research.ku.edu/sites/research.ku.edu/files/docs/EESE_EthicalDecisionmakingFramework.pdf

---

RONALD DUSKA, PHD, served The American College as The Charles Lamont Post Chair of Ethics and the Professions and as director of The American College Center for Ethics in Financial Services, from 1996 until 2011. Currently he is a business ethics consultant, President of the Society for Business Ethics, and an adjunct professor of business ethics at Villanova and St. Joseph's Universities.

Article   Prepared by: Eric Teoro, *Lincoln Christian University*

Good Morning! Your Moral Fiber Is Eroding by the Minute

DRAKE BENNETT

Learning Outcomes

After reading this article, you will be able to:

- Understand how an individual's ethical self-control is depleted throughout the day.

- Recognize the need to recharge one's ability to exercise ethical self-control.

- Structure your day to deal with ethical challenges at the optimal time.

Right now, as I write this, I am at peak integrity, but with every minute that passes, my moral fiber is weakening, like a cereal flake in milk. I don't notice it, but if there are decisions or tasks requiring personal discipline, I should take care of them quickly—by this afternoon, I will be defenseless against my baser instincts.

So say Maryam Kouchaki and Isaac Smith, researchers into organizational behavior, in a new paper in the journal *Psychological Science.* The idea that people can be more or less moral at different times goes back to the earliest recorded stories people told about each other: Achilles is both merciless killer and tender friend, Dr. Jekyll is Mr. Hyde. What's notable about the hypothesis Kouchaki and Smith set out to prove is that a person's moral upstandingness erodes over the course of each day, broken down in a process as regular and as ineluctable as digestion.

The paper sets out to show the effects on moral decision making of a phenomenon called "ego depletion," an influential explanation of human behavior first advanced by the psychologist Roy Baumeister. The basic insight is that a person's store of self-control is finite, and can be depleted. Like a muscle, our self-control weakens when we use it and is restored when we rest it. In one of his best-known studies, Baumeister had subjects sit in a room with a bunch of chocolate cookies. Some

of them got to eat the cookies, others had to eat radishes. The subjects were later given a difficult math problem to solve, and the radish-eaters gave up sooner than the cookie-eaters. Concentration requires willpower, and they had already run down their willpower resisting the sweets.

It isn't just in artificially torturous situations dreamt up by psychologists that we exhaust our willpower, though. It happens all the time in real life. Every decision, no matter how small, uses up some of it—what to wear to work, what to eat for breakfast, whether to tell a white lie about why you're late for a meeting. A person can minimize those decisions in an attempt to husband one's decision-making capacity—President Obama, citing the ego depletion literature, wears only gray or blue suits for this reason—but one can't escape all of them. Moving through one's day, there are inevitably a host of small decisions demanding to be made.

To the extent that acting ethically is a matter of mastering the temptation to do the wrong thing, Baumeister's radish-eaters would also be more likely to cheat or lie than those who hadn't already had to resist gustatory temptation. Or if they had less of a chance to replenish their reserves of self-control: Other research has shown that less sleep is correlated with less-ethical behavior in a workplace.

Kouchaki and Smith's study set out to see whether that steady onslaught of small daily decisions means that people are inevitably more moral in the morning, when their self-regulatory resources haven't yet been taxed, than they are in the afternoon. To a dramatic extent, the researchers found that they were. In one study, test subjects were randomly divided into a morning group and an afternoon group and given a chance to lie to earn more money. The participants in the afternoon group were 50 percent more likely to lie than those in the morning group. Given a math test on which they could easily cheat, subjects in a second study cheated on nearly twice as many questions if they took the test in the afternoon than if they took it in the morning.

Good Morning! Your Moral Fiber Is Eroding by the Minute by Drake Bennett

25

Asked on the phone if he has changed anything in his own life because of his finding, Smith said he hasn't. Still, he thinks there are ways to mitigate the effect. He points out that work by Baumeister and others has shown that, just as it does with real muscles, eating—like rest—helps replenish the strength of our decision muscle, so naps and snacks can help slow the transition to afternoon's Mr. Hyde. Also in the paper, he and Kouchaki suggest that "morally relevant tasks should be deliberately ordered throughout the day. Perhaps organizations, for instance, need to be more vigilant about combating the unethical behavior of customers (or employees) in the afternoon than in the morning."

Critical Thinking

1. What do you think of the hypothesis that one's ability to make ethical decisions or to behave ethically can be depleted throughout the day? Defend your position.

2. What steps can you take to recharge your ethical "muscles"? What steps can organizations take to recharge the ethical muscles of their members?

3. Think of ethical challenges you typically face. What specific changes should you make to improve your ethical decision-making and behavior regarding those challenges?

Create Central

www.mhhe.com/createcentral

Internet References

American Psychological Association
   https://www.apa.org/helpcenter/willpower-overview.aspx

The New York Times: Magazine
   http://www.nytimes.com/2011/08/21/magazine/do-you-suffer-from-decision-fatigue.html?pagewanted=all&_r=2&

Article   Prepared by: Eric Teoro, *Lincoln Christian University*

Stealing a Pen at Work Could Turn You On to Much Bigger Crimes

EMILY COHN

Learning Outcomes

After reading this article, you will be able to:

- Recognize the personal effects of minor ethical breaches.
- Recognize the danger of justifying unethical behavior.

Steal a pen from your office and you could find yourself on a path toward becoming the next Bernie Madoff.

That's the warning of a new study, called "The Slippery Slope: How Small Ethical Transgressions Pave The Way For Larger Future Transgressions," by David Welsh of the University of Washington, Lisa Ordóñez of the University of Arizona, Deirdre Snyder of Providence College, and Michael Christian of the University of North Carolina at Chapel Hill. According to the study, which was published in the *Journal of Applied Psychology,* minor unethical behavior at work, if undetected, puts workers on a "slippery slope" that could lead to worse behavior over time.

To most of us, fairly innocuous sins like taking a pen from work or neglecting to refill the office coffee pot are much easier to justify than, say, racking up $2 billion in trading losses. But over time, the researchers found, those minor misdeeds make it easier to justify more and bigger evils in the long run.

"People rationalize their behavior to justify it," Ordóñez, one of the study's authors, said in a press release. "They might think 'No one got hurt,' or 'Everyone does it.' . . . they feel fine about doing something a little bit worse the next time and then commit more severe unethical actions."

The researchers tested this theory by watching subjects in a number of different situations. One interesting experiment found that subjects who were given 25 cents for doing a minor unethical thing were much more likely to take $2.50 to do something more egregious later on than those who were offered $2.50 to do a big no-no at the start. According to the researchers, this shows that people are less likely to commit what they call "abrupt and large dilemmas" when they haven't already committed gradual, small transgressions.

The study cites Madoff, who was sentenced to 150 years in prison for orchestrating the largest Ponzi scheme in history and spoke of this phenomenon to his longtime secretary, according to Vanity Fair: "Well, you know what happens is, it starts out with you taking a little bit, maybe a few hundred, a few thousand. You get comfortable with that, and before you know it, it snowballs into something big."

So what can you do to prevent yourself from becoming the next Jeff Skilling? The researchers offer a number of tips to discourage the minor stuff, like putting in place a firm set of ethical guidelines and calling workers out for the small things, like taking home too many office supplies.

"The ideal is for employees to recognize when they've committed a minor transgression and check themselves," Michael S. Christian, one of the paper's coauthors, wrote.

Critical Thinking

1. Do you think minor ethical breaches are serious enough to warrant attention? Why or why not?
2. Provide examples of minor ethical breaches that occur in the workplace.
3. How would you respond to someone who is trying to justify a minor ethical breach?

Create Central

www.mhhe.com/createcentral

Internet References

European Molecular Biology Labrotory
http://www.embl.de/aboutus/science_society/discussion/discussion_2004/ref14may04.pdf

Houston Chronicle
http://smallbusiness.chron.com/catch-thief-workplace-19098.html

University of North Carolina—Chapel Hill: Kenan-Flagler Business School
http://www.kenan-flagler.unc.edu/news/2014/06/Slippery-Slope

Article   Prepared by: Eric Teoro, *Lincoln Christian University*

Three Simple Rules to Stop Yourself from Lying

Natalie Kitroeff

Learning Outcomes

After reading this article, you will be able to:

- Recognize that "small" lies can lead to more serious ethical breaches.

- Describe several basic steps to avoid lying.

Start by being honest when someone has something in their teeth.

The squirmiest part of Yael Melamede's new documentary about lying comes about 30 minutes in, when a 2007 news report about the resignation of the dean of admissions at MIT is featured. The dean had just resigned after lying for 28 years about having a college degree, reported NBC anchor Brian Williams. Viewers can watch Williams recount her ethical breach with a weird kind of clairvoyance. In February of this year (2015), the anchor was suspended from NBC for repeating a fabricated tale about taking fire while in a helicopter during the 2003 U.S. invasion of Iraq.

The idea that everyone lies is not surprising. It's still interesting to hear people explain the first lie in a string of lies that sent them to jail or see a fibber tell the world about the demise of another fibber. Melamede's documentary, *(Dis)Honesty—The Truth About Lies,* which began showing at film festivals in April and is now available to stream on demand, delivers all of the above scenes, with an assist from Duke behavioral economist Dan Ariely.

Melamede takes a tour through Ariely's research, which shows, broadly, that when people can justify it to themselves or see others behaving similarly, they have no qualms about lying. The movie features a wife who started cheating on her husband out of boredom, a pro cyclist who doped out of

necessity, and an accountant who fudged his company's books first out of fear and then out of greed. Watching people unspool their lies will not make you feel better about yourself. It will make you feel as though you're one lie away from being very publicly humiliated.

Most of the liars interviewed in *(Dis)Honesty* did not make huge mistakes from the get-go. They started small, with a quick visit to AshleyMadison.com or a conversation with a friend about how to get faster on a bike. The disgraced MIT admissions dean, Marilee Jones, said that at first, she simply didn't bother correcting people who assumed that she was a PhD Brian Williams said his memory failed him and that he confused the plane he was traveling on with another one. Ariely, who has spent his career studying lies, says that's typical: Often people who get into major trouble for dishonesty were at one point relatively low-key liars.

Bloomberg asked Ariely how people who tell little lies can keep from turning into people whose lies land them on television. He offered a couple of easy strategies. For a friend.

1. Stop telling people you want to meet up with them if you don't.

    The classic "let's meet up" lie, where two people pretend that they are planning on hanging out, can spiral out of control, Ariely says.

    "You basically don't want to tell this person that you aren't interested in meeting each other again," Ariely says. "It is really similar to other kinds of lies. We don't want to deal with unpleasantness right now, so we end up worse down the road."

    Telling someone that you must do drinks, then canceling drinks and repeating that process for months is the kind of habitual lie that Ariely says "lead you to be a bigger liar."

It also costs you time, causes guilt, and doesn't actually make the person on the other end of the line feel better. The next time you run into an old friend whom you would rather not see on purpose, preempt your desire to please them.

"Saying something like, 'I'm really buried at work for the next month, if things change I will let you know'," is a better approach, Ariely says.

That may be untrue, but unlike "let's meet up," a fib about your workload is unlikely to set off a chain reaction of untruths. "That's the kind of lie that doesn't cost you as much."

2. Tell your friends when you don't like the person they're dating.

Do you hate your bestie's bae? Make it known. "It's one of those things that people don't say enough. We don't get enough feedback," says Ariely. Offering a dispassionate opinion about something so subjective can help your pals and might also make you less self-delusional.

"When we are in our own little realm, it is very hard for us to see past our emotions and past our immediate incentives. When you give advice to someone else, you take the outside view. We do think more long-term," Ariely says. Facing an inconvenient opinion head on by blurting it out can make you more likely to take an objective stance about your own problems. Just be strategic about how significant of an other you target.

"Married without kids, go for it; married with kids, don't go for it," says Ariely.

3. Make easy-to-follow rules.

"I am a big believer in rules, because they help us be who we want without having to contemplate it every time," Ariely says. For example, he decided always to tell someone when they had something in their teeth. "Before that, it was 'should I say something? Should I not?'" he says. Now he realizes he should never have hesitated. "One hundred percent of the time people are grateful. They realize I am not going to be the last person they talk to."

Sure, answering "bloated" when someone asks how you're feeling, or saying "no" when they ask to hang out is uncomfortable. Do it anyway. Even Omar Little had a code.

Critical Thinking

1. Describe a time when you lied. Why did you do so? How did you justify it?
2. Develop several concrete steps you can take to avoid lying.
3. Is lying ever ethical? Why or why not?

Internet References

About.com
http://philosophy.about.com/od/Philosophical-Questions-Puzzle/a/The-Ethics-Of-Lying.htm
Harvard University
http://dash.harvard.edu/bitstream/handle/1/3209557/Korsgaard_Two ArgumentsLying.pdf?sequence=2
Santa Clara University
http://www.scu.edu/ethics/publications/iie/v6n1/lying.html
The (Dis)honesty Project
http://thedishonestyproject.com/

Article   Prepared by: Eric Teoro, *Lincoln Christian University*

A Time for Ethical Self-Assessment

Peter Drucker's literature on business scruples and the Ethics of Prudence is newly timely, and not just because of the holidays.

RICK WARTZMAN

Learning Outcomes

After reading this article, you will be able to:

- Understand the importance and value of answering the following question: When you look in the mirror in the morning, what kind of person do you want to see?

- Recognize that management deals with the nature of "Man, and with Good and Evil."

This may be the season of giving, but it sure feels like everybody is suddenly on the take.

Siemens (SI), the German engineering giant, agreed this month to pay a record $1.6 billion to US and European authorities to settle charges that it routinely used bribes and kickbacks to secure public works contracts across the globe. Prominent New York attorney Marc Dreier—called by one US prosecutor a "Houdini of impersonation and false documents"—has been accused by the feds of defrauding hedge funds and other investors out of $380 million.

And then, of course, there's financier Bernard L. Madoff, who is said to have confessed to a Ponzi scheme of truly epic proportions: a swindle of $50 billion, an amount roughly equal to the GPD of Luxembourg.

All told, it begs the question that Peter Drucker first raised in a provocative 1981 essay in the journal *The Public Interest* and that later became the title of a chapter in his book, *The Ecological Vision*: "Can there be 'business ethics'?"

Drucker didn't pose this to suggest that business was inherently incapable of demonstrating ethical behavior. Nor was he positing that the workplace should somehow be exempt from moral concerns. Rather, his worry was that to speak of "business ethics" as a distinct concept was to twist it into something that "is not compatible with what ethics always was supposed to be."

What Drucker feared, specifically, was that executives could say they were meeting their social responsibilities as business leaders—protecting jobs and generating wealth—while engaging in practices that were plainly abhorrent. "Ethics for them," Drucker wrote, "is a cost-benefit calculation . . . and that means that the rulers are exempt from the demands of ethics, if only their behavior can be argued to confer benefits on other people."

It's hard to imagine that a Madoff or a Dreier would even attempt to get away with such tortured logic: an ends-justify-the-means attitude that Drucker labeled "casuistry." But we all know managers who've tried to rationalize an unscrupulous act by claiming that it served some greater good.

The Mirror Test

In his book *Resisting Corporate Corruption*, Stephen Arbogast notes that when Enron higher-ups sought an exemption from the company's ethics policy so that they could move forward with certain dubious financial dealings, the arrangement was made to "seem a sacrifice for the benefit of Enron." Reinhard Siekaczek, a former Siemens executive, told *The New York Times* (NYT) that the company's showering of foreign officials with bribes "was about keeping the business unit alive and not jeopardizing thousands of jobs overnight."

For Drucker, the best way for a business—indeed, for any organization—to create an ethical environment is for its people to partake in what he came to call in a 1999 article "the mirror test." In his 1981 piece, Drucker had a fancier name for this idea: He termed it "The Ethics of Prudence." But either way, it boils down to the same thing: When you look in the mirror in the morning, what kind of person do you want to see?

The Ethics of Prudence, Drucker wrote, "does not spell out what 'right' behavior is." It assumes, instead, "that what is wrong behavior is clear enough—and if there is any doubt, it is 'questionable' and to be avoided." Drucker added that "by following prudence, everyone regardless of status becomes a leader" and remains so by "avoiding any act which would make one the kind of person one does not want to be, does not respect."

Drucker went on: "If you don't want to see a pimp when you look in the shaving mirror in the morning, don't hire call girls the night before to entertain congressmen, customers, or salesmen. On any other basis, hiring call girls may be condemned as vulgar and tasteless, and may be shunned as something fastidious people do not do. It may be frowned upon as uncouth. It may even be illegal. But only in prudence is it ethically relevant. This is what Kierkegaard, the sternest moralist of the 19th century, meant when he said that aesthetics is the true ethics."

Time to Reflect

Drucker cautioned that the Ethics of Prudence "can easily degenerate" into hollow appearances and "the hypocrisy of public relations." Yet despite this danger, Drucker believed that "the Ethics of Prudence is surely appropriate to a society of organizations" in which "an extraordinarily large number of people are in positions of high visibility, if only within one organization. They enjoy this visibility not, like the Christian Prince, by virtue of birth, nor by virtue of wealth—that is, not because they are personages. They are functionaries and important only through their responsibility to take right action. But this is exactly what the Ethics of Prudence is all about."

Now is the time of year when many of us find ourselves sitting in church or in synagogue, or, if we're not religious, simply taking stock of who we are and where we want to be as the calendar turns.

But what's even more critical is that we continue this sort of honest self-assessment when we return to our jobs in early 2009.

"I have learned more theology as a practicing management consultant than when I taught religion," Drucker once said. This, he explained, is because "management always deals with the nature of Man and (as all of us with any practical experience have learned), with Good and Evil as well."

So take the mirror test now—and then keep taking it well after the Christmas ornaments have been packed away and the Hanukkah candles have burned down to the nub. In the meantime, happy holidays to all.

Critical Thinking

1. Explain the meaning of Drucker's question "can there be business ethics?"
2. Defend the position that there can be business ethics.
3. What is the mirror test?
4. What is the ethics of prudence?
5. What is meant by "aesthetics is the true ethics"?

Create Central

www.mhhe.com/createcentral

Internet References

American Management Association
   http://www.amanet.org/training/articles/Ethical-Leadership-Self-Assessment-How-Machiavellian-Are-You.aspx

National Association Medical Staff Services
   http://www.namss.org/Portals/0/Ethics%20Files/Self-assessment%20Tool.pdf

RICK WARTZMAN is the director of the Drucker Institute at Claremont Graduate University.

Unit 2

UNIT

Prepared by: Eric Teoro, *Lincoln Christian University*

Corporate Social Responsibility and the Nature of Business

Contemporary businesses face several significant challenges in today's global marketplace. World trends are changing the expectations that individuals and whole societies have of business. No longer is the traditional product or service value proposition considered sufficient; today's company must also demonstrate values and a commitment to social good if it is to engender trust. Corporate Social Responsibility (CSR) refers to the obligation that a business has to operate in a manner that will benefit society at large.

As several articles demonstrate, when companies engage in charitable activities, activities that reflect constructive corporate citizenship, they engage employees at deeper levels, attract better talent, and build positive reputations. Companies engaged in Corporate Responsibility take sustainability seriously, not only with respect to environmental issues, but also with respect to human capital development. They adhere to fiduciary principles, recognizing their responsibility to create lasting value for all their stakeholders, and by so doing, practice "Conscious Capitalism."

Some of the authors, however, counter popular notions of CSR. They ask why offering a product or service that improves the quality of lives, treating employees fairly, conducting business dealings honestly, cleaning up one's own messes, following laws, and paying taxes are not sufficient, in and of themselves, to constitute a socially responsible company. The authors recognize the inherent worth of business, even defending high salaries awarded to effective executives. They question the ability, even the rightness, of executives at publically traded companies to focus on issues other than profit maximization, assuming such a focus remains within ethical norms. In essence, they ask why the normal operations of business are not considered sufficiently ethical in themselves. The unit concludes with examining consumer orientation toward ethical and sustainability concerns.

Article   Prepared by: Eric Teoro, *Lincoln Christian University*

Doing More Good

Here are several ways your company can become a better corporate citizen.

JODI CHAVEZ

Learning Outcomes

After reading this article, you will be able to:

- Describe the business benefits of good corporate citizenship.
- Describe steps for implementing corporate social responsibility.

Today's challenging economic climate has forced many organizations to reduce spending, release workers, and raise fees to consumers. The result is that businesses of all shapes and sizes are being painted in an unfavorable light, inviting criticism from the public and politicians alike.

But the picture being painted—that of a business culture that abandons the public in pursuit of profits—isn't an accurate one. The most effective counter to this depiction is the rise of corporate responsibility initiatives.

The Committee Encouraging Corporate Philanthropy (CECP), an international forum of business leaders focused on measuring and encouraging corporate philanthropy, recently released its *Giving in Numbers* report for 2011. In the report, the CECP noted that one out of every two businesses had actually increased the amount of funds contributed to charity or community organizations since the onset of the recession in 2007. As a matter of fact, a quarter of companies reported increasing their giving by more than 25 percent. Furthermore, the CECP tracked aggregate total contributions for 110 high-performing companies in 2007–2010 and found that aggregate total giving rose by 23 percent.

Clearly, many successful businesses are actually augmenting their contributions to society and taking the challenge of good corporate citizenship seriously. But why? Of course, the ability to "do more good" for more people carries intrinsic value and tremendous appeal. Yet there are other significant business benefits that arise out of doing more good.

Here we'll explore some of these benefits, and I'll offer practical ways you can begin to make a difference in your company and, ultimately, society.

The Business Case for Being Charitable

The rise of corporate responsibility and citizenship has been two decades in the making. As detailed in "Responsibility: The New Business Imperative," published in the May 2002 issue of *The Academy of Management Executive*, during the 1990s: "Numerous exposés of labor practices in global supply chains pressured multinational brands and retailers to adopt corporate codes of conduct. Later in the decade, pressure—and expectations—increased further, driving firms not only to introduce codes but also to ensure compliance with these codes by their suppliers." Finally, the fall of businesses like Enron and the recent financial collapse and mortgage crisis forced businesses to reexamine their "anything goes" approach to profitability.

All these are crucial steps in the evolution of corporate responsibility. But today the most important driver of corporate responsibility is the belief that good citizenship makes good business sense.

There are several ways it can give you a competitive advantage.

Building a reputation: Companies large and small impact the neighborhoods, cities, and countries they do business in. By aligning your goals with the goals of the community in which you operate, you're more likely to build a mutually beneficial relationship with potential stakeholders, including employees, customers, investors, suppliers, and business partners.

Setting your company apart: Like an innovative product or a new service offering, a strong record of corporate responsibility is a competitive advantage that you can leverage against others in your industry.

Attracting investment: Businesses with strong records of corporate responsibility generate more interest from investors when compared with apathetic competitors. In a study titled "Institutional and Social Investors Find Common Ground," originally published in the *Journal of Investing* and later cited in the comprehensive article "The Business Case for Corporate Social Responsibility" in the *International Journal of Management Review,* author Timothy Smith lays out why this is the case. "Many institutional investors 'avoid' companies or industries that violate their organizational mission, values, or principles . . . [They also] seek companies with good records on employee relations, environmental stewardship, community involvement, and corporate governance."

Reducing costs and risks: Companies that make a concerted effort to contribute to and advance society are more likely to avoid potential penalties or exposure to legal fines and government intervention. This is especially important in a climate of increased regulation and scrutiny. A strong record of corporate citizenship can also help you avoid harm to your reputation and sales that may arise without notice.

Attracting better talent: Great people want to work for great companies. By demonstrating your strong commitment to teamwork, responsibility, community, etc., you can attract employees who share those same values. Furthermore, now may be the opportune time to start reevaluating your corporate responsibility profile so you can connect with future leaders. Research indicates that the Millennial generation, currently entering the workforce in record numbers, is particularly civic minded. Members of this generation want more from their job than just a paycheck—they want an opportunity to make a difference. Why not give it to them and give yourself an edge in the process?

Increasing motivation and retention: In addition to attracting new talent, a demonstrated commitment to corporate responsibility can enhance engagement across your current workforce. It can also help you identify leaders who want to spearhead these important initiatives. This can help you reduce the expenses inherent in high turnover, including recruiting, training, and onboarding, and eliminate productivity gaps that occur when an employee leaves your company.

The Millennial generation wants more from their job than just a paycheck—they want an opportunity to make a difference.

Fostering innovation: By looking beyond the walls of your buildings and understanding the wider impact of your business, you can open your eyes to new opportunities and new avenues for growth. A primary example of this is Xerox, which has shown a continued commitment to sustainability and citizenship in designing "waste free" products and investing in "waste free" facilities. This commitment has led to the development of new products that appeal to corporations, fuel profitability, and set Xerox apart in the marketplace. Toyota is another example of a company that recognized the impact of its business—vehicle emissions—and built a profitable solution to the problem in the form of the popular Prius hybrid. Though other auto manufacturers have followed suit, the development of the Prius and its status as the first commercially viable hybrid gave Toyota a competitive advantage and a leg up on the competition. No matter what product or service you offer, a new perspective gleaned from a commitment to corporate responsibility can help you do the same.

Putting Responsibility into Action

Today, corporate responsibility encompasses many forms, including education about social issues and advancement of different cultures (social responsibility), ensuring the health of the environment (sustainability), and donating funds or time to charitable causes (philanthropy). Corporate responsibility is also concerned with the health and safety of the workforce and providing good working conditions for employees.

With corporate responsibility taking on so many facets, it may be difficult to determine how your company can begin making an impact. The International Institute for Sustainable Development (IISD) recently published *Corporate Social Responsibility: An Implementation Guide for Business* to help companies adapt and facilitate corporate social responsibility. Here is their recommended framework for implementation.

Conduct a corporate social responsibility (CSR) assessment: Gather and examine relevant information about your products, services, decision-making processes, and activities to determine your current CSR activity. An effective assessment should give you an accurate understanding of your values and ethics, the CSR issues that are affecting your business now or in the future, key stakeholders, and your leadership's ability to deliver a more effective CSR approach.

Develop a CSR strategy: Using your assessment as a starting point, begin to determine your objectives. Develop a realistic strategy that can help you reach your goals. The IISD recommends these five steps to developing an effective strategy:

- Build support with the CEO, senior management, and employees.
- Research what others (including competitors) are doing.
- Prepare a matrix of proposed CSR actions.
- Develop options for proceeding and the business case for them.
- Decide on direction, approach, boundaries, and focus areas.

Develop commitments: Create a task force to review your objectives and finalize your strategy. The task force should solicit input from key stakeholders—the CEO, department heads, top management, etc.—to gauge their interest and ensure future participation. Using this feedback, prepare a preliminary draft of your CSR commitment, and review this again with those employees who will be affected or who can help effect change. At this point, you can revise and publish your commitments for your internal audience, customers, investors, and potential employees.

Implement CSR commitments: This is the phase where your planning begins to give way to reality. Though each company should approach this critical step in accordance with its unique values and culture, the IISD offers these universal best practices:

- Prepare a CSR business plan.
- Set measurable targets, and identify performance measures.
- Engage employees and others to whom CSR commitments apply.
- Design and conduct CSR training.
- Establish mechanisms for addressing resistance.
- Create internal and external communications plans.
- Make commitments public.

Document progress: It's imperative that you're able to communicate the impact of your efforts to internal and external stakeholders. Reporting tools provide insight into the costs of your initiatives as well as the hard and soft benefits derived from your corporate responsibility program.

Reporting on responsibility initiatives has actually given rise to an entirely new financial model called social accounting. Social accounting is the process of measuring, monitoring, and reporting to stakeholders the social and environmental effects of an organization's actions. Social accounting is conducted by accountants who employ the same tools and knowledge used in traditional financial reporting. Though many larger organizations utilize social accounting, all businesses can benefit from being able to demonstrate the true value of their actions.

In fact, robust social accounting and responsibility reporting is fast becoming the standard for businesses, not the exception. KPMG conducted an *International Survey of Corporate Responsibility Reporting 2011* to review trends of 3,400 companies worldwide, including the top 250 global companies (the G250). The survey indicated that corporate responsibility reporting is undertaken by 95 percent of the G250 and 64 percent of the 100 largest companies across the 34 countries surveyed.

"[Corporate responsibility] has moved from being a moral imperative to a critical business imperative. The time has now come to enhance [corporate responsibility] reporting information systems to bring them up to the level that is equal to financial reporting, including a comparable quality of governance controls and management," said Wim Bartels, global head of KPMG's Sustainability Assurance.

Evaluate and improve: Using the reports and metrics generated, continue to refine your corporate responsibility initiatives. This is critical. Evaluate your performance objectively, identify opportunities for improvement, and engage key stakeholders to plot a course for the future.

The reality of today's economic, political, and social climate necessitates that business leaders rise above their bottom lines and look to make an impact outside their organization. Doing so presents an opportunity to elevate others while elevating your organization.

Critical Thinking

1. If a company focuses on the business benefits of good corporate citizenship, is it, in fact, being a good corporate citizen? Why or why not?

2. Describe a company that you believe is a good corporate citizen. Justify your belief.

3. What steps can you take as an employee to promote good corporate citizenship?

Internet References

CSRwire
   http://www.csrwire.com/pdf/JustGoodBusinessCSRwireExcerpt.pdf

Forbes
   http://www.forbes.com/sites/richardlevick/2012/01/11/corporate-social-responsibility-for-profit/

Journal of Economics, Business, and Management
   http://www.joebm.com/index.php?m=content&c=index&a=show&catid=43&id=535

Jodi Chavez is senior vice president of Accounting Principals.

Article   Prepared by: Eric Teoro, *Lincoln Christian University*

Doing Good to Do Well

Corporate Employees Help and Scope Out Opportunities in Developing Countries.

ANNE TERGESEN

Learning Outcomes

After reading this article, you will be able to:

- Describe initiatives by companies sending "volunteers" overseas to address social needs.

- Recognize the value to companies and employees in engaging in meeting social needs.

Last fall, Laura Benetti spent 4 weeks in rural India, helping women examine stitchery and figure out prices for garments to be sold in local markets.

After working nine-hour days, she and nine colleagues would sleep in a lodge frequented by locals that had spotty access to hot water and electricity. Ms. Benetti, a 27-year-old customs and international trade coordinator for Dow Corning Corp., considered it a plum assignment.

Dow Corning is among a growing number of large corporations—including PepsiCo Inc., FedEx Corp., Intel Corp., and Pfizer Inc.—that are sending small teams of employees to developing countries such as India, Ghana, Brazil, and Nigeria to provide free consulting services to nonprofits and other organizations. A major goal: to scope out business opportunities in hot emerging markets.

Despite the promise of long workdays in less-than-cushy surroundings, many employees consider the stints prize postings. There are usually many more applicants than spaces: Intel, for example, says about 5 percent of its applicants win spots in its Education Service Corps.

Though referred to as "volunteer" posts, employees usually continue to receive their regular salaries during the stints, which typically last 2 to 4 weeks. They appeal to employees looking to develop new skills and donate time and expertise to those in need—or simply take a break from their routines.

"It gives more meaning to your career," Ms. Benetti says.

At least 27 Fortune 500 companies currently operate such programs, up from 21 in April and six in 2006, according to a survey by CDC Development Solutions, a Washington, DC, nonprofit that designs and manages these programs.

At a cost of $5,000 to over $20,000 per employee, the programs require a significant investment. It costs International Business Machines Corp., which has the largest such corporate volunteer operation, roughly $5 million a year.

IBM has sent 1,400 employees abroad with its Corporate Service Corps since 2008. Its projects have produced plans to reform Kenya's postal system and develop an eco-tourism industry in Tanzania.

IBM credits its program with generating about $5 million in new business so far, including a contract, awarded in April 2010, to manage two public service programs for Nigeria's Cross River State, says Stan Litow, vice president for corporate citizenship.

Silicone supplier Dow Corning plans to evaluate 15 new business-related ideas generated by the 20 employees it has sent to India since September 2010, says Laura Asiala, director of corporate citizenship. Ms. Asiala declined to discuss specifics, but says the company has "identified opportunities" in affordable housing, energy, and other sectors, thanks to volunteers' observations.

The programs drum up good public relations, both internally and externally, via positive media coverage and blogs many participants write from the field.

Companies "gain local name recognition" in the markets they wish to break into, says Deirdre White, president and CEO of CDC Development Solutions.

Company officials also say the popular programs can help them recruit in-demand talent and retain valued employees.

Dow Corning accepted about 10 percent of the approximately 200 prospective volunteers who applied online for the trips it sponsored in 2010 and 2011. The company says it selects those with strong performance evaluations, and seeks a diverse mix of participants with varying tenure.

The overseas assignments can act as a training ground for future leaders. Caroline Roan, vice president of corporate responsibility and president of the Pfizer Foundation, says some of the 270 people the pharmaceutical giant has sent abroad describe the experience "as a mini-MBA."

"They build skills, in part because they are sometimes thrust into situations outside of their comfort zone, which tends to make people more creative," she says.

Chris Marquis, an associate professor at Harvard Business School, was hired by IBM in 2009 to survey its volunteers. His subsequent research shows that alumni of the program remain on the job longer than peers with similar performance and tenure.

"These are the stars at IBM," he says. "If by offering something like this they can retain these people for longer, it is a very smart investment."

Critical Thinking

1. Develop a brief report about the good-works projects of one of the companies named in the article. How do the good-works projects help the company to do well in the marketplace?

2. The article mentions that a major goal of sending employees abroad on good-works projects is "to scope out business opportunities in hot emerging markets." What do you think of this goal? Develop arguments defending the goal as well as denouncing the goal. Bring your arguments to class for class discussion.

3. Beyond the example given in the article of the various good-works projects, can you think of other good things companies might do in order to do well in the marketplace? Make a list of the other good things and bring your list to class discussion.

Create Central

www.mhhe.com/createcentral

Internet References

Fast Company Co.Exist
http://www.fastcoexist.com/1679510/corporate-volunteerism-should-be-part-of-corporate-social-responsibility
Itasca Project
http://www.theitascaproject.com/
Points of Light
http://www.pointsoflight.org/corporate-institute

Article   Prepared by: Eric Teoro, *Lincoln Christian University*

Necessary but Not Sufficient

An Exploration of Where CR Begins—and Ends

PETER A. SOYKA

Learning Outcomes

After reading this article, you will be able to:

- Understand the argument that CSR is good for business.

- Describe various facets of CSR and sustainability.

- Recognize the role of governance and values in promoting CSR and sustainability.

Recent years have witnessed a proliferation of corporate social responsibility (CSR) and corporate responsibility (CR) programs in many industries, along with media, graduate programs and institutes, and other resources to support and promote them. The underlying concept of CSR/CR is deeply rooted in the conviction that corporations have a variety of obligations to their host societies that go well beyond meeting shareholders' expectations of financial returns. A problem, however, complicates reliance on such an approach to guide the behavior of the organization. Setting aside the CR programs that lack substance and appear to be mainly about public relations (we count more than a few), it is not clear within the CR construct how far the responsibility to address environmental, social, and governance (ESG) concerns extends. Nor is it clear how such concerns should be balanced against the need for the corporation to satisfy the demands of its customers and earn the rate of return required by its owners and other capital providers.

The general rule of thumb appears to be to meet certain required minima (e.g., legal compliance, no use of unreasonable labor practices) and as many other "good" things as resources allow, with the proviso that virtually any demand made by a major customer will receive careful consideration. That is, CSR/CR as commonly understood does not provide a clear means for striking the appropriate balance between obligation

and opportunity, nor does it place sufficient emphasis on incenting the desired behaviors from companies and their employees. The concept of sustainability, as defined in this article (and more fully in my recent book), provides these missing elements. My concept of sustainability combines CSR/CR and related concepts with aggressive, financially driven assessment of opportunities. Such a balanced approach is the only viable way to get United States business at large on a more sustainable path.

Sustainability Defined

In my view, sustainability is a value set, philosophy, and approach that is rooted in the belief that organizations (corporate and otherwise) can and must materially contribute to the betterment of society. Sustainable organizations must balance their needs, aspirations, and limitations against the larger interests of the societies in which they operate. Only organizations that provide goods and/or services that are of value to people and/or society more generally, and are dedicated to excellence, interested in the full development of human potential, and committed to fairness, are likely to be durable (sustainable) over the long term. Fundamentally, sustainable organizations are purpose-driven, with the purpose being an overarching objective larger and less tangible than self-gratification or profit maximization. Indeed, they accept that their conduct and all their activities in totality must yield an overall benefit-to-cost ratio greater than unity. Accordingly, in my formulation of the concept, sustainable organizations are:

- Mission-driven;
- Aware of and responsive to societal and stakeholder interests;
- Responsible and ethical;
- Dedicated to excellence;

- Driven to meet or exceed customer/client expectations; and
- Disciplined, focused, and skillful.

This view places the conventional emphasis on the "three legs of the stool" (economic prosperity, environmental protection, and social equity) within a larger, more integrative context. It also recognizes that each is a key dimension of any coherent concept of sustainable organizations, past or present. The importance of each of the three major elements of sustainability depends on the organization's nature and purpose. Public sector and nonprofit organizations have been formed and structured specifically to provide some combination of products and services that benefit society, whether that involves forecasting the weather, teaching children, or defending the country from military threats. With the exception of agencies and nongovernmental organizations (NGOs) specifically focused on some aspect of sustainability—such as the United States Environmental Protection Agency (EPA) or the Sierra Club—most such organizations have a primary mission to fulfill that is not directly related to either environmental protection or social equity. Nonetheless, by adopting sustainability as a guiding principle, such organizations commit themselves at the very least to ensuring that they limit any adverse impacts of their operations on the environment and treat all stakeholders fairly. Many public sector organizations, including the federal government and its many parts, have been moving decisively in recent years to institute more sustainable behavior.

Only organizations that provide goods and/or services that are of value to people and/or society more generally, and are dedicated to excellence, interested in the full development of human potential, and committed to fairness, are likely to be durable (sustainable) over the long term.

Corporations are in quite a different place. They are not explicitly supported by and accountable to the American taxpayer and have not (generally) been formed to pursue a mission eligible for tax-exempt status as a nonprofit. Some observers believe that in contrast to the work done by the government and nonprofit sectors, the legitimate role of business is to make money for its owners (shareholders), and the more the better. In this view of the world, time and money invested in improving environmental performance, providing safer working conditions, supporting local communities through philanthropic activity, and other such CR behaviors are an unwarranted and unproductive use of the firm's assets. This view, which has been held and promoted with great conviction by many in the business community and academia, is increasingly being challenged.

Recognizing important sustainability issues and acting on them in an enlightened and sophisticated way has been shown to increase revenue growth and earnings and to strengthen firm positions in terms of the factors that drive long-term financial success.

Corporate leaders should accept and, ideally, embrace the concept of sustainability, for two fundamental reasons. One is that United States corporations, as distinct entities holding enumerated legal rights and receiving numerous public benefits, have an obligation not only to comply with all applicable laws and regulations but also to ensure that their conduct does not harm the broader societies of which they are a part and on which they depend for survival. (Unfortunately, many people in the business community and press seem not to recognize how many benefits the United States federal and state governments provide, and how different this largesse is from the situation in many other countries.) The other is that, increasingly, recognizing important sustainability issues and acting on them in an enlightened and sophisticated way has been shown to increase revenue growth and earnings and to strengthen firm positions in terms of the factors that drive long-term financial success. In other words, the argument for embracing corporate sustainability (above and beyond CR) has two elements: It is the right thing to do, and it is the smart thing to do.

Beyond Environment and Philanthropy

Each of these other, more limited concepts has considerable merit. However, none is new or sufficient to both address the needs and interests of the broad set of stakeholders to which most organizations are accountable and to position the firm to avail itself of all related opportunities.

Sustainability is often framed in the media as a campaign to "green" the world or "save the planet." When viewed from an appropriately broad perspective, however, sustainability extends beyond the currently fashionable focus on "greening." Greening is, after all, simply the latest manifestation of public interest in the environment, which has come back into vogue during the past 3 or 4 years following a multiyear hiatus. As an interested party who has watched several incarnations of a growing public/business interest in improving the environmental performance of organizations (and individuals), I find it both heartening and, in some ways, disturbing to observe the eagerness with which many are now embracing everything "green." Greening sounds and feels admirable, but public interest in this topic tends to wax and wane over time. My fear is that it will again fall out of fashion, unless the renewed focus on environmental performance improvement is coupled with considerations of social equity and both are underlain by rigorous economic analysis. Sustainability, defined in this way, provides the only theoretical and practical environmental improvement framework that can be fully justified and maintained during both good and challenging economic times. Therefore, it is robust and "sustainable" enough for the long haul.

My concerns with the terms CSR and CR are somewhat different. Although in most formulations they include the three "legs of the stool," they really are about delineating and acting on the obligations of the modern corporation to society at large. In contrast, and as highlighted above, sustainability should be considered an imperative that applies to all organizations and political entities (countries, states, municipalities). Each of these is challenged to understand and address the broad conditions under which it operates and its relationships with other entities and the natural world. Each also must chart a course on which it can thrive without undermining its asset base or unfairly precluding or limiting the sustainable success of others. In that context, CR can be thought of as one element of a corporate strategy to address the sustainability imperative. Such an element can, for example, identify the concerns of external stakeholders and define and execute processes to ensure that these external interests are respected as the firm pursues its broader business goals. In other words, CR and its analogues can be an important part of (but in any case are a subset of) an organization's approach to sustainability. In particular, CR can, and often does, comprise an organization's efforts to respond to the imperative to promote sustainable development. Similarly, CR can be used to appropriately target a company's philanthropic activities. Or the firm might separately deploy a strategic philanthropy campaign. But by its nature any such activity is far narrower in scope and effect than organizational sustainability. The two should not be confused or, in my view, ever be used interchangeably.

These distinctions are not trivial. Indeed, understanding and resolving them has proven difficult for many organizations and practitioners. Regardless of what words you choose to employ, the key point is that pursuing sustainability at the organizational level is more complex, more important, and more difficult than simply greening the organization to some arbitrary but comfortable level, or becoming more attentive to particular stakeholders and their views. However, substantial rewards can accompany taking on this greater level of difficulty.

Sustainability has emerged directly from the environmental movement and is often focused on key environmental issues and challenges. However, important opportunities exist for corporate leaders to examine social equity and economic issues in parallel with the environmental aspects of their organizations. The concept of sustainability provides an integrative framework to facilitate this thought process. Moreover, in practice, synergies and scale economies often make it possible to address issues having both environmental and social aspects more effectively and economically than would be possible by pursuing separate, unrelated approaches.

Of Governance and Values

Many stakeholders want assurance that the people at the top of the organization have thought through its important environmental and social issues and that they have developed and deployed effective programs, systems, and practices to address them. Sustainability provides an integrating structure that can both guide and explain how corporate leaders meet these expectations and do so in a way that is far more streamlined, sophisticated, and ultimately less time-consuming than would be possible otherwise.

Environmental and social improvement initiatives are continually underused when they are not seen as contributing to core business drivers or creating financial value in any tangible way.

Illegal and, increasingly, unethical behavior is not well tolerated by regulators, customers, suppliers, and other business partners. Such behavior can have severe financial consequences, both immediately and in the longer term. Understanding what is legal requires competence and vigilance on the part of one's general or outside counsel, but understanding what is ethical requires a set of organizational values and business norms. It is now widely understood that well-run companies have a core "DNA" or identity that embodies shared values and aspirations and is independent of any individual. This attribute enables the organization to remain strong and vibrant over an extended period even as people enter and depart from it. Moreover, this type of organizational identity provides many advantages under normal circumstances but is especially critical during crisis situations, when people need to know how to act as well as what to do. Sustainability can serve as a common, unifying principle to guide the thinking and behaviors of all members of the organization. This is important when different members are called on to execute their unique functions, some of which may be in conflict. Moreover, sustainability provides the needed flexibility to address the following realities:

- Environmental, social, and economic considerations must be balanced.
- The way in which they are balanced will differ according to the organization, issue, and circumstance in question.
- This balance will likely change over time.

The complexities of, and interrelationships among, ESG issues require a management approach that combines and considers all these disciplines. Such an approach should address all significant needs and requirements (particularly compliance), surface and resolve conflicts among them, provide consistency and predictability, and be both effective and efficient. In other words, some sort of overarching concept and management structure is required, and sustainability provides the "umbrella" under which many organizations are now organizing their previously disparate internal functions. I am unaware of any competing or alternative concept that has been shown to be workable while providing similar benefits.

The best way to pursue sustainability is to consider the three primary determinants of value for any business enterprise:

- The revenue stream and the customer base that generates it;
- Earnings or, in the case of public sector organizations, effective control of costs and management of capital; and
- Adequate understanding and management of risk.

A sensible sustainability strategy embodies careful consideration of how new initiatives or changes to existing programs might affect all three of these determinants of value. History has shown that absent this orientation, environmental and social improvement initiatives are continually underused because they are not seen as contributing to core business drivers or creating financial value in any tangible way. By the same token, a properly specified sustainability approach imposes a new measure of financial discipline on both internal and external proponents of new "greening" ideas and prospective investments in projects or activities having primarily a social orientation.

My fear is that "greening" will again fall out of fashion, unless the renewed focus on environmental performance improvement is coupled with considerations of social equity, with both underlain by rigorous economic analysis.

Entering the Mainstream

EHS issues have in many cases been managed tactically in United States corporations and public sector agencies. Historically, EHS functions were often housed within, and directed by, the organization's legal department because the focus then was on understanding legal requirements and ensuring compliance. More recently, EHS people have reported through various administrative functions (such as human resources), facility maintenance, or manufacturing management. In short, with few exceptions, EHS has been managed primarily as a facility-based tactical function, rather than as a strategic issue or source of potential broad-spectrum financial value creation. Adopting a sustainability framework can help disrupt, and might even compel, dissolution of organizational silos that exist in many companies. This can create the conditions needed for people across the organization to reach out to one another. They can identify and manage environmental and social issues in ways that limit risk, build brand and market value, and generate new cash flows. In an organization actively pursuing sustainability, achieving better environmental performance or more equitable dealings with stakeholders is not a task to be delegated to someone else. It is an integral part of everyone's job (if only in a small way), from the boardroom to the shop floor.

Critical Thinking

1. What is the relationship of sustainability and corporate responsibility?
2. Using the Internet, identify firms with strong sustainability programs and good corporate responsibility results.
3. For the firms you identified in answering question 2, analysis at least two of those firms on the basis of the six attributes of a sustainable organization presented in the article. Explain how the two firms you chose either exhibit or do not exhibit attributes of a sustainable organization.
4. What is the relationship of ethics and sustainability? To be an ethical firm, does the firm need a sustainability program? Why or why not?

Create Central

www.mhhe.com/createcentral

Internet References

Cranfield University School of Management
http://www.som.cranfield.ac.uk/som/p16919/Knowledge-Interchange/Management-Themes/Corporate-Responsibility-and-Sustainability

Forbes
http://www.forbes.com/sites/brucerogers/2014/04/07/corporate-responsibility-and-sustainability-is-a-competitive-advantage-for-capgemini/

PETER SOKA is founder and president of Soyka & Company. This is the first in a series of excerpts from his new book, *Creating a Sustainable Organization: Approaches for Enhancing Corporate Value Through Sustainability,* reprinted with permission from FT Press, a division of Pearson.

Fiduciary Principles: Corporate Responsibilities to Stakeholders by Susan C. Atherton, Mark S. Blodgett, and Charles A. Atherton

45

Article

Prepared by: Eric Teoro, *Lincoln Christian University*

Fiduciary Principles: Corporate Responsibilities to Stakeholders

SUSAN C. ATHERTON, MARK S. BLODGETT, AND CHARLES A. ATHERTON

Learning Outcomes

After reading this article, you will be able to:

- Describe the history of fiduciary theory and court opinion.
- Understand the relationship between fiduciary and corporate social responsibilities.

Introduction

The lack of trust in American corporations and in corporate management over the recent scandals and financial crisis has increased public and legislative outcry for accountability in business decisions. Frustration is rampant, with "seemingly unending examples of mismanagement, ethical misconduct, and patterned dishonesty of a society dubbed 'the cheating culture.'"[1] International competition created tremendous risks and rewards but forced companies to attract investors through creative accounting practices to raise share value. As a result, three decades of corporate greed, inappropriate financial risk-taking and personal misconduct eroded trust in corporate decision-making.[2]

Corporate governance reform initiatives beginning in 2002 were designed to increase financial disclosure and responsibility; however, such legislation is insufficient to rebuild public trust in business. Restoring trust requires that those individuals who manage corporations, that is, the board of directors and senior officers, comply with requirements for greater accountability and transparency, *and* abide by the legal norms to which boards of directors and management are already subject, as directors and officers are legally bound as fiduciaries owing duties of care and loyalty to the corporation.[3] However, centuries of legal and religious formalization and codification have diminished the actual meaning and

purpose of fiduciaries, with the result that modern corporate fiduciaries have limited responsibility toward stakeholders and the greater society. Restoring the original definitions and roles of fiduciaries may legitimize and guide the corporation in developing new relationships with stakeholders.

This paper does not focus on illegal conduct by corporate individuals, although many criminal violations of fiduciary norms involve intentional assessment of the risk of penalties versus potential profits.[4] Rather, the paper examines the limitations of today's corporate fiduciary duties given the original intent of the fiduciary relationship. In particular, we examine the definitions of fiduciaries and fiduciary responsibilities to determine the extent to which formalization and codification have led to avoidance of corporate responsibility. We then revisit the historical and religious origins of fiduciaries in commercial transactions that defined and shaped the integration of moral and ethical duties in business today yet were so narrowly defined that corporate liability became increasingly limited. We propose a modest but well-defined, consistent and universal definition of "fiduciary duties," that could offer corporate managers guidance in developing new approaches to stakeholder relationships—relationships built on expectations of corporate trust and decision-making that maximize shareholder wealth while protecting stakeholders.

The Modern Fiduciary

Most business students and executives today are introduced to the concept of a "fiduciary" in the context of agency law, where a fiduciary is defined as "one who has a duty to act primarily for another person's benefit," and agency is generally defined as "the fiduciary relation that results from the manifestation of consent by one person (a 'principal') to another (an 'agent') that the agent shall act on the principal's behalf and subject to the principal's control, and the agent manifests or otherwise consents so to act."[5] Restatement (Third) of Agency states that proof of an agency relationship requires the existence of the manifestation by the principal that the agent shall act for him; the agent's acceptance of the undertaking; and, the understanding that the principal is in control of the undertaking. The agency relationship that results is founded on trust, confidence, and good faith by one person in the integrity and fidelity of another, creating certain duties owed by each party established in the agency agreement and implied by law.[6] Within the relationship, fiduciaries have a duty of loyalty—the duty to act primarily for another in matters related to the activity and not for the fiduciary's own personal interest.

Fiduciaries also have a duty of good faith—the duty to act with scrupulous good faith and candor; complete fairness, without influencing or taking advantage of the client. The fiduciary relationship, as defined by history and case law, exists in every business transaction. Moreover, the relationship is defined by the specific role or function of the agent toward the principal, that is, the relationship of corporate management and boards of directors to shareholders, lawyer to client, or broker to client, and governed by the laws associated with those transactions, including criminal and labor law, securities and corporate law, contracts, partnerships, and trusts.[7] The roles of trustees, administrators, and bailees as fiduciaries were of ancient origin, whereas agents appeared only at the end of the eighteenth century.[8] Partners, corporate boards of directors, and corporate officers held fiduciary duties originating with the formation of modern partnerships and corporations, as did majority shareholders, while union leaders held fiduciary roles only when unions were granted power by statute to represent workers in negotiations with management.[9] While modern definitions of these duties remain intact, the scope of the duties greatly varies based on the fiduciary's role, which increases the complexity of analysis required to understand violations of those duties.

The modern definition of "agent" as a fiduciary was first rationalized and clarified as a legal doctrine in 1933:[10] "When the person acting is to represent the other in contractual negotiations, bargainings or transactions involved in business dealings with third persons, or is to appear for or represent the other in hearings or proceedings in which he may be interested, he is termed an 'agent,' and the person for whom he is to act is termed the 'principal.'" The element of continuous subjection to the will of the principal distinguishes the agent from other fiduciaries and the agency agreement from other agreements.[11] This implies that corporate officers and directors are also agents. However, in law and practice today, the fiduciary roles of corporate officers and directors are not "continuous subjection to the will of the principal (shareholders)" but more flexible as officers and directors make many decisions not approved by shareholders.

Further, the duties of officers and directors are distinct from those of other corporate employees. Corporate officers and directors owe fiduciary duties to shareholders (as defined by state case law and Delaware corporate law) while employees as agents owe duties to employers, suppliers, vendors, or customers in a wide variety of relationships involving trust.[12] This distinction has created a two-tiered definition of fiduciaries, each with different duties, and varying liabilities for breaches of those duties, and is supported by economic theory. Such differentiation in fiduciary roles does not appear to be the intention, either historically or in modern corporate law. In 1928, Judge Benjamin Cardozo, then Chief Judge of the New York Court of Appeals, eloquently recognized the significance and sanctity of fiduciary principles in *Meinhard v. Salmon*:[13]

> [J]oint adventurers, like copartners, owe to one another . . . the duty of the finest loyalty . . . and the level of conduct for fiduciaries has been kept at a higher level than that trodden by the crowd. It will not consciously be lowered by any judgment of this court.

Cardozo's opinion reflects three important principles that reinforce a long line of precedent in defining a *special level of fidelity for all fiduciaries:* (1) fiduciary matters demand a higher standard than normal marketplace transactions; (2) exceptions to the fiduciary standard undermine the duty of loyalty; and (3) neither courts nor regulators who interpret, enforce or modify the fiduciary standard should consciously weaken it.[14] Supreme Court Justice Brandeis later noted that a fiduciary "is an occupation which is pursued largely for others and not merely for oneself . . . in which the amount of financial return is not the accepted measure of success."[15]

Fiduciary Duties: The Required Triad

The Delaware Supreme Court, renowned for its corporate governance decisions and the source of the primary legal standards for the duties and liabilities of corporate officers, ruled in 1993, reaffirmed in 2006, and again in 2010, that the "triad" of duties includes the duty of loyalty, due care and good faith, where "good faith" and "full and fair disclosure" are considered to be the essential elements of, or prerequisites for proper conduct, by a director.[16] Violation of the duty of good faith could remove directors' protections from liability. The Delaware Court also ruled that corporate officers owe the same fiduciary duties as corporate directors, noting that it is not possible to discharge properly either the duty of care or the duty of loyalty without acting in good faith with respect to the interests of the companies' constituents.[17] Major legislation such as The Sarbanes-Oxley Act of 2002,[18] or The Dodd–Frank Act[19] of 2010 support these legal standards *and* require that directors and their corporations return to these fundamental principles to which they were formally subject already: individual integrity and responsibility in corporate governance; and, accountable and transparent disclosure of important financial and other information on which investors and the stability of the capital markets depend.[20]

The Court has long held that the board of directors is ultimately responsible for the management of the corporation,[21] although boards often delegate major decisions to corporate officers with more expertise and information on a particular subject. Under Delaware corporate law, officers are granted titles and duties through the corporation's bylaws or the board's resolutions and employees who are not granted this power are deemed agents.[22] Additionally, Delaware law dictates that the terms "officers" or "agents" are by no means interchangeable: officers are the corporation, but an agent is an employee and does not have the equivalent status of an officer.[23] Agents' specific duties include loyalty, performance, obedience, notification, and accounting.

Again, we see this distinction between officers as managers of the corporation and agents as employees as contrary to the historical and case law definitions espoused by two leading Chief Justices. It is noteworthy that agents as employees (and fiduciaries) are not required to act in a manner that ensures that organizational activities are conducted in good faith and with care for stakeholder's interests. Also noteworthy is the omission in corporate law of the duty of obedience (to obey the law), which appeared to occupy a recognized place in corporations through 1946 but eventually was eliminated. As recent courts have made clear that corporate actors cannot consciously violate, or permit the corporation to violate, corporate and noncorporate norms, even when it may be profitable for the corporation, this duty may be resurfacing.[24] The recent *Disney* decision specifically defines the current required triad of fiduciary duties.[25]

The Duty of Loyalty

"[T]he duty of loyalty mandates that the best interests of the corporation and its shareholders takes precedence over any interest possessed by a director, officer or controlling shareholder and . . . is not limited to cases involving a financial or other cognizable fiduciary conflict of interest. It also encompasses cases where the fiduciary fails to act in good faith."[26] The duty of loyalty is often described as a obligation of directors to protect the interests of the company and its stockholders, to refrain from decisions that would injure the company or deprive the company of profit or an advantage that might properly be brought to the company for it to pursue, and to act in a manner that he or she believes is in good faith to be in the best interests of the company and its stockholders.[27] Recent case law also adds that the duty of loyalty requires boards to act *"affirmatively and in good faith."*[28]

The Duty of Care

The duty of care is defined as " . . . that amount of care which ordinarily careful and prudent men would use in similar circumstances."[29] Courts review the standard of care in directors' decision-making *process,* not the substance of decisions thus limiting director liability for failure in risky decisions. A breach of the duty of care may be found when a director is grossly negligent if the substance of the board's informed decision cannot be "attributed to any rational business purpose."[30] In response to the financial crisis, legislation has specifically addressed the need for increased risk assessment in our financial institutions, requiring increased disclosure to ensure that effective reporting systems are in place and that all relevant information has been evaluated to ensure financial and economic stability. The duty of care is often perceived as a minimal standard, but addressing the impact of risk could increase the importance of this standard.

The Duty to Act in Good Faith

In the *Disney* case, the court stated that "Good faith has been said to require an 'honesty of purpose,' and a genuine care for the fiduciary's constituents . . ."[31] A director acts in "subjective bad faith" when his actions are "motivated by an actual intent to do harm" to the corporation, and bad faith can take different forms with varying degrees of culpability.[32] The court clearly ruled that the duty of good faith cannot be satisfied if directors act in subjective bad faith, consciously disregard their duties, actually intend to harm the corporation, or cause the corporation to knowingly violated the law.[33]

Most legal scholars disagree as to the practical importance of the duty of good faith, but proponents of managerial accountability in corporate governance look to the doctrine of good faith because the traditional duties of care and loyalty do very little to discipline boards, even if allegations of self-dealing were made (i.e., violations of duty of loyalty).[34] The Disney decision was critical for corporate governance since the court recognized that conduct that benefits the corporation must be done with proper motives in order to satisfy the duty of good faith, thus making boards and senior managers more accountable for their decisions. Implicit in these recent cases is the assumption that new rules of "conduct" may be useful in restoring trust to a doubting public. To more fully understand these new rules of ethical conduct we must turn to the historical origins of fiduciary principles.

Origins of Fiduciary Principles
Biblical and Early History

If you would understand anything, observe its beginning and its development.

Aristotle, 4th Century BCE [35]

The historical definition of a "fiduciary" was stated in terms of "an essential code of conduct for those who have been entrusted to care for other peoples' property," carry out transactions, work for another, or aid persons who were vulnerable and dependent upon others.[36] The breadth and complexity of early trust relationships is implicit in today's corporate organizational structure and business relationships. As early as 1790 B.C., the Code of Hammurabi (a Babylonian code of laws) established rules of law governing business conduct, or fiduciary considerations, for the behavior of agents (employees) entrusted with property.[37] For example, a merchant's agent was required to keep receipts and to pay triple damages for failing to provide promised goods, although an exception was allowed if losses were due to enemy attack during a journey.[38] The insightful research of several scholars traces the religious roots of the fiduciary principle to the Old and New Testaments.[39] For example, the Lord told Moses that it is a sin not to restore that which is delivered unto a man to keep safely, and penalties must be paid for the violation,[40] (i.e., duties of loyalty and due care); the right to fair treatment in the marketplace,[41] implying a responsibility to conduct transactions in good faith; and the unjust steward who, expecting to be fired, curries favor with his master's debtors by allowing them to repay less than their full debts, illustrating the precept that one cannot serve two masters.[42] Additionally, the law on pledges obligates everyone to establish his own trustworthiness by carrying out the agreements he has made and by being sensitive to the needs of those who depend on him to meet their needs (i.e., loyalty of master to servant, employer to employee, seller to buyer, powerful to vulnerable).[43]

Fiduciary roles were likened to the roles of stewards in early religious and business history as well as in later corporate development. In this context, "Fiduciary law secularized a particular religious tradition and applied it to commercial pursuits," where the shepherd tending his flocks may be likened to a fiduciary (steward or employer) or an agent (servant or employee) tending the sheep for the owner of the flock.[44] The "steward," may be described as a moral agent or representative of "God," a corporate partner or stakeholder whose profits could be distributed by the steward to the poor at year's end.[45] Also, the King (as steward) was described as God's representative responsible for administering the covenant (agreements) for the people, and who must avoid preoccupation with the trappings of office while observing the law.[46] Thus, the king may be described as a model of godliness to the people by governing in a way that conforms to the requirements of the covenant.[47]

The increasing complexity in fiduciary relationships over time is equated to the increasing complexity in the relationship between man and God (as owner) in early biblical history. The relationships change as a function of the increase in the complexity of the duties demanded of the steward (manager of covenants). Similarly, the steward is the precursor to the modern professional fiduciary as well as to those corporate directors or officers who owe a duty of care to the owners (shareholders) of the corporation as well as a duty of loyalty to all stakeholders and to the larger society. Stewards, or fiduciaries, "hold offices with authority, power and privileges set by law or custom, separate from individual personalities, and such office demands moral duties in private conduct, requiring new decision-making habits and reflective capacities that transcend selfishness."[48] Similar to the descriptions of fiduciaries by Justices Cardozo and Brandeis, the description of stewards implies an inherent willingness to serve others (a moral duty), and a willingness to subordinate one's interests to that of others by acceptance of the duty to serve. Both in early law and today, the fiduciary, or steward, is evaluated and compensated for his performance and understands that failure to fulfill his duties will result in penalties. While today's corporations seldom attribute morality to a deity in fiduciary law, acceptance of fiduciary duties does require selflessness and a willingness to subordinate the fiduciary's interests to that of another. Aristotle, who lived from 384 B.C. to 322 B.C., influenced the development of fiduciary principles, recognizing that in economics and business, people must be bound by high obligations of loyalty, honesty and fairness, and that when such obligations aren't required or followed, society suffers.[49]

Fiduciaries in Ancient Law

Modern fiduciary law is traceable to developments in Ancient Roman law and early English law. Ancient Roman law defined fiduciary relationships as both moral and legal relationships of trust. For centuries until the end of the eighteenth century, Roman law refined and formalized fiduciary law, recognizing various "trust" (*fiducia*) contracts in which a person held property in safekeeping or otherwise acted on another's behalf (the core duties of loyalty and due care), and acted in good "faith" (*fides*) (core duties of honesty, full disclosure and applied diligence). Failure to uphold such trust could result in monetary penalties as well as a formal "infamy" (*infamia*), in which one lost rights to hold public office or to be a witness in a legal case.[50] These fiduciary relationships in early Roman law were later incorporated into British courts of equity and then into Anglo-American law, providing standards for modern corporate law.[51]

Early English law established the role of steward or agent with the granting of the Magna Carta, an English legal charter issued in 1215 which allowed the King to grant charters (companies) yet retain sovereignty (ownership) in the charter while recognizing the recipient's limited rights.[52] The King served as steward, with fiduciary rights (ownership) in the management of his property but was required to place the interests of his subjects (inferior rights) above his own—a fiduciary relationship. Increasing population growth caused the King to transfer his role as steward to town leaders, creating an early form of agency (master to servant). Scholars describe the king's stewardship duties as similar to the legal or fiduciary duties ascribed primarily to boards of directors and senior officers.[53] Town leaders were similar to "agents" or employees who owed duties to their "stewards" or employers (managers). The continued development of Charter companies and later private companies, during the era of industrialization and specialization in business of the 1700s–1800s, formalized the role of fiduciaries and their specific duties.

Early common law separated management from ownership (investors), creating the office of "manager" to protect the interests of investors and to prevent corporate self-dealing.[54] Subsequently, fiduciary duties were attached to such office, and stewardship duties were borrowed from early law and applied to positions of responsibility to promote financial goals. Thus, although a "fiduciary" is a term described by legal statute, case law or professional codes of conduct, this term also describes ethical obligations and duties in a wide variety of business and personal activities and encompasses a "legal or moral recognition of trust, reliance, or dependence and of responsibility often ignored." [55]

A Modest Proposal: New Rules of Fiduciary Conduct

Legal standards for management behavior can be traced to "deeply rooted moral standards" that shaped the "fiduciary principle, a principle of natural law incorporated into the Anglo-American legal tradition underlying the duties of good faith, loyalty and care that apply to corporate directors and officers."[56] Scholars examined early fiduciary history as a potential solution to understanding corporate misconduct, suggesting that revisiting those early fiduciary principles might answer the questions: To what standards should managers be held? What are the historical and conceptual bases for these standards?[57] Alternatively, if one assumes that fiduciaries are responsible to the company's shareholders as well as to a wider set of constituents, one might ask questions such as: In whose interests does the company presently function? In whose interests should it function in the future?[58] The latter set of questions not only asks who is served by the company, but also suggests that stakeholders bear some general rights as citizens, and should be protected against an abuse of power or violation that causes injury, as citizens.

If the role of a fiduciary is ascribed only to corporate boards and officers or to licensed professionals, corporate misconduct at other levels may go undetected. Despite this, corporate management argues that directors and officers are responsible only to shareholders, and that corporate management cannot serve two masters, that is multiple groups of stakeholders. To the contrary, history has demonstrated that fiduciary duties have been and can be the responsibility of all corporate members, and these duties may be extended to all stakeholders and the larger society. Research supports the theory that the corporation

should have one set of duties for multiple stakeholders, an argument made by managers in the 1990s that managers had the skills and independence to mediate fairly among the firm's stakeholders, and could assemble innovative teams capable of expanding wealth and economic opportunity.[59] Managers sustained this claim well into the 1990s, both within their firms and within their major business associations but by 1997 pressure from the global commodity and national financial markets persuaded managers to revise their stakeholder standard. The perception is that managers moved from a focus on a single duty of loyalty to shareholders, to a narrower focus on making their principals (shareholders) and themselves rich, while disassociating themselves from the ideal of widening economic opportunity and improving living standards for the many.[60] The Clarkson Principles, a set of principles for stakeholder management, are considered to be a critical academic effort to revive the idea that managers should be obligated to expand material opportunities for the many through economic growth.[61] Additionally, compliance with fiduciary duties can reduce the principal's costs of monitoring and disciplining agents and lessens the need for government regulation.[62]

Today, although most major corporations support the idea of corporate social responsibility (CSR), and believe that CSR and profit maximization work together, they continue to support the Freidman view that "The social responsibility of business is to increase its profits."[63] A top executive of a major oil company illustrates this view in the comment that "a socially responsible way or working is not . . . a distraction from our core business. Nor does it in any way conflict with our promise and our duty to deliver value to our shareholders."[64]

We propose that adherence to a *new understanding and rule* of fiduciary principles goes hand in hand with CSR and profit maximization and is perhaps the missing link in today's corporate governance. The essential definition of a fiduciary does not change—a fiduciary is a person who has a duty to act primarily for the benefit of another. However, the role of the fiduciary should extend to all corporate members, and the duties of the fiduciary should not differ regardless of the specific function or distinction in roles. The primary focus of all corporate members continues to be to the shareholders (owners of the corporation), but duties toward other stakeholders should be consistent with those duties to shareholders. Any differentiation lowers the high standard of fidelity required of fiduciaries. Thus, the duties of loyalty, good faith, due care and obedience to the law should be incorporated fully into all fiduciary relationships, regardless of role or function within the corporation.

Concluding Thoughts

"Many of the most shocking examples of corporate misbehaviors involve conduct that violates existing law."[65] This result occurs when most cost-benefit analysis weighs the potential harm and subsequent penalties against the potential profits, resulting in an ethical question often ignored because of the focus on maximizing shareholder profitability. Therefore, reform initiatives for boards of directors and corporate governance "without proper attention to ethical obligations will likely prove ineffectual."[66] Schwartz et al. found that board and officer leadership by example and action are roles central to the overall ethical and governance environment of their firms, a leadership role that is reinforced by board members' legal responsibilities to provide oversight of the financial performance of their firms—based on the assumption that ethical corporate leadership results in the best long-term interests of the firm.

Thus, Schwartz et al.'s study of corporate boards of directors demonstrated that boards have a professional duty expressed as a fiduciary duty to make ethics-based decisions. We contend that ethics and morals in line with fiduciary principles *must* permeate the entire corporate culture, if corporate governance reform is to succeed. A return to those central values inherent in ethical and fiduciary duties extended to the greater community as well as to shareholders may provide more socially responsible guidelines for corporations in this period of stakeholder demand for increased government regulation. Defining and providing examples of fiduciary values of honesty, loyalty, integrity responsibility, fairness, and citizenship can provide guidance for corporate fiduciary relationships with all stakeholders, and provide a more efficient voluntary control mechanism. Thus, we contend that consistent fiduciary principles should be implemented throughout the firm, regardless of the corporate member's function or role.[67] This view is consistent with Friedman's view, that a corporate executive is an employee of the owners of the business, owes responsibility to his employers to conduct the business in accordance with their desires, which generally will be to make as much money as possible while conforming to the basic rules of society, embodied both in law and ethical custom.[68]

Our review of the historical and religious origins of fiduciary relationships demonstrates that the concept of fiduciary was intended to be both a societal and a legal principle, and this is consistent with Friedman's view of obeying the law and social custom. The leaders of organizations, as stewards, were responsible to the whole organization, and to society, not just to themselves or shareholders. Perhaps a revitalization of the stewardship principle is part of the new perspective required to create sustainable competitive advantage in today's economy. We believe that there is room for stakeholder-focused management that does no harm to shareholder interests while also benefiting a larger constituency, *and* that fiduciary duties require the exercise of care, loyalty, obedience, and good faith with regard to shareholders as well as to all stakeholders and the larger community.[69]

References

1. See David Callahan, *The Cheating Culture: Why More Americans are Doing Wrong to Get Ahead* (Florida: Harcourt, Inc., 2004), 12.
2. See LaRue Tone Hosmer, *The Ethics of Management, 6th Ed.* (New York: McGraw-Hill, 2008).
3. Peter C. Kostant, *Meaningful Good Faith: Managerial Motives and the Duty to Obey the Law,* 55 N.Y.L.S.L. Rev., 421 (2010).
4. Alan R. Palmiter, *Duty of Obedience: The Forgotten Duty,* 55 N.Y.L.S.L. Rev., 457 (2010).
5. Restatement (Third) of Agency, 3rd Ed. §1(1). (2006), Restatement Third of Agency is a set of principles issues by the American Law Institute, frequently cited by judges as well as attorneys and scholars in making legal arguments.
6. Nancy Kubasek et al., *Dynamic Business Law* (New York: McGraw-Hill/Irwin, 2009), 856,857.
7. Tamar Frankel, *Fiduciary Law,* 71 Cal. L. Rev. 795, 797–802 (1983).
8. See Tamar Frankel, *Fiduciary Law,* 71 Cal. L. Rev., 801–802.
9. See note 8.
10. Deborah A. DeMott, "The First Restatement of Agency: What Was the Agenda?," 32 *S. Ill. U.L.J.,* (2007). Restatement (Second) of Agency, 1958, the American Law Institute, is now out of print and has been completely superseded and replaced by Restatement of the Law Third, Agency, 2006. However, some courts will continue to cite to The Restatement of the Law Second, Agency.
11. Deborah A. DeMott, "The First Restatement of Agency: What Was the Agenda?," 31.
12. Kenneth M. Rosen, *Meador Lecture Series 2005–2006: Fiduciaries,* 58 Ala. L. Rev., 1041 (2007).
13. Kenneth M. Rosen, *Meador Lecture Series 2005–2006: Fiduciaries,* citing *Meinhard v. Salmon,* 164 N.E. 545 (N.Y. 1928).
14. Kenneth M. Rosen, *Meador Lecture Series 2005–2006: Fiduciaries,* 1041.
15. See Kenneth M. Rosen, "*Meador Lecture Series 2005–2006: Fiduciaries.*"
16. *See In re* Walt Disney Co. Deriv. Litig., 907 A.2d 693, 753–57 (Del. Ch. 2005) (identifying possible duty of good faith), *aff'd,* 906 A.2d 693 (Del. 2006) (affirming the decision of the Chancellor).
17. Michael Follett, "Note: *Gantler V. Stephens:* Big Epiphany or Big Failure? A look at the current state of officers' fiduciary duties and advice for potential protection," *35 Del. J. Corp. L.,* 563 (2010).
18. Sarbanes-Oxley Act of 2002, PL 107–204, 116 Stat 745. Sarbanes-Oxley requires corporate officers to be responsible for earnings reports, prohibits accounting firms from acting as consultants to accounting clients (a conflict of interest) and increases penalties for fraud.
19. The Dodd-Frank Wall Street Reform and Consumer Protection Act, Pub.L. 111–203, H.R. 4173, (2010).

Fiduciary Principles: Corporate Responsibilities to Stakeholders by Susan C. Atherton, Mark S. Blodgett, and Charles A. Atherton

51

20. Kilpatrick Stockton LLP, *Directors Fiduciary Duties After Sarbanes-Oxley* (Atlanta: Kilpatrick Stockton LLP), 2003.

21. Delaware General Corporation Law section 141(a) provides that "[t]he business and affairs of every corporation organized under this chapter shall be managed by or under the direction of a board of directors, except as may be otherwise provided in this chapter or in its certificate of incorporation." DEL. CODE ANN. Tit. 8, § 141(a)(2006).

22. See Michael Follett, note 57.

23. Michael Follett, note 57.

24. Alan R. Palmiter, citing *Stone v. Ritter,* 911 A.2d 362, 364–65 (Del. 2006), *Graham V. Allis-Chalmers Mfg. Co.,* 188 A.2d 125, 130 (Del. 1963), and *Caremark Int'l Inc. Deriv. Litig.,* 698 A.2d 959, 971 (Del. Ch. 1996), where directors breached the duty of care for "sustained or systematic failure" to assure existence of reporting systems that identify illegal corporate conduct, for example, medical referral kickbacks, 459.

25. *In re* Walt Disney Co. Deriv. Litig., 907 A.2d 693, 753 (Del. Ch. 2005), aff'd. 906 A.2d 27 (Del. 2006).

26. Thomas A. Uebler, "Shareholder Police Power: Shareholders' Ability to Hold Directors Accountable for Intentional Violations of Law," 33 Del. J. Corp. L., 199 (2008).

27. Thomas A. Uebler, "Shareholder Police Power: Shareholders' Ability to Hold Directors Accountable for Intentional Violations of Law," 201.

28. See Thomas A. Uebler.

29. *In re* Walt Disney Co. Deriv. Litig., 907 A.2d 693, 753–57 (Del. Ch. 2005), *aff'd,* 906 A.2d 693 (Del. 2006) .

30. *In re* Walt Disney Co. Deriv. Litig., 907 A.2d 693, 753 (Del. Ch. 2005), aff'd. 906 A.2d 27 (Del. 2006)), quoting *Sinclair Oil Corp. v. Levien,* 280 A.2d 717, 720 (Del. 1971), and *Smith v. Van Gorkom,* 488 A.2d 858, 873 (Del. 1985),

31. *In re* Walt Disney.

32. *In re* Walt Disney, at 55.

33. Peter C. Kostant , "Meaningful Good Faith: Managerial Motives and the Duty to Obey the Law," 424,426.

34. See Peter C. Kostant, 426–427.

35. Amanda H. Podany, "Why Study History? A View from the Past," Presented at The History Summit I, California State University Dominguez Hills, May 29, 2008.

36. See Kenneth Silber, "Fiduciary Matters," www.AdvisorOne .com/article/fiduciarymatters, June 28, 2011.

37. Joseph F. Johnston, Jr., "Natural Law and the Fiduciary Duties of Managers," *Journal of Markets & Morality* (2005), 8:27–51.

38. Kenneth Silber, "Fiduciary Matters."

39. See Brian P. Schaefer, "Shareholders Social Responsibility," *Journal of Business Ethics* (2008), 81:297–312; and Stephen B. Young, "Fiduciary Duties as a Helpful Guide to Ethical Decision-Making in Business," *Journal of Business Ethics* (2007), 74:1–15.

40. John H. Walton, Deuteronomy: An Exposition of the Spirit of the Law, *Grace Theological Journal* 8, 2(1987), 213–25, quoting Leviticus 6:2–5.

41. See John H. Walton, quoting Deuteronomy 25:13–16.

42. John H. Walton notes that the precept that one cannot serve two masters in Luke 16:1–13 was later cited by scholar Austin Scott in an influential 1949 paper "The Fiduciary Principle," which describes boards' and officers' responsibility to shareholders and not to other constituents.

43. John H. Walton, "Deuteronomy: An Exposition of the Spirit of the Law," quoting Deuteronomy 24:14–15.

44. See Stephen B. Young, "Fiduciary Duties as a Helpful Guide to Ethical Decision-Making in Business."

45. Sarah Key, "Toward a New Theory of the Firm: A Critique of Stakeholder 'Theory'," *Management Decision* (1999), 37:317–328.

46. John H. Walton, quoting Deuteronomy 17:14–20, 216.

47. Stephen B. Young details the link between fiduciary and ethical duties in the four covenants, or agreements, between God and man in the Old Testament that establishes and expands man's duties of care. These covenants allow stewards to impose ethical duties on those who obey them (i.e., agents or employees) and reflect the core of modern agency and fiduciary relationships: (1) The first covenant establishes Noah as steward of God's will to care for creation, and if Noah and his descendents take good care of creation it would not be destroyed (duty of care for the owner's property); (2) The second covenant requires Abraham to accept the duty to behave according to a code of holy behavior in return for protection (protection from liability for accepting the responsibilities of duty of loyalty and care); (3) The third covenant requires the children of Israel to behave morally with religious devotion in return for protection of all of society (extending fiduciary duties of loyalty and care from an individual to society, i.e., to all stakeholders); and (4) The fourth covenant expanded these promises–if the conduct of all mankind is ethical and moral and not based on material temptations, Jesus will protect them on earth and grant them entry into heaven (fiduciary duties are deeply rooted in moral principles).

48. See Stephen B. Young and Joseph F. Johnston, Jr.

49. John H. Walton, "Deuteronomy: An Exposition of the Spirit of the Law."

50. See Kenneth Silber, "Fiduciary Matters."

51. See Kenneth M. Rosen, *Meador Lecture Series 2005–2006: Fiduciaries.*

52. See Stephen B. Young, "Fiduciary Duties as a Helpful Guide to Ethical Decision-Making in Business."

53. See Kenneth M. Rosen, "Meador Lecture Series 2005–2006: Fiduciaries."

54. Richard Marens and Andrew Wicks, "Getting Real: Stakeholder Theory, Managerial Practice, and the General Irrelevance of Fiduciary Duties Owed to Shareholders," *Business Ethics Quarterly* (1999), 273–293.

55. Sarah W. Holtman, "Fiduciary Relationships," in The Encyclopedia of Ethics, 2nd Ed, eds. Lawrence C. Becker and Charlotte B. Becker (NY: Routledge, 2001), 545–49.

56. See Joseph F. Johnston, Jr., "Natural Law and the Fiduciary Duties of Business Managers."

57. See Joseph F. Johnston, Jr. "Natural Law and the Fiduciary Duties of Business Managers."

58. Sheldon Leader, "Participation and Property Rights," *Journal of Business Ethics* 21:97–109, (1999), 98–99.

59. Allan Kaufman, "Managers' Double Fiduciary Duty," *Business Ethics Quarterly* 12:189–214 (2002), 189.

60. Allan Kaufman, "Managers' Double Fiduciary Duty," 190.
61. Allan Kaufman, "Managers' Double Fiduciary Duty," 190–193.
62. Kaufman, "Managers' Double Fiduciary Duty."
63. See Peter C. Kolstad, 137–138, citing Milton Friedman, "The Social Responsibility of Business is to Increase Its Profits," The New York Times Magazine (New York: 1970).
64. See Allan Kaufman, 192.
65. See David Callahan, "The Cheating Culture: Why More Americans are Doing Wrong to Get Ahead."
66. Mark S. Schwartz et al., "Tone at the Top: An Ethics Code for Directors?," Journal of Business Ethics (2005), 58:79–100.
67. R. Edward Freeman, in "The Politics of Stakeholder Theory: Some Future Directors," Business Ethics Quarterly (1994) 4:409–421, suggested that "multi-fiduciary stakeholder analysis is simply incompatible with widely-held moral convictions about the special fiduciary obligations owed by management to stockholders. At the center of the objections is the belief that the obligations of agents to principals are stronger or different in kind from those of agents to third parties." This view is not supported by historical development of the fiduciary principle, and may be perceived more as a function of corporate management choosing those functions that support personal, not fiduciary, goals.
68. See Milton Friedman, 51.
69. Bradley R. Agle and Ronald K. Mitchell, "Introduction: Recent Research and New Questions," in Agle et al., "Dialogue: Toward Superior Stakeholder Theory," Business Ethics Quarterly (2008), 18:153–190.

Critical Thinking

1. Describe the fiduciary duties of officers and directors? of managers? of employees?
2. What safeguards should be employed to assure the fulfillment of the above fiduciary duties?
3. What ethical principles undergird fiduciary principles?

Internet References

Business for Social Responsibility
http://www.bsr.org/reports/BSR_AW_Corporate-Boards.pdf
Forbes
http://www.forbes.com/sites/csr/2010/10/28/friend-or-foe-fiduciary-duties-meet-sociallyresponsible-investments/
United States Department of Labor
http://www.dol.gov/ebsa/publications/fiduciaryresponsibility.html

Article   Prepared by: Eric Teoro, *Lincoln Christian University*

The CSR Litmus Test

Ask yourself some questions before blithely tossing around the term "Corporate Social Responsibility."

CHRIS MACDONALD

Learning Outcomes

After reading this article, you will be able to:

- Understand your own definition of corporate social responsibility (CSR).

- Question the value of CSR as a concept.

- Question what responsibilities businesses should fulfill.

I've complained *ad nauseum* about the fact that there's no clear, agreed-upon definition of CSR (Corporate Social Responsibility). Many definitions say something about "social contribution" or "giving back to the community." But just what that amounts to is up for grabs. It might mean something trivial, or it might mean something unfairly burdensome. In a forthcoming short article in *Canadian Business,* I riff on a recent *Globe and Mail* story about a South African winery that is working hard to face up to its slave-holding past. The winery's story serves as a nice example. The Solms-Delta winery's owners have done things like set up a museum in its wine cellar, and establish a trust for the benefit of workers. This is clearly admirable; other South African wineries generally prefer to sweep the past under a rug. But your particular reaction to the story of Solms-Delta is also a good way to delve into your own understanding of the term "Corporate Social Responsibility." Consider: Is highlighting the past as the company is doing an *obligation* owed to the winery's current employees? If so, then Solms-Delta is simply meeting its ethical obligations. But if this is not something owed to current employees, then it seems better cast as a matter of *social responsibility*. Right? To push this theme

further, let's move from the Solms-Delta example and consider a hypothetical company. Here's a litmus test to help you figure out your own views about CSR, and what those views imply. So imagine a company that does all of the following, with reasonable consistency:

- . . . makes a decent product that people feel improves their lives in some small but meaningful way;
- . . . treats employees fairly;
- . . . deals honestly with suppliers;
- . . . tries to do a decent job of building long-term shareholder value;
- . . . cleans up their messes, environmental, or otherwise;
- . . . does its best to follow all applicable laws, and trains and rewards employees suitably;
- . . . pays its taxes, making use of all relevant exemptions but not cynically seeking loopholes.

Next, if you consider yourself a fan of CSR, ask yourself this question: Would such a company count as a *socially responsible* company, in your books? Or is there something more it needs to do in order to garner that designation? Is the company ethically obligated to do something further? If your answer is "Yes, that's a socially responsible company!" then good for you. That's a very reasonable answer. But then you should ask yourself two questions. One, why are you attached to the label "CSR"? Why not just call them a company that does right, or that acts ethically? Why try to shoehorn all the good stuff listed above into a specific little box called "social responsibility"? If your answer is "No, they're still not giving back to the community!" then next you need to ask yourself *what more* and *why*. The company described above is engaging in voluntary, mutually advantageous transactions with customers, making those customers better off (by their own lights). It is doing something good in the world, and being conscientious about how it does it. That seems pretty decent. And whatever your answer is, taking this test should clarify both what your own views are, and perhaps why the term "CSR" is far less useful than it is popular. And whenever two people *think* they agree on the importance of CSR, each of them ought to doubt—or ask—whether they really share the *same understanding* of what social responsibility really means.

Critical Thinking

1. What responsibilities to the broader community do businesses have beyond providing their specific goods and services? Why?

2. As an employee, what, if any, social responsibilities are you obligated to fulfill? Why?

3. Debate with a fellow student/employee that businesses are obligated to give more to communities than their specific goods and services.

Create Central

www.mhhe.com/createcentral

Internet References

Houston Chronicle: Small Business
http://smallbusiness.chron.com/social-responsibility-advertising-52880.html

International Institute for Sustainable Development
https://www.iisd.org/business/issues/sr.aspx

Article   Prepared by: Eric Teoro, *Lincoln Christian University*

The Four Principles of 'Conscious Capitalism'

R. MICHAEL ANDERSON

Learning Outcomes

After reading this article, you will be able to:

- Recognize that doing business the "right way" is not incompatible with being profitable.

- Describe the four principles of Conscious Capitalism.

If you had a chance to implement a system that would bring in 10 times more profit than similar firms in your market, would your first thought be about what you'd have to give up to do so? What part of your soul you'd have to sell?

The truth is that by doing business the right way—being truly authentic, sticking wholeheartedly to your ethics and morals, and caring more about your customers and employees than your shareholders—you can achieve that gain *without* losing your soul.

Conscious Capitalism is the system that lets you do this. I know, because we launched Conscious Capitalism San Diego last week (disclosure: I'm president of the board of directors). As the 20th local chapter worldwide, the results are clear: Conscious Capitalism companies don't only outperform the market by 10.5 times, they even outperformed the Good to Great companies such as Fannie Mae and Walgreens by 300 percent—by doing business the "right way."

Imagine that: you don't have to give anything up to become a market leader.

In fact, you can be the good guy.

There are four principles of Conscious Capitalism.

1. Conscious leadership

Organizations mirror the actions and personality of the individual at the top. This is the kind of person people want to follow. The authentic, open person. Conscious Leaders are the ones who inspire loyalty and consistent high performance in their teams.

2. Stakeholder orientation

Conscious leaders know the importance of taking into account *all* of their stakeholders. You're never going to become a premium brand by only focusing on the shareholders. The really important factors for long-term business success are the employees and customers, and often the vendors and community as well. Take care of them and they will take care of you.

3. Conscious culture

A values-based culture is one that is intentional about how people act and perform. When a culture is not defined and enforced, your people aren't all moving in the same direction.

For example, Greg Koch, the CEO of Stone Brewing Co. and one of the speakers at our inaugural event, talked about how he would rather leave a key position unfilled than bring in someone not 100 percent aligned with his firm's values and mission. He explained that not having that position filled hurt, but it was better than the alternative. Stone Brewing Co. is now one of the top micro-brewing house[s] in the U.S.—it's even expanding into Germany.

4. Higher purpose

Finally, the company should be in business to do more than just make money. Great leaders realize that in order to become successful over the long term, you must provide true value. That comes from passionate people getting inspired about their work. How inspiring is your company's purpose? For example, would you want to work for a company whose mission it is to "deliver maximum value to the shareholders"?

I wouldn't either.

Coach John Wooden famously never talked about winning. He talked about doing your best. And you know what? He won. More than anyone.

That's what we're talking about with Conscious Capitalism. Quit trying to play someone else's game. Be true to yourself, your customers, your employees. And you will be rewarded.

Those who chase the almighty dollar never find it.

Andrew Hewitt of Game Changers 500, another speaker at the launch, puts it in perspective: "A 2013 Cone Communications-Echo study found that only 20 percent of brands worldwide are seen to meaningfully and positively impact people's lives, yet 91 percent of global consumers would switch brands if a different brand of similar price and quality supported a good cause."

"With this huge gap between societal values and corporate values it's no wonder that purpose-driven organizations are far outperforming the pack. Doing good has become good business, not only because of changing consumer values but also because good companies are attracting the top talent, particularly millennials who are estimated to make up 75 percent of the global workforce by 2025."

The fact is, many business leaders are already living these principles without even knowing it. If you're one of them, now you know you're not alone.

It isn't just the "right" thing to do.

It's also the *profitable* thing to do.

Critical Thinking

1. What does it take to become a conscious leader?
2. What values would characterize a conscious corporate culture?
3. Choose five companies in five different industries. Write higher purpose statements for each company.

Internet References

Bloomberg Business
   http://www.bloomberg.com/news/articles/2015-02-19/container-store-conscious-capitalism-and-the-perils-of-going-public

Fast Company
   http://www.fastcompany.com/3031509/the-future-of-work/5-myths-about-the-freshest-iteration-of-capitalism

Forbes
   http://www.forbes.com/sites/danschawbel/2013/01/15/john-mackey-why-companies-should-embrace-conscious-capitalism/

Article

Prepared by: Eric Teoro, *Lincoln Christian University*

Business Rx: Here's Why, Ethically, You Should Stop Bashing Business

RAJSHREE AGARWAL

Learning Outcomes

After reading this article, you will be able to:

- Appreciate the value that business leaders offer society.
- Describe five lessons regarding value creation.

Society appreciates athletes and entertainers. When they use their talents to get rich, fans applaud their success. The opposite happens when business leaders use their brains and industry to earn equally big paychecks.

Rather than receiving thanks for expanding economic opportunity, successful business leaders face suspicion and sometimes scorn. Many people view them, not as givers who create value, but as takers who exploit human and natural resources.

The tension grows as corporate salaries increase. People root for underdogs struggling to launch start-ups in their parents' garage. But as soon as these risk takers achieve wealth—precisely because they are productive—then public sentiment sours and these entrepreneurs often find themselves lumped in with the perceived evil establishment of business.

Few dare to speak up as champions of enterprise in such an environment. Even within business schools, some professors view profit as a necessary evil—or worse—even while teaching aspiring managers the pragmatics of how to make money with finance, marketing and strategy.

Instead of all the handwringing and guilt, business schools should teach their students to celebrate accomplishment. This can be done, in part, by supplementing the core curriculum with a broader foundation in ethics.

Business students already learn about the need for honesty and integrity. But they also need to be given historical and philosophical perspectives to help them understand the role of enterprise and markets in both the creation of value and its distribution.

Far too many of our ethical lessons these days are focused on how value ought to be distributed, while not thinking about the principles required to create value in the first place. What follows are five often-overlooked lessons that future business leaders need to know.

1. **Don't substitute money for purpose.** Author Dan Pink lays out the research on what really motivates high performers when they tackle complex problems. Their real objectives are threefold: Autonomy, the ability to be self-directed; mastery, the ability to get better at something; and purpose, the ability to make a meaningful contribution. People focused on these motivators use business to organize their time and create value. They earn self-esteem and lead a rich life, in more ways than one. Aspiring executives who are focused on money alone typically perform worse or burn out when challenges arise.

2. **Keep it win-win.** Ethical business is based on voluntary trade. Nothing is forced. Internally, companies create social structures that allow people to pursue their passions to the best of their abilities. Engineers, accountants and sales managers have different talents, but they can all find their places within the same organization and do what they enjoy while contributing to corporate profits. Employees and shareholders both win. Externally, customers choose where they spend their time and money. They get what they want, and so do the companies that serve them. When one side loses—or when participation becomes coerced—then results are not sustainable. Business leaders who want long and satisfying careers cannot take shortcuts.

3. **Business combats poverty.** The unproductive rich do not need capitalism. Through cronyism and the purchase of political favors, they will thrive. The poor lack access to these backroom deals and generally suffer when government decides to pick economic winners and losers. History is filled with examples. The poor have the most to gain when businesses are allowed to trade freely, because only then can they flourish based on merit and upward mobility rather than privilege and status-quo. As businesses thrive, economic conditions improve for everyone. I have seen this firsthand in my native India, where conditions of extreme poverty have softened in the post-liberalization era. Many politicians don't like to acknowledge it, but voluntary trade combats poverty better than government programs—even the ones established in the name of fighting poverty.

4. **Philanthropy is not penance.** Productive business leaders tend to be benevolent. When they see a need, they want to provide solutions. This mindset extends to their philanthropy. Yet instead of thanking them for their giving, many beneficiaries view philanthropy as an obligation or form of penance for extracting profits from society. People who hated Bill Gates as chief executive of Microsoft love his work with the Gates Foundation. This line of thinking discounts the value that comes through core commercial activities—regardless of what gets designated as "corporate social responsibility." In terms of economic impact, Microsoft has improved more lives than the Gates Foundation. Business also generates the profits that make philanthropy possible, giving society a second layer of benefits. So give thanks and expect it in return, both for the initial creation of value and the philanthropy that often follows.

5. **You are worth it.** Many people can sing, dance or play sports, but only elite performers merit lucrative contracts. All-Pros such as New England Patriots quarterback Tom Brady earn more than players on the practice squad—regardless of who works the hardest—because the NFL has short supply and high demand for great play callers. The same principle applies in business. Markets generally pay people what they are worth based on supply and demand. Companies pay big salaries to executives because they bring rare talent to the C suite, where decisions affect entire organizations. One bad leader can destroy a company, while good leaders can create enduring value. Think about the contributions of Henry Ford, Thomas Edison and Steve Jobs. These innovators are no longer alive to collect income, but society still benefits from their work. So if your paycheck has several figures after the dollar sign, congratulations! You probably earned it. If not, beware. The market will soon catch up to you like a one-hit wonder or NFL draft bust.

Critical Thinking

1. Debate with a classmate the legitimacy of high corporate salaries.

2. Choose three businesses in different industries. Describe how they generate value for society through their products or services.

3. Describe how business fights poverty.

Internet References

Fast Company
    http://www.fastcompany.com/resources/columnists/vgct/071904.html

Norfund
    http://www.norfund.no/businesses-poverty-alleviation/category449.html

The Business Ethics Blog
    http://businessethicsblog.com/2011/10/18/are-ceo-salaries-too-high/

Rajshree Agarwal, PhD, is academic director of the Ed Snider Center for Enterprise and Markets at the University of Maryland's Robert H. Smith School of Business.

Agarwal, Rajshree, "Business Rx: Here's Why, Ethically, You Should Stop Bashing Business," *The Washington Post*, March 18, 2015. Copyright © 2015 by Rajshree Agrawal. Used with permission.

Article   Prepared by: Eric Teoro, *Lincoln Christian University*

The Social Responsibility of Business Is to Increase Its Profits

MILTON FRIEDMAN

Learning Outcomes

After reading this article, you will be able to:

- Describe Friedman's position regarding the primary responsibility of a corporate executive.
- Describe Friedman's concerns regarding the popular understanding of social responsibility.

When I hear businessmen speak eloquently about the "social responsibilities of business in a free-enterprise system," I am reminded of the wonderful line about the Frenchman who discovered at the age of 70 that he had been speaking prose all his life. The businessmen believe that they are defending free enterprise when they declaim that business is not concerned "merely" with profit but also with promoting desirable "social" ends; that business has a "social conscience" and takes seriously its responsibilities for providing employment, eliminating discrimination, avoiding pollution and whatever else may be the catchwords of the contemporary crop of reformers. In fact they are—or would be if they or anyone else took them seriously—preaching pure and unadulterated socialism. Businessmen who talk this way are unwitting puppets of the intellectual forces that have been undermining the basis of a free society these past decades.

The discussions of the "social responsibilities of business" are notable for their analytical looseness and lack of rigor. What does it mean to say that "business" has responsibilities? Only people can have responsibilities. A corporation is an artificial person and in this sense may have artificial responsibilities, but "business" as a whole cannot be said to have responsibilities, even in this vague sense. The first step toward clarity in examining the doctrine of the social responsibility of business is to ask precisely what it implies for whom.

Presumably, the individuals who are to be responsible are businessmen, which means individual proprietors or corporate executives. Most of the discussion of social responsibility is directed at corporations, so in what follows I shall mostly neglect the individual proprietors and speak of corporate executives.

In a free-enterprise, private-property system, a corporate executive is an employee of the owners of the business. He has direct responsibility to his employers. That responsibility is to conduct the business in accordance with their desires, which generally will be to make as much money as possible while conforming to the basic rules of the society, both those embodied in law and those embodied in ethical custom. Of course, in some cases his employers may have a different objective. A group of persons might establish a corporation for an eleemosynary purpose—for example, a hospital or a school. The manager of such a corporation will not have money profit as his objective but the rendering of certain services.

In either case, the key point is that, in his capacity as a corporate executive, the manager is the agent of the individuals who own the corporation or establish the eleemosynary institution, and his primary responsibility is to them.

Needless to say, this does not mean that it is easy to judge how well he is performing his task. But at least the criterion of performance is straight-forward, and the persons among whom a voluntary contractual arrangement exists are clearly defined.

Of course, the corporate executive is also a person in his own right. As a person, he may have many other responsibilities that he recognizes or assumes voluntarily—to his family, his conscience, his feelings of charity, his church, his clubs, his city, his country. He may feel impelled by these responsibilities to devote part of his income to causes he regards as worthy, to refuse to work for particular corporations, even to leave his job, for example, to join his country's armed forces. If we wish, we may refer to some of these responsibilities as "social responsibilities." But in these respects he is acting as a principal, not an agent; he is spending his own money or time or energy, not the money of his employers or the time or energy he has contracted to devote to their purposes. If these are "social responsibilities," they are the social responsibilities of individuals, not of business.

What does it mean to say that the corporate executive has a "social responsibility" in his capacity as businessman? If this statement is not pure rhetoric, it must mean that he is to act in some way that is not in the interest of his employers. For example, that he is to refrain from increasing the price of the product in order to contribute to the social objective of preventing inflation, even though a price increase would be in the best interests of the corporation. Or that he is to make expenditures on reducing pollution beyond the amount that is in the best interests of the corporation or that is required by law in order to contribute to the social objective of improving the environment. Or that, at the expense of corporate profits, he is to hire "hardcore" unemployed instead of better qualified available workmen to contribute to the social objective of reducing poverty.

In each of these cases, the corporate executive would be spending someone else's money for a general social interest. Insofar as his actions in accord with his "social responsibility" reduce returns to stockholders, he is spending their money. Insofar as his actions raise the price to customers, he is spending the customers' money. Insofar as his actions lower the wages of some employees, he is spending their money.

The stockholders or the customers or the employees could separately spend their own money on the particular action if they wished to do so. The executive is exercising a distinct "social responsibility," rather than serving as an agent of the stockholders or the customers or the employees, only if he spends the money in a different way than they would have spent it.

But if he does this, he is in effect imposing taxes, on the one hand, and deciding how the tax proceeds shall be spent, on the other.

This process raises political questions on two levels: principle and consequences. On the level of political principle, the imposition of taxes and the expenditure of tax proceeds are governmental functions. We have established elaborate constitutional, parliamentary and judicial provisions to control these functions, to assure that taxes are imposed so far as possible

in accordance with the preferences and desires of the public—after all, "taxation without representation" was one of the battle cries of the American Revolution. We have a system of checks and balances to separate the legislative function of imposing taxes and enacting expenditures from the executive function of collecting taxes and administering expenditure programs and from the judicial function of mediating disputes and interpreting the law.

Here the businessman—self-selected or appointed directly or indirectly by stockholders—is to be simultaneously legislator, executive and jurist. He is to decide whom to tax by how much and for what purpose, and he is to spend the proceeds—all this guided only by general exhortations from on high to restrain inflation, improve the environment, fight poverty and so on and on.

The whole justification for permitting the corporate executive to be selected by the stockholders is that the executive is an agent serving the interests of his principal. This justification disappears when the corporate executive imposes taxes and spends the proceeds for "social" purposes. He becomes in effect a public employee, a civil servant, even though he remains in name an employee of a private enterprise. On grounds of political principle, it is intolerable that such civil servants—insofar as their actions in the name of social responsibility are real and not just window-dressing—should be selected as they are now. If they are to be civil servants, then they must be elected through a political process. If they are to impose taxes and make expenditures to foster "social" objectives, then political machinery must be set up to make the assessment of taxes and to determine through a political process the objectives to be served.

This is the basic reason why the doctrine of "social responsibility" involves the acceptance of the socialist view that political mechanisms, not market mechanisms, are the appropriate way to determine the allocation of scarce resources to alternative uses.

On the grounds of consequences, can the corporate executive in fact discharge his alleged "social responsibilities?" On the other hand, suppose he could get away with spending the stockholders' or customers' or employees' money. How is he to know how to spend it? He is told that he must contribute to fighting inflation. How is he to know what action of his will contribute to that end? He is presumably an expert in running his company—in producing a product or selling it or financing it. But nothing about his selection makes him an expert on inflation. Will his holding down the price of his product reduce inflationary pressure? Or, by leaving more spending power in the hands of his customers, simply divert it elsewhere? Or, by forcing him to produce less because of the lower price, will it simply contribute to shortages? Even if he could answer these questions, how much cost is he justified in imposing on his stockholders, customers and employees for this social purpose? What is his appropriate share and what is the appropriate share of others?

And, whether he wants to or not, can he get away with spending his stockholders', customers' or employees' money? Will not the stockholders fire him? (Either the present ones or those who take over when his actions in the name of social responsibility have reduced the corporation's profits and the price of its stock.) His customers and his employees can desert him for other producers and employers less scrupulous in exercising their social responsibilities.

This facet of "social responsibility" doctrine is brought into sharp relief when the doctrine is used to justify wage restraint by trade unions. The conflict of interest is naked and clear when union officials are asked to subordinate the interest of their members to some more general purpose. If the union officials try to enforce wage restraint, the consequence is likely to be wildcat strikes, rank-and-file revolts and the emergence of strong competitors for their jobs. We thus have the ironic phenomenon that union leaders—at least in the U.S.—have objected to Government interference with the market far more consistently and courageously than have business leaders.

The difficulty of exercising "social responsibility" illustrates, of course, the great virtue of private competitive enterprise—it forces people to be responsible for their own actions and makes it difficult for them to "exploit" other people for either selfish or unselfish purposes. They can do good—but only at their own expense.

Many a reader who has followed the argument this far may be tempted to remonstrate that it is all well and good to speak of Government's having the responsibility to impose taxes and determine expenditures for such "social" purposes as controlling pollution or training the hard-core unemployed, but that the problems are too urgent to wait on the slow course of political processes, that the exercise of social responsibility by businessmen is a quicker and surer way to solve pressing current problems.

Aside from the question of fact—I share Adam Smith's skepticism about the benefits that can be expected from "those who affected to trade for the public good"—this argument must be rejected on the grounds of principle. What it amounts to is an assertion that those who favor the taxes and expenditures in question have failed to persuade a majority of their fellow citizens to be of like mind and that they are seeking to attain by undemocratic procedures what they cannot attain by democratic procedures. In a free society, it is hard for "evil" people to do "evil," especially since one man's good is another's evil.

I have, for simplicity, concentrated on the special case of the corporate executive, except only for the brief digression on trade unions. But precisely the same argument applies to the newer phenomenon of calling upon stockholders to require corporations to exercise social responsibility (the recent G.M crusade, for example). In most of these cases, what is in effect involved is some stockholders trying to get other stockholders (or customers or employees) to contribute against their will to "social" causes favored by the activists. Insofar as they succeed, they are again imposing taxes and spending the proceeds.

The situation of the individual proprietor is somewhat different. If he acts to reduce the returns of his enterprise in order to exercise his "social responsibility," he is spending his own money, not someone else's. If he wishes to spend his money on such purposes, that is his right and I cannot see that there is any objection to his doing so. In the process, he, too, may impose costs on employees and customers. However, because he is far less likely than a large corporation or union to have monopolistic power, any such side effects will tend to be minor.

Of course, in practice the doctrine of social responsibility is frequently a cloak for actions that are justified on other grounds rather than a reason for those actions.

To illustrate, it may well be in the long-run interest of a corporation that is a major employer in a small community to devote resources to providing amenities to that community or to improving its government. That may make it easier to attract desirable employees, it may reduce the wage bill or lessen losses from pilferage and sabotage or have other worthwhile effects. Or it may be that, given the laws about the deductibility of corporate charitable contributions, the stockholders can contribute more to charities they favor by having the corporation make the gift than by doing it themselves, since they can in that way contribute an amount that would otherwise have been paid as corporate taxes.

In each of these—and many similar—cases, there is a strong temptation to rationalize these actions as an exercise of "social responsibility." In the present climate of opinion, with its widespread aversion to "capitalism," "profits," the "soulless corporation" and so on, this is one way for a corporation to generate goodwill as a by-product of expenditures that are entirely justified on its own self-interest.

It would be inconsistent of me to call on corporate executives to refrain from this hypocritical window-dressing because it harms the foundation of a free society. That would be to call on them to exercise a "social responsibility"! If our institutions, and the attitudes of the public make it in their self-interest to cloak their actions in this way, I cannot summon much indignation to denounce them. At the same time, I can express admiration for those individual proprietors or owners of closely held corporations or stockholders of more broadly held corporations who disdain such tactics as approaching fraud.

Whether blameworthy or not, the use of the cloak of social responsibility, and the nonsense spoken in its name by influential and prestigious businessmen, does clearly harm the foundations of a free society. I have been impressed time and again by the schizophrenic character of many businessmen. They are capable of being extremely far-sighted and clearheaded in matters that are internal to their businesses. They are incredibly short-sighted and muddle-headed in matters that are outside their businesses but affect the possible survival of business in general. This shortsightedness is strikingly exemplified in the calls from many businessmen for wage and price guidelines or controls or income policies. There is nothing that could do more in a brief period to destroy a market system and replace it by a centrally controlled system than effective governmental control of prices and wages.

The short-sightedness is also exemplified in speeches by businessmen on social responsibility. This may gain them kudos in the short run. But it helps to strengthen the already too prevalent view that the pursuit of profits is wicked and immoral and must be curbed and controlled by external forces. Once this view is adopted, the external forces that curb the market will not be the social consciences, however highly developed, of the pontificating executives; it will be the iron fist of Government bureaucrats. Here, as with price and wage controls, businessmen seem to me to reveal a suicidal impulse.

The political principle that underlies the market mechanism is unanimity. In an ideal free market resting on private property, no individual can coerce any other, all cooperation is voluntary, all parties to such cooperation benefit or they need not participate. There are no values, no "social" responsibilities in any sense other than the shared values and responsibilities of individuals. Society is a collection of individuals and of the various groups they voluntarily form.

The political principle that underlies the political mechanism is conformity. The individual must serve a more general social interest—whether that be determined by a church or a dictator or a majority. The individual may have a vote and say in what is to be done, but if he is overruled, he must conform. It is appropriate for some to require others to contribute to a general social purpose whether they wish to or not.

Unfortunately, unanimity is not always feasible. There are some respects in which conformity appears unavoidable, so I do not see how one can avoid the use of the political mechanism altogether.

But the doctrine of "social responsibility" taken seriously would extend the scope of the political mechanism to every human activity. It does not differ in philosophy from the most explicitly collectivist doctrine. It differs only by professing to believe that collectivist ends can be attained without collectivist means. That is why, in my book *Capitalism and Freedom,* I have called it a "fundamentally subversive doctrine" in a free society, and have said that in such a society, "there is one and only one social responsibility of business—to use its resources and engage in activities designed to increase its profits so long as it stays within the rules of the game, which is to say, engages in open and free competition without deception or fraud."

Critical Thinking

1. Do you agree with Friedman's position? Why or why not?

2. Does Friedman advocate maximizing profits regardless of cost or behavior? Defend your answer.

3. Would Friedman support popular notions of corporate social responsibility if such behaviors maximized profits? Why or why not?

Internet References

Becker Friedman Institute (University of Chicago)
https://bfi.uchicago.edu/feature-story/corporate-social-responsibilty-friedmans-view

Huffington Post
http://www.huffingtonpost.com/john-friedman/milton-friedman-was-wrong_b_3417866.html

PhilPapers
http://philpapers.org/archive/COSDMF.pdf

Article   Prepared by: Eric Teoro, *Lincoln Christian University*

Can This Startup Make the Ultimate Ethical T-Shirt?

ADELE PETERS

Learning Outcomes

After reading this article, you will be able to:

- Describe Zady's business model, and relate it to ethical concerns.

- Understand some of the ethical challenges in the garment industry.

Zady is trying to prove that it's possible to manufacture clothing that's good for workers and the environment—and at a reasonable cost.

How do you make a T-shirt that does no harm?

It's not a simple challenge. Growing cotton uses more pesticides than any other crop in the world, and processing the fabric typically involves dumping polluted wastewater into rivers. Garment factories are notorious for the type of negligence that led to the 2013 building collapse in Bangladesh and the death of over 1,000 people—all working on the latest fast fashion, likely to quickly fall apart and end up in a landfill.

A startup called Zady is trying to rethink the entire system and prove that it's possible to do things differently.

"The bottom line of it all is that it's really hard to un-know things once you discover them," says Maxine Bedat, who co-founded Zady with Soraya Darabi. "That was kind of why we have ventured down this crazy but incredibly exciting path."

Every step of the production process happens in the U.S., so the company can better track what's happening—and rely on stricter U.S. regulations. Zady's new T-shirt is made from cotton grown organically in Texas on farms that use compost as fertilizer and natural dips in temperature to kill bugs and defoliate the crops. The bales are sent to small towns in

North Carolina—part of the last vestiges of the former American apparel industry—for spinning, knitting, and non-toxic dyeing. A worker-owned factory sews the shirt.

"It's working entirely backwards from how the industry developed over the past 20 years," says Bedat. "But as a result of going through the reverse process—starting with the farm and working our way forward—we actually were able to make not just a more sustainable product, but a better quality product."

By working domestically, the brand can stay in better communication with the factories, and better monitor quality and design issues. They're also automatically forced into long relationships with suppliers, since so few American apparel manufacturers are left.

"Part of the problem in the fashion industry is that the fashion brands will be with one factory one season, the next season they'll be with the next—it's just kind of the lowest cost provider," she says. "And we're finding that we can develop a much better product by building these relationships over the long term."

They can also easily see how workers are being treated, and avoid a common problem in the industry: A factory in a place like Bangladesh might outsource orders to another factory with human rights issues. "So you have this great relationship with the factory, and a brand might go and take a picture of that factory, but little did you know that the factory is outsourcing somewhere else that doesn't look as pretty or have the same standards," Bedat says.

The fledgling brand has also designed a socially responsible sweater from scratch, using wool from a ranch in Oregon with a carbon management plan. While most industrial sheep ranching—in places like Chinese and Australian deserts—relies on scarce water supplies to irrigate land for grazing, the ranch in Oregon uses rainwater. The wool is cleaned and dyed without the typical polluting processes (a typical wool cleaning plant might create as much daily waste as the sewage from a town of 50,000).

All of these details mean extra production costs. Still, the final product isn't outrageously expensive—the T-shirt is $36, more than you'd pay at Gap, but less than you might spend at some boutiques. And the company is betting that people will pay for the quality and the story.

"It's a challenge when we're competing against people who are paying non-living wages, and we're paying living wages," says Bedat. "But it's about getting a better quality product. And at the end of the day, people—especially in our generation—we have enough clothing. So when we're buying something, we're buying it for a reason."

They're offering a range of clothing from other small, sustainable producers, along with their own brand. They hope to target people beyond those who might already shop at Whole Foods and be well-versed on the challenges of the apparel supply chain.

"We're not just looking at those people who are kind of the do-gooders," she says. "I have to admit I wasn't one. I very readily bought fast fashion brands and incorporated that without any knowledge."

The company's mission, as much as selling clothes, is helping open eyes to the problems. "There are parallels with the tobacco industry," says Bedat. "All of that information was hidden from us, but then once that information came out about what it does to our bodies, the trend kind of changed. The same can happen with apparel. We see we're at the beginning stages of that whole movement. There has been an industry that has hidden this information."

Critical Thinking

1. Do you think Zady's business model is sustainable? Why or why not?
2. Do you think customers will support Zady's mission given the price of its clothing? Why or why not?
3. If Zady's business model is unsustainable due to competition, is it ethical? Why or why not?

Internet References

Ethical Fashion Forum
http://www.ethicalfashionforum.com/the-issues

Wall Street Journal
http://www.wsj.com/articles/made-in-america-from-sheep-to-shelf-zadys-feel-good-sweater-1416847912

Article   Prepared by: Eric Teoro, *Lincoln Christian University*

Price Is Most Important Factor For Consumers, Whatever They May Say About Ethics

Liz Nelson

Learning Outcomes

After reading this article, you will be able to:

- Recognize that there can be a stark difference between the values espoused by consumers and their purchasing behavior.

- Recognize the role of emotional components of behavior when promoting ethical purchasing behavior.

London, July 30, 2014—80 percent of consumers believe it is important for companies and brands to behave ethically, however the most significant factors when shopping are price, value and quality.

Research from online sourcing and optimisation specialists Trade Extensions on UK and US consumers' attitudes towards ethics and sustainability and how they affect purchasing decisions suggests consumers display a 'do as I say, not as I do' attitude towards ethics and sustainability in that they recognise its importance but are ultimately swayed by price.

The ethical behaviour of companies and brands is relevant to consumers and, when asked in isolation, four out of five consumers regard it as important, however it becomes less so when ranked alongside other factors. When asked to rank the three most important attributes when shopping, the most important factor is price—40 percent of consumers ranked this number one. The second most important factor is value for money—30 percent ranked this number one. And the third most important factor is quality—16 percent ranked this number one.

Convenience is more important for shoppers than ethics with 'easy to find/ shop/ delivered' appearing in the top three rankings of 17 percent of consumers compared with ethics appearing in the top three of 12 percent of consumers. Choosing an ethical company or brand when shopping is the most important factor and ranked number one for 2 percent of UK and US consumers.

Despite consumers' relatively low ranking of ethical and sustainability concerns, over 70 percent say they are more likely or much more likely to buy from companies with strong and proven policies on sustainability and ethics. UK and US consumers also say they are willing to pay a premium for sustainably sourced and ethically produced goods and over 60 percent will pay up to 10 percent more. Not all consumers are willing to pay more for ethically produced goods and of the 10 percent of UK consumers who say they will not pay any extra, 73 percent are men.

The opinions of US and UK consumers are broadly similar although there are some notable differences. For example, nearly twice as many US consumers, 14 percent against 8 percent in the UK, say they will never buy a product or service from a company with a poor record on ethics or sustainability. Also, UK men are 40 percent more likely 'not to care about ethics and sustainability' than US men. And of the 5 percent of UK consumers who 'do not care' about ethics and sustainability, 81 percent were men.

Consumers opinions also reflect a degree of scepticism regarding companies' communication of ethical and sustainability policies with only 2 percent of UK consumers 'always' believing what companies tell them on these topics and approximately one third feeling "a lot of companies just say stuff like this to impress but they don't actually do anything."

Behaviour change and research expert, Dr Liz Nelson OBE, said "It's critical to understand the differences between what people think—their attitudes—and what they actually do—their behaviour. The fact they say they care about ethics and sustainability is important and it might make a difference given two otherwise equal choices. But this research shows that only a small number will actively go out of their way to act on those feelings. So the challenge for those trying to change behaviour towards ethical purchasing is to find what can prompt a behaviour change. To do this, businesses have to understand the emotional components of behaviour, and that demands they develop a greater understanding of their consumers' attitudes."

Trade Extensions online sourcing and optimisation platform is used in complex procurement projects and many of its customers are now including 'ethical and sustainability' criteria in projects in order to find sourcing solutions that take these criteria into account while identifying the best solution in terms of price and quality.

Trade Extensions, CEO, Garry Mansell said, "The research shows a desire from consumers to buy ethically but ultimately price, value and quality are the deciding factors. These areas can now be addressed together and the beauty of our platform is that when companies collect ethical and sustainability data from their suppliers it can be included in their final decision making just as they would consider price, quality and any other criteria."

Critical Thinking

1. Describe your purchasing behavior. How often do you consider ethical issues? When do you do so?

2. How can a company influence consumer behavior to include, and pay for, ethical considerations?

Internet References

Ethical Consumer
http://www.ethicalconsumer.org/commentanalysis/consumerism/thepriceofethics.aspx

Guardian
http://www.theguardian.com/sustainable-business/2014/sep/10/consumer-behaviour-sustainability-business

Policy Innovations
http://www.policyinnovations.org/ideas/briefings/data/000199

Dr Liz Nelson OBE FMRS is a pioneer of market research and co-founded market research company Taylor Nelson in 1965. She is a Board Member of the Market Research Society; a Trustee of the Tavistock Institute and is Executive Chairman of Fly Research.

Unit 3

UNIT

Prepared by: Eric Teoro, *Lincoln Christian University*

Building an Ethical Organization

Ethos can be defined as the fundamental character, spirit, or disposition of an individual, group, or culture. It informs, and is manifested in, one's beliefs, customs, aspirations, or practices. For business ethics ultimately to be meaningful, it must transcend momentary reactions or responses to ethical scandals. For business ethics ultimately to be meaningful, it must become part of an organization's ethos. It should guide member behavior on a daily, on-going basis. It should impact strategic decision-making, and shape an organization's inter-actions with all stakeholders. Business ethics should start at the top of an organization, and filter its way throughout every level. It is not a tactic to prevent legal action against an organization, though it might result in fewer lawsuits or govern-mental regulations and interventions. By its nature, business ethics should be proactive and normative, promoting the good for its own sake.

The articles in this unit explore how an organization can embed ethics into its corporate ethos. Authors ask how com-panies measure the success of their ethics and compliance programs. Do they address the seven levels of an ethical orga-nization, inculcating the necessary values at each level? Do business leaders recognize the ambiguity that surrounds many business decisions, equipping their employees to do the right thing? Do they consider issues regarding fairness, expect hon-esty on the part of their employees, and establish incentive and control systems to ensure honest behavior? What types of questions do hiring managers ask during interviews? Do they reinforce the company's position on ethical standards? What messages do CEOs communicate to their workforce through their actions, words, and espoused and enacted values? How can companies utilize technology such as social media to undergird and promote ethics and compliance?

Article   Prepared by: Eric Teoro, *Lincoln Christian University*

Creating an Ethical Culture

Values-based ethics programs can help employees judge right from wrong.

DAVID GEBLER, JD

Learning Outcomes

After reading this article, you will be able to:

- Describe the seven levels of corporate values and how they relate to each other.

- Develop a program for creating an ethical corporate culture.

While the fate of former Enron leaders Kenneth Lay and Jeffrey Skilling is being determined in what has been labeled the "Trial of the Century," former WorldCom managers are in jail for pulling off one of the largest frauds in history.

Yes, criminal activity definitely took place in these companies and in dozens more that have been in the news in recent years, but what's really important is to take stock of the nature of many of the perpetrators.

Some quotes from former WorldCom executives paint a different picture of corporate criminals than we came to know in other eras:

"I'm sorry for the hurt that has been caused by my cowardly behavior."
—*Scott Sullivan, CFO*

"Faced with a decision that required strong moral courage, I took the easy way out. . . . There are no words to describe my shame."
—*Buford Yates, director of general accounting*

"At the time I consider the single most critical character-defining moment of my life, I failed. It's something I'll take with me the rest of my life."
—*David Myers, controller*

These are the statements of good people gone bad. But probably most disturbing was the conviction of Betty Vinson, the senior manager in the accounting department who booked billions of dollars in false expenses. At her sentencing, US District Judge Barbara Jones noted that Vinson was among the lowest-ranking members of the conspiracy that led to the $11 billion fraud that sank the telecommunications company in 2002. Still, she said, "Had Ms. Vinson refused to do what she was asked, it's possible this conspiracy might have been nipped in the bud."

Judge Jones added that although Ms. Vinson "was among the least culpable members of the conspiracy" and acted under extreme pressure, "that does not excuse what she did."

Vinson said she improperly covered up expenses by drawing down reserve accounts—some completely unrelated to the expenses—and by moving expenses off income statements and listing them as assets on the balance sheet.

Also the company's former director of corporate reporting, Vinson testified at Bernie Ebbers's trial that, in choosing which accounts to alter, "I just really pulled some out of the air. I used some spreadsheets." She said she repeatedly brought her concerns to colleagues and supervisors, once describing the entries to a coworker as "just crazy." In spring 2002, she noted, she told one boss she would no longer make the entries. "I said that I thought the entries were just being made to make the income statement look like Scott wanted it to look."

Standing before the judge at her sentencing, Vinson said: "I never expected to be here, and I certainly won't do anything like this again." She was sentenced to 5 months in prison and 5 months of house arrest.

Pressure Reigns

While the judge correctly said that her lack of culpability didn't excuse her actions, we must carefully note that Betty

Vinson, as well as many of her codefendants, didn't start out as criminals seeking to defraud the organization. Under typical antifraud screening tools, she and others like her wouldn't have raised any red flags as being potential committers of corporate fraud.

Scott Sullivan was a powerful leader with a well-known reputation for integrity. If any of us were in Betty Vinson's shoes, could we say with 100 percent confidence that we would say "no" to the CFO if he asked us to do something and promised that he would take full responsibility for any fallout from the actions we were going to take?

Today's white-collar criminals are more likely to be those among us who are unable to withstand the blistering pressures placed on managers to meet higher and tougher goals. In this environment, companies looking to protect themselves from corporate fraud must take a hard look at their own culture. Does it promote ethical behavior, or does it emphasize something else?

In most companies, "ethics" programs are really no more than compliance programs with a veneer of "do the right thing" messaging to create an apparent link to the company's values. To be effective, they have to go deeper than outlining steps to take to report misconduct. Organizations must understand what causes misconduct in the first place.

We can't forget that Enron had a Code of Ethics. And it wasn't as if WorldCom lacked extensive internal controls. But both had cultures where engaging in unethical conduct was tacitly condoned, if not encouraged.

Building the Right Culture

Now the focus has shifted toward looking at what is going on inside organizations that's either keeping people from doing the right thing or, just as importantly, keeping people from doing something about misconduct they observe. If an organization wants to reduce the risk of unethical conduct, it must focus more effort on building the right culture than on building a compliance infrastructure.

The Ethics Resource Center's 2005 National Business Ethics Survey (NBES) clearly confirms this trend toward recognizing the role of corporate culture. Based on interviews with more than 3,000 employees and managers in the United States the survey disclosed that, despite the increase in the number of ethics and compliance program elements being implemented, desired outcomes, such as reduced levels of observed misconduct, haven't changed since 1994. Even more striking is the revelation that, although formal ethics and compliance programs have some impact, organizational culture has the greatest influence in determining program outcomes.

The Securities & Exchange Commission (SEC) and the Department of Justice have also been watching these trends. Stephen Cutler, the recently retired SEC director of the Division of Enforcement, was matter of fact about the importance of looking at culture when it came to decisions of whether or not to bring an action. "We're trying to induce companies to address matters of tone and culture. . . . What we're asking of that CEO, CFO, or General Counsel goes beyond what a perp walk or an enforcement action against another company executive might impel her to do. We're hoping that if she sees that a failure of corporate culture can result in a fine that significantly exceeds the proverbial 'cost of doing business,' and reflects a failure on her watch—and a failure on terms that everyone can understand: the company's bottom line—she may have a little more incentive to pay attention to the environment in which her company's employees do their jobs."

Measuring Success

Only lagging companies still measure the success of their ethics and compliance programs just by tallying the percentage of employees who have certified that they read the Code of Conduct and attended ethics and compliance training. The true indicator of success is whether the company has made significant progress in achieving key program outcomes. The National Business Ethics Survey listed four key outcomes that help determine the success of a program:

- Reduced misconduct observed by employees,
- Reduced pressure to engage in unethical conduct,
- Increased willingness of employees to report misconduct, and
- Greater satisfaction with organizational response to reports of misconduct.

What's going to move these outcomes in the right direction? Establishing the right culture.

Most compliance programs are generated from "corporate" and disseminated down through the organization. As such, measurement of the success of the program is often based on criteria important to the corporate office: how many employees certified the Code of Conduct, how many employees went through the training, or how many calls the hotline received.

Culture is different—and is measured differently. An organization's culture isn't something that's created by senior leadership and then rolled out. A culture is an objective picture of the organization, for better or worse. It's the sum total of all the collective values and behaviors of all employees, managers, and leaders. By definition, it can only be measured by criteria that reflect the individual values of all employees, so understanding cultural vulnerabilities that can lead to ethics issues requires knowledge of what motivates employees in the organization. Leadership must know how the myriad human behaviors and interactions fit together like puzzle pieces to create a whole picture. An organization moves toward an ethical culture only if it understands the full range of values and behaviors needed to meet its ethical goals. The "full-spectrum" organization is one that creates a positive sense of engagement and purpose that drives ethical behavior.

Leadership must know how the myriad human behaviors and interactions fit together like puzzle pieces to create a whole picture. An organization moves toward an ethical culture only if it understands the full range of values and behaviors needed to meet its ethical goals.

Why is understanding the culture so important in determining the success of a compliance program? Here's an example: Most organizations have a policy that prohibits retaliation against those who bring forward concerns or claims. But creating a culture where employees feel safe enough to admit mistakes and to raise uncomfortable issues requires more than a policy and "Code training." To truly develop an ethical culture,

the organization must be aware of how its managers deal with these issues up and down the line and how the values they demonstrate impact desired behaviors. The organization must understand the pressures its people are under and how they react to those pressures. And it must know how its managers communicate and whether employees have a sense of accountability and purpose.

Categorizing Values

Determining whether an organization has the capabilities to put such a culture in place requires careful examination. Do employees and managers demonstrate values such as respect? Do employees feel accountable for their actions and feel that they have a stake in the success of the organization?

How does an organization make such a determination? One approach is to categorize different types of values in a way that lends itself to determining specific strengths and weaknesses that can be assessed and then corrected or enhanced.

The Culture Risk Assessment model presented in Figure 1 has been adapted from the Cultural Transformation Tools® developed by Richard Barrett & Associates. Such tools provide a comprehensive framework for measuring cultures by mapping values. More than 1,000 organizations in 24 countries have used this technique in the past 6 years. In fact, the international management consulting firm McKinsey & Co. has adopted it as its method of choice for mapping corporate cultures and measuring progress toward achieving culture change.

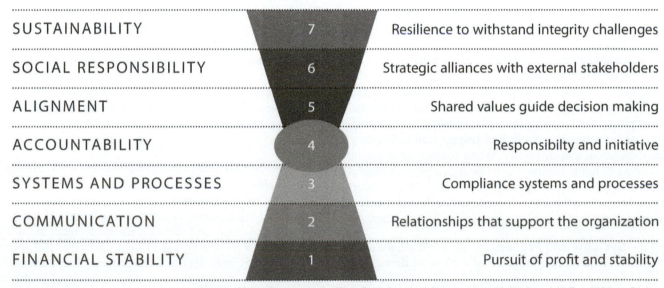

SUSTAINABILITY	7	Resilience to withstand integrity challenges
SOCIAL RESPONSIBILITY	6	Strategic alliances with external stakeholders
ALIGNMENT	5	Shared values guide decision making
ACCOUNTABILITY	4	Responsibilty and initiative
SYSTEMS AND PROCESSES	3	Compliance systems and processes
COMMUNICATION	2	Relationships that support the organization
FINANCIAL STABILITY	1	Pursuit of profit and stability

Based on Cultural Transformation Tools Seven Levels of Consciousness Model, Copyright Barrett Values Centre

Figure 1   Seven levels of an ethical organization.

The model is based on the principle, substantiated through practice, that all values can be assigned to one of seven categories:

Levels 1, 2, and 3—The Organization's Basic Needs

Does the organization support values that enable it to run smoothly and effectively? From an ethics perspective, is the environment one in which employees feel physically and emotionally safe to report unethical behavior and to do the right thing?

Level 1—Financial Stability. Every organization needs to make financial stability a primary concern. Companies that are consumed with just surviving struggle to focus enough attention on how they conduct themselves. This may, in fact, create a negative cycle that makes survival much more difficult. Managers may exercise excessive control, so employees may be working in an environment of fear.

In these circumstances, unethical or even illegal conduct can be rationalized. When asked to conform to regulations, organizations do the minimum with an attitude of begrudging compliance.

Organizations with challenges at this level need to be confident that managers know and stand within clear ethical boundaries.

Level 2—Communication. Without good relationships with employees, customers, and suppliers, integrity is compromised. The critical issue at this level is to create a sense of loyalty and belonging among employees and a sense of caring and connection between the organization and its customers.

The most critical link in the chain is between employees and their direct supervisors. If direct supervisors can't effectively reinforce messages coming from senior leadership, those messages might be diluted and confused by the time they reach line employees. When faced with conflicting messages, employees will usually choose to follow the lead of their direct supervisor over the words of the CEO that have been conveyed through an impersonal communication channel. Disconnects in how local managers "manage" these messages often mean that employees can face tremendous pressure in following the lead established by leadership.

Fears about belonging and lack of respect lead to fragmentation, dissension, and disloyalty. When leaders meet behind closed doors or fail to communicate openly, employees suspect the worst. Cliques form, and gossip becomes rife. When leaders are more focused on their own success, rather than the success of the organization, they begin to compete with each other.

Level 3—Systems and Processes. At this level, the organization is focused on becoming the best it can be through the adoption of best practices and a focus on quality, productivity, and efficiency.

Level 3 organizations have succeeded in implementing strong internal controls and have enacted clear standards of conduct. Those that succeed at this level are the ones that see internal controls as an opportunity to create better, more efficient processes. But even those that have successfully deployed business processes and practices need to be alert to potentially limiting aspects of being too focused on processes. All organizations need to be alert to resorting to a "check-the-box" attitude that assumes compliance comes naturally from just implementing standards and procedures. Being efficient all too often leads to bureaucracy and inconsistent application of the rules. When this goes badly, employees lose respect for the system and resort to self-help to get things done. This can lead to shortcuts and, in the worst case, engaging in unethical conduct under the guise of doing what it takes to succeed.

Level 4—Accountability

The focus of the fourth level is on creating an environment in which employees and managers begin to take responsibility for their own actions. They want to be held accountable, not micromanaged and supervised every moment of every day. For an ethics and compliance program to be successful, all employees must feel that they have a personal responsibility for the integrity of the organization. Everyone must feel that his or her voice is being heard. This requires managers and leaders to admit that they don't have all the answers and invite employee participation.

Levels 5, 6, and 7—Common Good

Does the organization support values that create a collective sense of belonging where employees feel that they have a stake in the success of the ethics program?

Level 5—Alignment. The critical issue at this level is developing a shared vision of the future and a shared set of values. The shared vision clarifies the intentions of the organization and gives employees a unifying purpose and direction. The shared values provide guidance for making decisions.

The organization develops the ability to align decision making around a set of shared values. The values and behaviors must be reflected in all of the organization's processes and systems, with appropriate consequences for those who aren't willing to walk the talk. A precondition for success at this level is building a climate of trust.

Level 6—Social Responsibility. At this level, the organization is able to use its relationships with stakeholders to sustain itself through crises and change. Employees and customers see that the organization is making a difference in the world through its products and services, its involvement in the local community, or its willingness to fight for causes that improve humanity. They must feel that the company cares about them and their future. Companies operating at this level go the extra mile to make sure they are being responsible citizens. They support and encourage employees' activities in the community by providing time off for volunteer work and/or making a financial contribution to the charities that employees are involved in.

Level 7—Sustainability. To be successful at Level 7, organizations must embrace the highest ethical standards in all their interactions with employees, suppliers, customers, shareholders, and the community. They must always consider the long-term impact of their decisions and actions.

Employee values are distributed across all seven levels. Through surveys, organizations learn which values employees bring to the workplace and which values are missing. Organizations don't operate from any one level of values: They tend to be clustered around three or four levels. Most are focused on the first three: profit and growth (Level 1), customer satisfaction (Level 2), and productivity, efficiency, and quality (Level 3). The most successful organizations operate across the full spectrum with particular focus in the upper levels of consciousness—the common good—accountability, leading to learning and innovation (Level 4), alignment (Level 5), social responsibility (Level 6), and sustainability (Level 7).

Some organizations have fully developed values around Levels 1, 2, and 3 but are lacking in Levels 5, 6, and 7. They may have a complete infrastructure of controls and procedures but may lack the accountability and commitment of employees and leaders to go further than what is required.

Similarly, some organizations have fully developed values around Levels 5, 6, and 7 but are deficient in Levels 1, 2, and 3. These organizations may have visionary leaders and externally focused social responsibility programs, but they may be lacking in core systems that will ensure that the higher-level commitments are embedded into day-to-day processes.

Once an organization understands its values' strengths and weaknesses, it can take specific steps to correct deficient behavior.

Starting the Process

Could a deeper understanding of values have saved WorldCom? We will never know, but if the culture had encouraged open communication and fostered trust, people like Betty Vinson might have been more willing to confront orders that they knew were wrong. Moreover, if the culture had embodied values that encouraged transparency, mid-level managers wouldn't have been asked to engage in such activity in the first place.

The significance of culture issues such as these is also being reflected in major employee surveys that highlight what causes unethical behavior. According to the NBES, "Where top management displays certain ethics-related actions, employees are 50 percentage points less likely to observe misconduct." No other factor in any ethics survey can demonstrate such a drastic influence.

So how do compliance leaders move their organizations to these new directions?

1. *The criteria for success of an ethics program must be outcomes based.* Merely checking off program elements isn't enough to change behavior.

2. *Each organization must identify the key indicators of its culture.* Only by assessing its own ethical culture can a company know what behaviors are the most influential in effecting change.

3. *The organization must gauge how all levels of employees perceive adherence to values by others within the company.* One of the surprising findings of the NBES was that managers, especially senior managers, were out of touch with how nonmanagement employees perceived their adherence to ethical behaviors. Nonmanagers are 27 percentage points less likely than senior managers to indicate that executives engage in all of the ethics-related actions outlined in the survey.

4. *Formal programs are guides to shape the culture, not vice versa.* People who are inclined to follow the rules appreciate the rules as a guide to behavior. Formal program elements need to reflect the culture in which they are deployed if they are going to be most effective in driving the company to the desired outcomes.

Culture may be new on the radar screen, but it isn't outside the scope or skills of forward-thinking finance managers and compliance professionals. Culture can be measured, and finance managers can play a leadership role in developing systematic approaches to move companies in the right direction.

Critical Thinking

1. Whose values should guide an organization? Senior management? Middle management? "Workers"? Investors?

2. What might happen in an organization that switched "resilience to withstand integrity challenges" and "pursuit of profit and stability" on the right hand side of the seven levels of an ethical organization, while leaving the left hand side as is?

Create Central

www.mhhe.com/createcentral

Internet References

AZ Central
http://yourbusiness.azcentral.com/ethical-behavior-culture-14949.html
Corporate Compliance Insights
http://www.corporatecomplianceinsights.com/guarding-the-slippery-slope-what-can-hr-do-to-create-an-ethical-culture/
Houston Chronicle
http://smallbusiness.chron.com/create-ethical-workplace-10543.html

DAVID GEBLER, JD, is president of Working Values, Ltd., a business ethics training and consulting firm specializing in developing behavior-based change to support compliance objectives. You can reach him at dgebler@workingvalues.com.

From *Strategic Finance*, May 2006, pp. 29–34. Copyright © 2006 by Institute of Management Accountants-IMA. Reprinted by permission via Copyright Clearance Center.

Article   Prepared by: Eric Teoro, *Lincoln Christian University*

Barclays Tells Staff to Uphold New Values or Leave

Margot Patrick

Learning Outcomes

After reading this article, you will be able to:

- Describe Barclays' CEO's position on upholding corporate values.

- Recognize that working for a given company is a choice—you can choose to leave if you find its policies disagreeable.

B arclays PLC's Chief Executive Antony Jenkins Thursday told staff they should uphold the company's new values or leave. The comments come 7 months after a scandal over trying to rig interest rates.

In a memorandum to employees, Mr. Jenkins said bonuses will now be based in part on how employees and business units uphold five values, rather than "just on what we deliver."

"We must never again be in a position of rewarding people for making the bank money in a way which is unethical or inconsistent with our values," Mr. Jenkins said.

Barclays is attempting to repair its reputation with regulators, investors, customers, and the broader public after acknowledging in June that some staff had tried to manipulate interest rates. It paid around $450 million in regulatory fines and its chief executive, chairman, and chief operating officer resigned. Mr. Jenkins became CEO in August after having run the group's global retail and business banks. He pledged to make reforms.

"Having a firm commitment throughout the business to strong values is not something I want to do for public relations or political benefit. It is simply how I will run Barclays," Mr. Jenkins told staff.

"There might be some who don't feel they can fully buy in to an approach which so squarely links performance to the upholding of our values," Mr. Jenkins said. "My message to those people is simple: Barclays is not the place for you. The rules have changed. You won't feel comfortable at Barclays and, to be frank, we won't feel comfortable with you as colleagues."

Mr. Jenkins is to address staff to expand upon the memo later Thursday and will present the outcome of a strategic review of the bank Feb. 12, the day Barclays is to report full-year results. He has previously said every part of the bank would be reviewed by considering its contribution to both returns and reputation.

He said there are plans to train more than 1,000 staff to spread the new values across the bank in an effort to "embed them throughout our business at every level."

The values are: respect, integrity, service, excellence and stewardship.

Critical Thinking

1. Would you like to work for Antony Jenkins? Why or why not?

2. Would you have taken a similar or different approach to what Jenkins did? Why?

3. Did Jenkins behave ethically in issuing his charge? Why or why not?

Create Central

www.mhhe.com/createcentral

Internet References

Barclays
   http://www.barclays.com/about-barclays/barclays-values.html
Choose
   http://www.choose.net/money/guide/features/how-ethical-banking.html

Designing Honesty into Your Organization by Christian Mastilak et al.

75

Article

Prepared by: Eric Teoro, *Lincoln Christian University*

Designing Honesty into Your Organization

CHRISTIAN MASTILAK ET AL.

Learning Outcomes

After reading this article, you will be able to:

- Understand how perceptions of fairness impact dishonest behavior in organizations.

- Understand how the framing of organizational processes can lead to dishonest behavior.

- Take concrete, actionable steps to facilitate honest behavior on the part of employees.

The past decade has provided ample evidence that some people don't behave honestly at work. While it's easy to blame individual factors, such as greed or lack of an ethical compass, recent academic research paints a different picture. As a leader in your organization, you may have more influence than you realize about whether your employees act honestly or not. You can design honest behavior into an organization by using fair and properly aligned reward systems and simple communication strategies.

We know dishonesty is costly, and it may be on the rise. The Ethics Resource Center reports that the following percentages of employees surveyed in 2009 had observed these behaviors in the previous year: company resource abuse (23 percent), lying to employees (19 percent), lying to outside stakeholders (12 percent), falsifying time or expenses (10 percent), and stealing (9 percent). The Association of Certified Fraud Examiners suggests United States organizations may have lost as much as $994 billion to occupational fraud in 2008, and a Pricewater-houseCoopers global survey in 2009 suggests that recent economic pressures have increased the likelihood of fraud taking place. But how can this common problem be reduced?

Research suggests that integrity testing goes only so far in predicting honesty in the workplace. It turns out that most employees are neither consistent truthtellers who can be completely trusted in the absence of controls nor consistent liars who can never be trusted. This means preventing dishonesty isn't just a matter of finding the right people. Some factors can motivate employees to be closer to the truthtelling end of the scale. Specifically, research shows that honest behavior is influenced by employees' beliefs about whether they are being treated fairly, whether expectations of honest behavior have been made explicit, and whether organizational control systems reward dishonest behavior. This suggests that honest behavior can be designed into—or out of—an organization. In this article, we first discuss some of the research findings, then draw on them to develop practical suggestions for how managers can create an environment that both discourages dishonest behavior and enables honest behavior.

Why Do Employees Behave Dishonestly?

We broadly define dishonest behavior as making a report known to contain lies or taking an action known to be unauthorized for personal gain. This excludes accidental errors but includes a variety of behaviors common to accounting and finance functions. Most research in accounting has focused primarily on budgeting behavior, such as padding requests in order to keep the extra funds. But research on more direct forms of theft, such as stealing company property, has led to similar conclusions about why employees steal.

Admittedly, the reasons for dishonest behavior are many and varied. Much has been written about the fraud triangle and how the presence of pressure, opportunity, and rationalization increases the chance of fraud. We can't do justice to the entire topic here, but we can discuss some organizational design and control choices that affect people's behavior. Two common themes that surface are *fairness* and *frame*.

Fairness

For years, economic theory has rested on the assumption that two important desires drive people's behavior: leisure and wealth. Business schools teach future managers to assume that employees will avoid working hard and will lie to increase their wealth. These assumptions then show up in practice as internal control systems are developed to help prevent and detect lack of effort and dishonesty.

Recent academic research has identified two other desires that influence behavior: honesty and fairness. So it isn't simply that people want to be as rich and put forth as little effort as possible; rather, most people also care about being honest and want to ensure that their treatment and outcomes are reasonable compared to the treatment and outcomes of others. More importantly, these desires affect honesty in the workplace.

When employees believe they haven't received what they are due, they will look for ways to recover what they believe they're owed.

Several studies provide examples of how tradeoffs among desires for wealth, honesty, and fairness play out in organizational settings. Coauthor Linda Matuszewski conducted one such study with funding from the IMA® Foundation for Applied Research (now called IMA Research Foundation). Appearing in the 2010 issue (Volume 22) of the *Journal of Management Accounting Research*, "Honesty in Managerial Reporting: Is It Affected by Perceptions of Horizontal Equity?" is one of several studies in accounting in which student participants played the role of managers reporting to their employer. Participants knew the amount of actual costs that would be incurred on a project and were asked to submit a budget request. The employer would never know the actual costs. If the participant lied and the budget request exceeded actual costs, the participants kept the difference. This difference was personal gain for participants—at the expense of their employers. That is, the greater the lie, the more money the participants received.

Overall, Matuszewski's results are consistent with "Honesty in Managerial Reporitng," a study by John Evans, Lynn Hannan, Ranjani Krishnan, and Donald Moser in the October 2001 issue of *The Accounting Review*. Matuszewski's study shows that only

a small proportion of people (15 percent) lied to maximize their wealth. A similar proportion of people were at the other end of the spectrum, with 19 percent behaving completely honestly. This left the vast majority (66 percent) in the middle—lying some and trading their desire to be honest against their desire for wealth.

At the two extremes, managers could assume the worst and develop expensive management controls to prevent and detect dishonesty, or they could assume the best and not develop any controls. Since most employees don't fall into either extreme, neither of these solutions is likely to be the most cost effective. Managers are left with the challenge of designing control systems for the majority of employees—those who have some desire to be honest but are also willing to lie to some extent. This is where the results of several other studies can be helpful, as they shed some light on factors within a company's control that influence whether an employee's behavior is closer to the honest or the dishonest end of the scale.

One factor is *vertical* fairness. This represents the relationship between employees and their organizations. In "Stealing in the Name of Justice: Informational and Interpersonal Moderators of Theft Reactions to Underpayment Inequity," Jerald Greenberg describes a study in which he promised two groups of research participants a certain level of pay for performing a low-skilled task (*Organizational Behavior and Human Decision Processes*, Volume 54, Issue 1, February 1993). Participants who were treated unfairly by being paid less than they were originally promised "stole" from the researcher, likely rationalizing that they were due the stolen amount. Participants who were given a reasonable explanation for why their pay was less than promised and received an apology from the researcher, however, stole less. Greenberg's work shows that an explanation and empathy can go a long way toward soothing hurt feelings—and reducing retaliation in firms.

Vertical fairness is critical—but it isn't the only element that matters. Look no further than *Strategic Finance's* Annual Salary Survey each June to know that horizontal fairness—how fairly people are treated compared to their peers—is also important. This was the main focus of Matuszewski's study, which demonstrated that participants' beliefs about changes in the *horizontal* fairness of their pay changed the honesty in their budgeting behavior. Participants in the study were paid a salary and received information about the salaries of other participants. When the horizontal fairness of pay declined, the change in honesty was the same, whether it occurred because of a decrease in the participant's own pay or an increase in others' pay. To make matters worse, this dishonest behavior is hard to undo. In Matuszewski's study, improvements in horizontal fairness resulting from decreases in others' pay didn't result in more honest behavior. Thus, being treated fairly right from the beginning is extremely important.

We aren't trying to minimize employees' personal responsibility for their actions. But research shows that when employees believe they haven't received what they are due, they will look for ways to recover what they believe they're owed. Accordingly, we believe that if top management designs fairness into its dealings with employees, it will eliminate this possible rationalization and cause employees to pursue honest behavior more frequently.

Frame

Another way to design honest behavior into organizations is to ensure that an organization clearly communicates that honesty is expected. When would an employee think that honest behavior isn't expected? Think of it this way: Imagine you're playing basketball. Is a head fake unethical? No, it's completely normal behavior because basketball is a competition, and misleading your opponent is expected. Imagine Kobe Bryant complaining that LeBron James cheated because he made a no-look pass. "Not fair! He looked the other way!" That isn't going to happen because Kobe understands they're competing against each other.

How is this relevant? Well, how often do your budgeting processes become framed as strategic competitions among employees and management rather than decisions with ethical implications? You're more likely to find dishonest behavior if employees believe that the budgeting process is expected to be competitive rather than collaborative, strategic rather than honest. That's what Frederick Rankin, Steven Schwartz, and Richard Young found in "The Effect of Honesty and Superior Authority on Budget Proposals" (*The Accounting Review,* July 2008). Participants completed a budgeting task similar to the task in Matuszewski's study. Those who were asked to honestly share their information about actual costs were more honest than those who were simply asked what portion of the profits should be returned to the company. This study suggests that, in the absence of formal controls, people will be more honest if you simply ask them to be!

Rankin, Schwartz, and Young's finding is particularly important given recent research about the costs and benefits of formal controls. In "When Formal Controls Undermine Trust and Cooperation," Margaret Christ, Karen Sedatole, Kristy Towry, and Myra Thomas suggest that employees sometimes view formal controls as a sign that employers question their competence and integrity, and this may undermine trust and cooperation (*Strategic Finance,* January 2008). To be clear, we aren't advocating doing away with all explicit formal controls. In circumstances in which formal controls aren't present or are too costly, Rankin, Schwartz, and Young show that some of the same benefits can be achieved by describing a task as an ethical dilemma, rather than a strategic competition, and asking for honesty.

Another effect that framing has in determining whether honest behavior is expected showed up in the large-scale fraud at Enron. Bennett Stewart suggests in "The Real Reasons Enron Failed" that Enron's managers were, in fact, paid to do dishonest things (*Journal of Applied Corporate Finance,* Volume 18, Issue, 2, Spring 2006). Stewart documents that performance at Enron was framed as an accounting game rather than as increasing the company's true economic value. In part, this involved manipulating internal performance measures to exclude any costs of capital. Stewart documents the use of EBITDA—the least accountable, most misleading indicator of corporate performance ever devised—by Enron executives who clearly knew better.

Why did they use this measure? Simple: Enron's performance measurement and compensation system, which included stock-based compensation, paid them to do so. Increases in Enron's stock price were driven in large part by—you guessed it—accounting performance. And we shouldn't be surprised when people do what firms pay them to do.

The greatest problem with poorly framed control systems is that, even when employees intend to be honest, a bad control system may discourage that employee from acting on that honest urge and *disable* that honesty. The challenge is for top managers to design control systems that *enable* honesty.

The Designed Honesty Model

Putting these research results together, we present the designed honesty model of organizational behavior (see Figure 1). The model shows that both fairness and frame contribute to designed honesty. Where should top management look to understand why employees aren't behaving honestly? That depends. If employees are grumbling about their working conditions or their pay—especially their pay relative to others within the organization—then they probably believe they aren't being treated fairly and may well be working the system to get what they believe is due them. On the other hand, if employees report conflicts between what they believe they should do and what they believe they're being asked and paid to do, then the culture and control system frame are probably the culprits, leading otherwise honest employees to feel like they are being encouraged to behave dishonestly.

The designed honesty model isn't intended to be complete—the factors that influence honesty and dishonesty are many and varied. As the research shows, most employees value honesty and fairness in addition to wealth and leisure and are influenced by all of these values when deciding whether to behave honestly. Since fairness and frame are within an organization's control to some extent, it's important for management to understand how these factors can contribute to honest behavior.

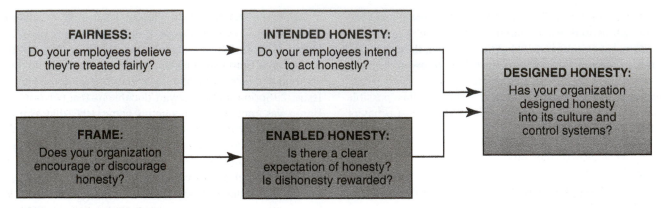

Figure 1 The designed honesty model.

Table 1 Six Key Steps toward Designing Honesty into Your Organization

1. Consider vertical and horizontal fairness when making compensation decisions
2. Fully explain compensation policies and procedures
3. Determine whether employees believe they are being paid fairly
4. Show (and feel!) empathy when tough compensation choices need to be implemented
5. Ask employees to be honest, and describe routine decisions as ethical dilemmas rather than strategic competitions
6. Review incentive plans to ensure they reward honest reporting of economic results

Therefore, in addition to attempting to hire the right people, we recommend that companies take the following steps to encourage employees to act on their intentions to be honest (see Table 1):

1. ***Consider vertical and horizontal fairness when making compensation decisions.***
   Employees consider the fairness of their compensation from two perspectives—relative to their exchange with the company (vertical) and relative to the compensation of their peers (horizontal). Managers may be able to get a sense of the perceptions about the vertical fairness of compensation by considering employees' alternative employment opportunities. In today's culture of high turnover, it's reasonable to assume that employees are keeping their eye on the job market and asking "What could I make elsewhere?" But how often do managers consider their subordinates' opportunities when making compensation decisions? Incorporating this practice into the firm's periodic performance review system could help avoid the costs of dishonesty motivated by perceptions of vertical unfairness.
   From the horizontal perspective, although firms often have policies that discourage peers from sharing information about pay, we believe managers should assume that employees know how much money

their peers are making so should make an effort to compensate employees fairly compared to their peers.

2. ***Fully explain compensation policies and procedures.***
   Fair doesn't necessarily imply equal. In cases where compensation isn't equal to an alternative employment opportunity or the pay a peer is receiving, detailed explanations may be especially important in helping employees evaluate whether their pay is fair. Communication strategies that help employees understand the justification for compensation policies can be extremely valuable. For instance, employees may be more likely to consider their compensation fair if managers explain the connection between the resources of their division and employee compensation.

3. ***Determine whether employees believe they are being paid fairly.***
   Most large companies have periodic performance review systems in place, and it's through these systems that compensation decisions get communicated. Yet how many of these systems are two-way communication devices designed to determine whether employees believe they are being paid fairly? This data may be challenging to get, especially if employees fear

retaliation if they admit they don't believe they are being paid fairly. Managers may need to put themselves in their employees' shoes and pursue indirect methods for answering this question, such as anonymous surveys or hotline methods.

4. *Show (and feel!) empathy when tough compensation choices need to be implemented.*
Of course, managers won't always have the resources to give employees the compensation they want and feel they deserve. But empathy can have an impact on honesty, even when employees face an outcome they believe is unfair.

5. *Ask employees to be honest, and describe routine decisions as ethical dilemmas rather than strategic competitions.*
A logical first step in making it clear that you expect employees to be honest is the establishment of a corporate code of ethics, but even the best code won't be effective unless employees can see the connection between the code and their everyday activities. Think of it this way: Corporate planning doesn't stop with the development of a vision statement. Firms work toward the vision by identifying core competencies, developing organizational strategies, and translating these strategies into operating plans. In the same way, a company must develop strategies for ensuring honest behavior. The research suggests that one successful strategy would be to identify tasks that provide employees with opportunities to benefit from dishonesty and describe these tasks as ethical dilemmas rather than strategic competitions.

This suggestion is consistent with the findings in two 2011 studies published in the *Journal of Business Ethics* that identify factors that contribute to the effectiveness of corporate codes of ethics. Muel Kaptein found in "Toward Effective Codes: Testing the Relationship with Unethical Behavior" (Volume 99, No. 2, March 2011) that the quality of communication regarding a corporate code of ethics has a greater impact on reducing unethical behavior than the quantity of communication about the code. Put simply, it isn't enough to establish a code and talk about it a lot. The code must be accessible, clear, easy to understand, and useful for decision making. In the other study, "Determinants of the Effectiveness of Corporate Codes of Ethics: An Empirical Study" (Volume 101, No. 3, July 2011), Jang Singh found that a code's impact on behavior is determined in part by whether the code guides strategic planning and is useful in resolving ethical dilemmas in the marketplace.

6. *Review incentive plans to ensure they reward honest reporting of economic results.*
Both Kaptein's and Singh's studies also provide insight into the steps managers should take to ensure that their incentive plans promote honesty in the workplace. Singh found that codes are more effective when compliance with their provisions is a part of performance reviews and when there are real consequences for violations. Kaptein found that the most important factor in reducing unethical behavior was senior and local management's embedding of the corporate code of ethics within an organization. More specifically, employees are more likely to be honest when their managers are approachable positive role models who set reasonable performance targets that promote, rather than undermine, compliance with the corporate code of ethics. In addition, it's important that managers don't authorize violations of the code to meet business goals, are aware of the extent to which employees comply with (or violate) the code, and respond to violations appropriately.

To prevent the kind of financial reporting dishonesty that occurred at Enron and many other companies, we suggest that managers should also consider whether performance targets based on economic results are using measures less subject to manipulation than traditional financial accounting measures may be.

Steps Will Go a Long Way

While we can't guarantee that these steps will eliminate all dishonesty in the workplace, we believe that paying attention to the fairness of employees' compensation and highlighting the ethical dimension of certain decisions will go a long way toward designing honesty into your organization.

Critical Thinking

1. Why do some people behave dishonestly at work?
2. Using the Designed Honesty Model presented in the article, develop your own model and explain its strengths and weaknesses compared to the model presented in the article.
3. Pick out one of the "six key steps" toward designing honesty in an organization. Build arguments for and against the key step.
4. If you are a student in a class, engage in a debate for/against with another student concerning the key step you selected.

Create Central

www.mhhe.com/createcentral

Internet References

Forbes

http://www.forbes.com/sites/joefolkman/2013/11/18/how-to-make-your-organization-more-honest/

Houston Chronicle: Small Business

http://smallbusiness.chron.com/managerial-ethics-36425.html

Switch and Shift

http://switchandshift.com/honesty-the-secret-to-successful-organizations

CHRISTIAN MASTILAK, PhD, is an assistant professor of accountancy and business law in the Williams College of Business at Xavier University and a member of the North Cincinnati Chapter of IMA. You can reach Christian at (513) 745-3290 or mastilakc@xavier.edu. LINDA MATUSZEWSKI, PhD, is an assistant professor of accountancy in the College of Business at Northern Illinois University and a member of the Rockford Chapter of IMA. You can reach Linda at (815) 753-6379 or lmatus@niu.edu. FABIENNE MILLER, PhD, is an assistant professor of accounting in the School of Business at Worcester Polytechnic Institute and a member of the Worcester Chapter of IMA. You can reach Fabienne at (508) 831-6128 or fabienne@wpi.edu. ALEXANDER WOODS, PhD, is an assistant professor of accounting in the Mason School of Business at The College of William & Mary. You can reach Alex at (757) 221-2967 or alex.woods@mason.wm.edu.

Mastilak, Christian; Matuszewski, Linda; Miller, Fabienne; Woods, Alexander. From *Strategic Finance*, December 2011. Copyright © 2011 by Institute of Management Accountants-IMA. Reprinted by permission via Copyright Clearance Center.

Article   Prepared by: Eric Teoro, *Lincoln Christian University*

Hiring Character

In their new book, *Integrity Works,* authors Dana Telford and Adrian Gostick outline the strategies necessary for becoming a respected and admired leader. In the edited excerpt that follows, the authors present a look at business leader Warren Buffett's practice of hiring people based on their integrity. For sales and marketing executives, it's a practice worth considering, especially when your company's reputation with customers—built through your salespeople—is so critical.

DANA TELFORD AND ADRIAN GOSTICK

Learning Outcomes

After reading this article, you will be able to:

- Describe the ethicality of Warren Buffet.

- Determine if résumés are accurate.

- Ask ethics-based questions during hiring interviews.

This chapter was the hardest for us to write. The problem was, we couldn't agree on whom to write about. We had a number of great options we were mulling over. Herb Brooks of the Miracle on Ice 1980 US hockey team certainly put together a collection of players whose character outshined their talent. And the results were extraordinary. We decided to leave him out because we had enough sports figures in the book already. No, we wanted a business leader. So we asked, "Who hires integrity over ability?"

The person suggested to us over and over as we bandied this idea among our colleagues was Warren Buffett, chairman of Berkshire Hathaway Inc.

Sure enough, as we began our research we found we had not even begun to tell Buffett's story. But we were reluctant to repeat his story. Buffett had played an important part in our first book. And yet, his name kept coming up. So often, in fact, that we finally decided to not ignore the obvious.

Perhaps more than anyone in business today, Warren Buffett hires people based on their integrity. Buffett commented, "Berkshire's collection of managers is unusual in several ways. As one example, a very high percentage of these men and women are independently wealthy, having made fortunes in the

businesses that they run. They work neither because they need the money nor because they are contractually obligated to—we have no contracts at Berkshire. Rather, they work long and hard because they love their businesses."

The unusual thing about Warren Buffett is that he and his longtime partner, Charlie Munger, hire people they trust—and then treat them as they would wish to be treated if their positions were reversed. Buffett says the one reason he has kept working so long is that he loves the opportunity to interact with people he likes and, most importantly, trusts.

Buffett loves the opportunity to interact daily with people he likes and, most importantly, trusts.

Consider the following remarkable story from a few years ago at Berkshire Hathaway. It's about R.C. Willey, the dominant home furnishings business in Utah. Berkshire purchased the company from Bill Child and his family in 1995. Child and most of his managers are members of the Church of Jesus Christ of Latter-day Saints, also called Mormons, and for this reason R.C. Willey's stores have never been open on Sunday.

Now, anyone who has worked in retail realizes the seeming folly of this notion: Sunday is the favorite shopping day for many customers—even in Utah. Over the years, though, Child had stuck to his principle—and wasn't ready to rejigger the formula just because Warren Buffett came along. And the formula was working. R.C.'s sales were $250,000 in 1954 when Child took over. By 1999, they had grown to $342 million. Child's determination to stick to his convictions was what attracted Buffett to him and his management team. This was a group with values and a successful brand.

Arnie Ferrin, longtime friend of Child, said, "I believe that [Child] is a man of extreme integrity, and I believe that Warren Buffett was looking to buy his business because he likes to do business with people like that, that don't have any shadows in their lives, and they're straightforward and deal above-board."

This isn't to say Child and Buffett have always agreed on the direction of the furniture store.

"I was highly skeptical about taking a no-Sunday policy into a new territory, where we would be up against entrenched rivals open seven days a week," Buffett said. "Nevertheless, this was Bill's business to run. So, despite my reservations, I told him to follow both his business judgment and his religious convictions."

Proving once again that he believed in his convictions, Child insisted on a truly extraordinary proposition: He would personally buy the land and build the store in Boise, Idaho—for about $11 million as it turned out—and would sell it to Berkshire at his cost if—and only if—the store proved to be successful. On the other hand, if sales fell short of his expectations, Berkshire could exit the business without paying Child a cent. This, of course, would leave him with a huge investment in an empty building.

You're probably guessing there's a happy ending to the story. And there is. The store opened in August of 1998 and immediately became a huge success, making Berkshire a considerable margin. Today, the store is the largest home furnishings store in Idaho.

Child, good to his word, turned the property over to Berkshire—including some extra land that had appreciated significantly. And he wanted nothing more than the original cost of his investment. In response, Buffett said, "And get this: Bill refused to take a dime of interest on the capital he had tied up over the two years."

And there's more. Shortly after the Boise opening, Child went back to Buffett, suggesting they try Las Vegas next. This time, Buffett was even more skeptical. How could they do business in a metropolis of that size and remain closed on Sundays, a day that all of their competitors would be exploiting?

But Buffett trusts his managers because he knows their character. So he gave it a shot. The store was built in Henderson, a mushrooming city adjacent to Las Vegas. The result? This store outsells all others in the R.C. Willey chain, doing a volume of business that far exceeds any competitor in the area. The revenue is twice what Buffett had anticipated.

As this book went to print, R.C. Willey was preparing to open its third store in the Las Vegas area, as well as stores in Reno, Nevada, and Sacramento, California. Sales have grown to more than $600 million, and the target is $1 billion in coming years. "You can understand why the opportunity to partner with people like Bill Child causes me to tap dance to work every morning," Buffett said.

Here's another example of Buffett's adeptness at hiring character. He agreed to purchase Ben Bridge Jeweler over the phone, prior to any face-to-face meeting with the management.

Ed Bridge manages this 65-store West Coast retailer with his cousin, Jon. Both are fourth-generation owner-managers of a business started 89 years ago in Seattle. And over the years, the business and the family have enjoyed extraordinary character reputations.

Buffett knows that he must give complete autonomy to his managers. "I told Ed and Jon that they would be in charge, and they knew I could be believed: After all, it's obvious that [I] would be a disaster at actually running a store or selling jewelry, though there are members of [my] family who have earned black brits as purchasers."

Talk about hiring integrity! Without any provocation from Buffett, the Bridges allocated a substantial portion of the proceeds from their sale to the hundreds of coworkers who had helped the company achieve its success.

Overall, Berkshire has made many such acquisitions—hiring for character first, and talent second—and then asking these CEOs to manage for maximum long-term value, rather than for next quarter's earnings. While they certainly don't ignore the current profitability of their business, Buffett never wants profits to be achieved at the expense of developing ever-greater competitive strengths, including integrity.

It's an approach he learned early in his career.

Warren Edward Buffett was born on August 30, 1930. His father, Howard, was a stockbroker-turned-congressman. The only boy, Warren was the second of three children. He displayed an amazing aptitude for both money and business at a very early age. Acquaintances recount his uncanny ability to calculate columns of numbers off the top of his head—a feat Buffett still amazes business colleagues with today.

At only 6 years old, Buffett purchased six-packs of Coca-Cola from his grandfather's grocery store for 25 cents and resold each of the bottles for a nickel—making a nice five-cent profit. While other children his age were playing hopscotch and jacks, Buffett was already generating cash flow.

Buffett stayed just 2 years in the undergraduate program at Wharton Business School at the University of Pennsylvania. He left disappointed, complaining that he knew more than his professors. Eventually, he transferred to the University of Nebraska–Lincoln. He managed to graduate in only 3 years despite working full time.

Then he finally applied to Harvard Business School. In what was undoubtedly one of the worst admission decisions in history, the school rejected him as "too young." Slighted, Buffett applied to Columbia where famed investment professor Ben Graham taught.

Professor Graham shaped young Buffett's opinions on investing. And the student influenced his mentor as well. Graham bestowed on Buffett the only A+ he ever awarded in decades of teaching.

While Buffett tried working for Graham for a while, he finally struck out on his own with a revolutionary philosophy: He would research the internal workings of extraordinary companies. He could discover what really made them tick and why they held a competitive edge in their markets. And then he would invest in great companies that were trading at substantially less than their market values.

Ten years after its founding, the Buffett Partnership assets were up more than 1,156 percent [compared to the Dow's 122.9 percent], and Buffett was firmly on his way to becoming an investing legend.

In 2004, Warren Buffett was listed by Forbes as the world's second-richest person (right behind Bill Gates), with $42.9 billion in personal wealth. Despite starting with just $300,000 in holdings, Berkshire's holdings now exceed $116 billion. And Buffett and his employees can confidently say they have made thousands of people wealthy.

We often ask business leaders one simple question: Which is more dangerous to your firm—the incompetent new hire or the dishonest new hire? It's the part of our presentation where attendees sit up straight and start thinking.

We always follow the question with an exercise on identifying and hiring integrity. Though it becomes obvious that many of the executives and managers haven't given employee integrity much thought, most of the CEOs in the audiences are increasingly concerned about hiring employees with character.

So, how do you hire workers with integrity? It's possible, but not easy. It is important to spend more time choosing a new employee than you do picking out a new coffee machine. Here are a few simple areas to focus on:

It is important to spend more time choosing a new employee than you do picking out a new coffee machine.

First, ensure educational credentials match the resume. Education is the most misrepresented area on a resume. Notre Dame football coach George O'Leary was fired because the master's degree he said he had earned did not exist, the CEO of software giant Lotus exaggerated his education and military service, and the CEO of Bausch & Lomb forfeited a bonus of more than $1 million because he claimed a fictional MBA.

Job candidates also often claim credit for responsibilities that they never had. Here's a typical scenario:

Job candidate: "I led that project. Saved the company $10 million." Through diligent fact checking, you find an employee at a previous employer who can give you information about the candidate:

Coworker: "Hmm. Actually, Steve was a member of the team, but not the lead. And while it was a great project, we still haven't taken a tally of the cost savings. But $10 million seems really high."

How do you find those things out? Confer with companies where the applicant has worked—especially those firms the person isn't listing as a reference. Talk to people inside the organization, going at least two levels deep (which means you ask each reference for a couple more references). Talk to the nonprofit organizations where the person volunteers. Tap into alumni networks and professional associations. Get on the phone with others in the industry to learn about the person's reputation. Check public records for bankruptcy, civil, and criminal litigation (with the candidate's knowledge). In other words, check candidates' backgrounds carefully (but legally, of course).

We find that most hiring managers spend 90 percent of their time on capability-related questions, and next to no time on character-based questions. In your rush to get someone in the chair, don't forget to check backgrounds and be rigorous in your interviewing for character. Hiring the wrong person can destroy two careers: your employee's—and your own.

Ask ethics-based questions to get to the character issue. We asked a group of executives at a storage company to brainstorm a list of questions they might ask candidates to learn more about their character. Their list included the following questions:

- Who has had the greatest influence on you and why?
- Who is the best CEO you've worked for and why?
- Tell me about your worst boss.
- Who are your role models and why?

- How do you feet about your last manager?
- Tell me about a time you had to explain bad news to your manager.
- What would you do if your best friend did something illegal?
- What would your past manager say about you?
- What does integrity mean to you?
- If you were the CEO of your previous company, what would you change?
- What values did your parents teach you?
- Tell me a few of your faults.
- Why should I trust you?
- How have you dealt with adversity in the past?
- What are your three core values?
- Tell me about a time when you let someone down.
- What is your greatest accomplishment, personal or professional?
- What are your goals and why?
- Tell me about a mistake you made in business and what you learned from it.
- Tell me about a time when you were asked to compromise your integrity.

It's relatively easy to teach a candidate your business. The harder task is trying to instill integrity in someone who doesn't already have it.

Of course, we don't want to imply that it's impossible. Sometimes people will adapt to a positive environment and shine. Men's Wearhouse has certainly had tremendous success hiring former prison inmates, demonstrating everyone should have a second chance.

But integrity is a journey that is very personal, very individual. An outside force, such as an employer, typically can't prescribe it. It's certainly not something that happens overnight. That's one reason many of the CEOs we have talked with prefer promoting people from inside their organizations when possible.

Don Graham, chairman and CEO of the Washington Post Company, said, "There's a very good reason for concentrating your hires and promotions on people who already work in your organization. The best way to predict what someone's going to do in the future is to know what they've done in the past—watch how people address difficult business issues, how they deal with the people who work for them, how they deal with the people for whom they work. You may be able to put on a certain face for a day or even a week, but you're not going to be able to hide the person you are for five or ten years."

Graham tells a story about Frank Batten, who for years ran Landmark Communications and founded The Weather Channel. "Frank is a person of total integrity," Graham says. "Frank once said, 'When you go outside for hire you always get a surprise. Sometimes it's a good surprise. But you never hire quite the person you thought you were hiring.'"

What do you look for in a job applicant? Years of experience? College degree? Specific skill sets? Or do you look for character? If so, you're in good company.

Years ago, Warren Buffett was asked to help choose the next CEO for Salomon Brothers. "What do you think [Warren] was looking for?" Graham asks. "Character and integrity—more than even a particular background. When the reputation of the firm is on the line every day, character counts."

Don't like surprises? Then hire people who have integrity. Want to ensure a good fit with the people you hire? Then hire people who have integrity. Want to ensure your reputation with customers? Then hire people who have integrity.

Are we saying that nothing else matters? No. But we are saying that nothing matters more.

Critical Thinking

1. Describe Warren Buffett's hiring practices that assure he is hiring integrity.
2. What are the top three characteristics that an ethical leader must exhibit (from your perspective)?
3. What area in your life do you need to work on to become an ethical job candidate? What steps can you take to develop ethically in that area?

Internet References

Entrepreneur
   http://www.entrepreneur.com/article/235101
Montana State University Billings
   http://www.msubillings.edu/BusinessFaculty/larsen/MGMT452/HR%20Articles/Can%20You%20Interview%20for%20Integrity%20-%20Across%20the%20Board%20%28MarApr%2007%29.pdf
Recruiterbox
   http://recruiterbox.com/blog/what-warren-buffett-wants-to-know-before-he-hires-you/

From *Integrity Works: Strategies for Becoming a Trusted, Respected and Admired Leader* by **Dana Telford** and **Adrian Gostick**.

Article   Prepared by: Eric Teoro, *Lincoln Christian University*

Creating an Ethical Workplace

Business decisions aren't always black and white. How can you trust that your workers will do the right thing?

DORI MEINERT

Learning Outcomes

After reading this article, you will be able to:

- Describe steps that can be taken to foster ethical behavior in the workplace.

- Describe ethical danger signs.

JPMorgan Chase paid the federal government $13 billion last fall—the largest corporate settlement in U.S. history—to settle charges involving conduct that prosecutors say contributed to the mortgage meltdown. The bank acknowledged that it made serious misrepresentations to the public about numerous residential mortgage-backed securities.

In January, the bank agreed to another $2.6 billion in payments to resolve charges that it failed to adequately warn its clients about Bernard Madoff's multibillion-dollar Ponzi scheme.

JPMorgan's troubles are the latest in a series of high-profile corporate scandals to grab the headlines, damaging company reputations and employee morale.

Last year, 41 percent of U.S. workers said they observed unethical or illegal misconduct on the job, according to the Ethics Resource Center's 2013 National Business Ethics Survey (http://www.ethics.org/nbes/).

Not all of those incidents were major, budget-busting acts of wrongdoing. But ethical lapses tend to snowball. Once employees see others breaking rules without repercussions, they may believe it's OK for them to do so, as well. Or they may get fed up and leave the company.

In short, a culture where misconduct is tolerated—or, worse, encouraged—could result in higher turnover, lower productivity and, ultimately, a diminished reputation and profitability.

On the other hand, companies that work to build and maintain ethical workplace cultures are more financially successful and have more motivated, productive employees, studies have shown.

"If you look at the big picture, the livelihood of the company is at stake," says Holly Nowak, SPHR, director of HR for the Western New York division of Alcott HR (http://www.alcottgroup.com/), an HR outsourcing company with 50 employees based in Farmingdale, N.Y.

HR professionals are in a unique position to help build an ethical workplace culture because their involvement in hiring, training and evaluating employees allows them to influence their organizations at many levels.

They are—or should be—both guardians and champions of the ethical culture in their organizations, says Steven D. Olson, director of the Center for Ethics and Corporate Responsibility (http://ethics.robinson.gsu.edu/) at Georgia State University in Atlanta.

As guardians, they have a duty to protect their organizations' employees, customers and clients from unethical conduct. As champions, they can help their organizations flourish by promoting ethical values in daily operations and by building trust, says Olson, author of Shaping an Ethical Workplace Culture (https://www.shrm.org/about/foundation/products/documents/ 9-13%20ethics%20epg%20final.pdf), a SHRM Foundation report.

Changing Expectations

The 2008 financial crisis and recession tested people's faith in business leaders. Only 15 percent of Americans trust such leaders to tell the truth, according to the 2013 Edelman Trust Barometer (http://www.edelman.com/insights/intellectual-property/trust-2013/). Globally, only 28 percent of the more than 30,000 survey respondents believe that businesses follow ethical practices. The scandal-plagued banking and financial services industry garnered the least trust compared with other industries.

Before 2008, corporate reputations were largely determined by financial success. Today, businesses build trust by treating employees well, demonstrating ethical practices and placing customers ahead of profits, according to the Edelman survey. The rapid rise of social media also is pressuring organizations to be more transparent—or risk exposure of unethical practices.

Meanwhile, researchers have found that ethical workplace cultures make good business sense. From 1997 to 2013, the annualized stock market returns of the *Fortune 100 Best Companies to Work For* (http://www.greatplacetowork.com/best-companies/100-best-companies-to-work-for) in the U.S. were 11.8 percent compared with 6.4 percent for the Russell 3000 index and 6 percent for the Standard & Poor's 500 index, according to the Great Place to Work Institute (http://www.greatplacetowork.com/).

More organizations are recognizing the value of creating ethical workplace cultures. The percentage of companies with "strong" or "strongleaning" ethics cultures climbed to 66 percent last year, up from 60 percent in 2011, according to the National Business Ethics Survey of 6,420 employees.

When companies value ethical performance, misconduct is substantially lower. In 2013, only 20 percent of workers reported seeing misconduct in companies where ethical cultures are "strong," compared with 88 percent who witnessed wrongdoing in companies with the weakest cultures, according to the survey.

What Is an Ethical Culture?

Culture is often seen as abstract and tough to measure. It's more than all those carefully drafted corporate values statements and ethics codes—it's the way things really work. Workplace culture includes how employees dress, how they work with customers and how they interact with their bosses. HR professionals' initial challenge is defining an ethical workplace culture for business leaders who may doubt its effectiveness.

"What it means to me is an environment that makes it easy to do the right thing and makes it difficult to do the wrong thing," says Michael C. Hyter, senior partner, leadership and talent consulting, at Korn Ferry (http://www.kornferry.com/) in Washington, D.C.

In the SHRM Foundation report, Olson describes an ethical workplace culture as one that gives priority to employee rights, fair procedures, and equity in pay and promotion, and that promotes tolerance, compassion, loyalty and honesty in the treatment of customers and employees.

When employers respect the law and treat employees in a fair and consistent manner, employees begin to trust managers and internalize the company's values as their own. Once that happens, ethics become embedded in the workplace culture, he says.

Managers' Influence

Managers play a major role in determining whether employees embrace a company's values. If managers and top leaders don't model ethical behavior or enforce rules in a fair manner, employees lose trust. Studies also show that people are more likely to override their own ethical concerns if their manager doesn't share those concerns.

So, recent survey results that show managers are responsible for 60 percent of workplace misconduct are especially troubling, says Ethics Resource Center (http:www.ethics.org/) President Patricia J. Harned. Senior managers are more likely than lower-level managers to break the rules, the National Business Ethics Survey found.

When managers are involved in misconduct, "it really has an impact on people's perceptions of the culture altogether," says Harned, noting it was the first time the survey asked who was committing the misconduct.

More than 1 in 5 workers who reported misconduct said they suffered retaliation as a result, up from 12 percent in 2007. A third of those who declined to report the misconduct said they feared they would be punished for doing so.

Employees are quick to pick up on inconsistencies, says Rebecca Barnes-Hogg, SPHR, founder of YOLO Insights (http://yoloinsights.com/), an HR consulting company in Little River, S.C.

She recalls an incident involving a midlevel manager who was running a side business from work. He rationalized that it was OK as long as he was getting his job done. However, when he disciplined a staff member, the staffer complained to HR about the double standard: Managers could break rules, but others couldn't.

"A lot of these things happen because no one speaks up," Barnes-Hogg says. "If we had known a year earlier, we could have avoided a lot of bad morale and turnover."

At a different company, a high-level executive was caught viewing pornography on his work computer. Although he was a valuable asset, the chief executive officer made the right decision and let him go, she recalls. An announcement was made at an all-staff meeting. Without giving details, the CEO let employees know that he had taken action, she says.

"I think the employees felt 'These are people we can trust,'" she says.

Can You Teach Ethics?

HR professionals help lay out the expectations for employees by developing written standards of ethical workplace conduct, providing training to make sure everyone is aware of the expectations and equipping managers to reinforce the company's values through their actions.

When interviewing applicants, many HR professionals say they strive for a good "cultural fit," asking for examples of how potential hires have juggled competing values in the past or responded to unethical behavior in others.

The Six Elements of an Ethics and Compliance Program

- Written standards of ethical workplace conduct.
- Training on standards.
- Company resources that provide advice on ethics issues.
- A process to report potential violations confidentially or anonymously.
- Performance evaluations of ethical conduct.
- Systems to discipline violators.

Source: *2013 National Business Ethics Survey* (http://www.ethics.org/nbes/), Ethics Resource Center.

Although psychological assessments are an option, most focus on the behaviors that people see, says Joyce LeMay, SPHR, associate professor of HR at Bethel University in St. Paul, Minn. In a survey of 210 HR professionals she conducted last year, just 5 percent said they believed it was possible to hire an ethical person.

Once individuals are hired, ongoing training is critical to maintain a heightened level of awareness of ethical choices employees will face on the job, HR professionals say. Harned sees positive signs.

For example, the percentage of companies providing ethics training increased from 74 percent in 2011 to 81 percent in 2013, the National Business Ethics Survey found. Other key indicators of strong ethical workplace cultures: Two-thirds of companies include ethical conduct as a performance measure in employee evaluations, up from 60 percent in 2011, and almost 3 in 4 companies communicate internally about disciplinary actions when wrongdoing occurs.

Many companies provide online ethics training, which can be easier to administer and track, but live training is more memorable, says Denise Messineo, SPHR, senior vice president of HR at Dimension Data (http://www.dimensiondata.com/en-US), a global ITC solutions and services provider with U.S. headquarters in New York City.

Every other year, most of Dimension Data's 915 U.S. employees participate in a half-day ethics program, discussing how they would respond to various workplace scenarios.

"It just creates a great dialogue and awareness around what Dimension Data considers ethical behavior," Messineo says. "Because different people bring different things to the table based on their background, you can see some 'aha' moments as people talk through the different scenarios."

At Intuitive Research and Technology Corp (http://www.irtc-hq.com) in Huntsville, Ala., new employees are required to attend a session called "Let's Talk Ethics with Hal." In the session, the company's co-founder and president, Howard "Hal" Brewer, discusses specific examples of ethical decisions employees will face in doing business with the government and other entities and how important their actions are to the company.

"He makes it clear that he is the ethics officer," says Juanita Phillips, SPHR, director of HR at the engineering and analytical services company, which has 282 employees. "I am in on those meetings, so they know I am a resource as well."

"His strength is that he means every word of it, and he shows it in how he lives every day in terms of running the company," says Phillips, adding that she knows it makes an impression because she has heard employees later paraphrasing some of his advice.

Howard Winkler, SPHR, project manager for ethics and compliance at Southern Co. (http://www.southerncompany.com/) in Atlanta, says he's constantly changing his company's training program to keep its 25,000 employees engaged and attentive to ethics issues. He runs contests, produces videos and uses internal social media.

Two years ago, the company invited a convicted felon to speak to employees about how a good person can go astray. The former chief financial officer for a major health care company served five years in federal prison for fraud.

"It made an enormous impression," Winkler says. "This person didn't start out his career looking to commit fraud. The main message was that once you make the first ethical compromise, you are embarking on a path that can lead all the way to a prison cell."

Winkler recently replaced the company's mandatory online ethics training, which required employees to read the code of ethics and certify that they had done so. "When it's put online, it usually has all the charm and engagement of a software licensing agreement," he says.

He worked with his corporate communications department to hire actors and produce "a really nice uplifting video that lasts less than 10 minutes as a far more engaging alternative to simply scrolling through a lot of words."

This year, Southern Co. is kicking off an online video ethics training series to ensure that new front-line managers have the tools they need to step into their new roles, Winkler says. He also tries to create opportunities for senior executives to talk to employees about ethics, which he says helps elevate the issue in employees' eyes.

Beware of Ethical Danger Zones

Sometimes good people can get swept into unethical behavior, warns Steven D. Olson, director of the Center for Ethics and Corporate Responsibility at Georgia State University and author of *Shaping an Ethical Workplace Culture,* a SHRM Foundation report. Watch out for these danger signs:

Conflicting goals. If forced to cut corners to attain performance goals or given objectives that they believe are unattainable, employees may feel pressured to compromise ethical standards and lose trust in their managers.

Fear of retaliation. The fear of payback for doing the right thing is a powerful cause of inaction in organizations.

Avoidance. When bad things go unpunished or are ignored, that can lead to even worse behavior. It sends the message "We don't care."

Rationalization. The "Everybody's doing it" mindset can lead people into murky ethical waters.

Lowered thresholds. With each unethical decision, the next one becomes easier. It's a slippery slope.

Euphemisms. Using neutral terms to describe questionable actions (e.g., "creative accounting") is a subtle form of rationalization.

Evaluation Time

To gauge whether their efforts are successful, many HR professionals use employee surveys.

At Southern Co., last year 73 percent of employees said executive managers earn their trust "by consistently demonstrating high ethical behavior," up from 68 percent in 2009. The company also tracks employees' fear of retaliation when reporting a concern: 69 percent said they had no fear of retaliation, up from 60 percent in 2009.

"We'd like the scores to be higher, but the constant improvement is gratifying," Winkler says.

In addition, the company measures employees' understanding of what the company expects of them. Last year, 93 percent of employees said they understood that, along with their business results, the success of their career at the company

"depends on my ethical behavior." And 94 percent agreed that "I am personally responsible for reporting improper conduct."

FIS (http://www.fisglobal.com/), a global provider of banking technologies with 37,000 employees worldwide, has moved away from employee surveys because the results were too predictable, says Michael Oates, executive vice president, general counsel and chief human resources officer at company headquarters in Jacksonville, Fla.

Instead, the company's top executives conduct employee meetings and roundtable sessions several times a year. "We found we can keep a thumb on the pulse better that way," Oates says.

Many organizations include ethics or related values in employees' performance reviews. Others monitor complaints and turnover for signs of a deteriorating culture.

"You start to see a decline in productivity because the workforce isn't engaged. People don't want to produce for an organization that they don't feel is ethical and operating in a compliant manner," says Nowak of Alcott HR. Another red flag is when employees suddenly stop raising issues, she adds. More than likely, they have given up.

Of course, the ultimate distress signal is when the organization starts losing valuable people.

"When I have seen organizations stall—someone brings something to their attention, and it's not handled in a timely manner—what I see is almost an unraveling of the organization," Nowak says.

Particularly in smaller markets, "you're going to have a hard time recruiting people to replace the ones who have left" if the organization has a reputation for treating its employees unfairly, she says.

Talk About It—A Lot

Finally, ethics needs to be brought up regularly so that it stays at the top of employees' minds. Ask managers to raise ethics questions in meetings. Encourage top executives to speak to it, as well. Managers can't monitor employees' every move, but they can help them recognize the right thing to do when company priorities clash.

"When an ethical issue arises, it does not come gift-wrapped with a note that says, 'This is an ethical issue. Prepare to make an ethical decision.' It just comes across as another business problem that needs to be solved," Winkler says.

"So if we can keep the chatter up and keep ethics on the minds of our employees, they are more likely to recognize and identify a business problem as having ethical ramifications than they otherwise would. Psychologists call it priming," he says. "That's what an ethical culture is all about: It's a place where people are more likely to see issues as having ethical implications."

As guardians of their workplace culture, HR professionals can not only lead the charge for ethical values but also inspire and empower employees at all levels to do the right thing. And they'll create a stronger organization in doing so.

Critical Thinking

1. In addition to those mentioned in the article, describe concrete steps managers can take to encourage ethical behavior.

2. Describe forms of unethical behavior that you have witnessed or committed in organizational settings. What affects did such behavior have on you? On your attitude toward the organization?

3. Describe conflicting goals that could encourage unethical behavior.

Internet References

Graziadio Business Review (Pepperdine University)
https://gbr.pepperdine.edu/2010/08/creating-and-sustaining-an-ethical-workplace-culture/

Houston Chronicle: Small Business
http://smallbusiness.chron.com/effects-negative-corporate-culture-ethical-behavior-65787.html

Society for Human Resource Management
http://www.shrm.org/about/foundation/products/documents/9-13%20ethics%20epg%20final.pdf

True North Partnering
http://www.truenorthpartnering.com/sites/default/files/Unethical%20behavior%20and%20bad%20managers.pdf

Workplace Therapist
http://theworkplacetherapist.com/top-4-worst-corporate-cultures-1-"this-is-an-unethical-culture"/

Article   Prepared by: Eric Teoro, *Lincoln Christian University*

Using Social Media to Boost Ethics and Compliance

PAMELA BABCOCK

Learning Outcomes

After reading this article, you will be able to:

- Describe social media usage among employees.

- Describe steps an organization can take to utilize social media to improve ethics and compliance.

Organization leaders should take a cue from their employees and spend some time on social media, experts said.

Even though employees may misuse social media—and need to be trained on what is and is not acceptable—it is a powerful tool that companies can use to promote ethical practices and culture, a recent study found.

To more effectively engage employees, enhance ethics and compliance programs, and positively affect workplace culture, businesses should tap their employees' expertise and encourage workers to use social media, according to a July 17, 2103, report from the Ethics Resource Center (ERC) in Arlington, Va. The key is seizing the opportunity of having tech-savvy employees who are invested in the company while mitigating the risk of inappropriate postings.

"If you can't beat them, leverage them," quipped ERC President Patricia J. Harned, PhD, adding that active social networkers "have a really strong interest in the culture of the workplace. They are more likely to be responsive if you're making use of social networks to address company culture and employee concerns."

The report, *National Business Ethics Survey of Social Networkers: New Risks and Opportunities at Work* (http://www.ethics.org/nbes/download.html), is based on responses to a September 2012 online poll from 2,089 workers at U.S.-based companies. Respondents to the survey, sponsored by PwC and NAVEX Global, said they were active on at least one social networking site.

Andrea Falcione, J.D., PwC's managing director of risk assurance in Boston, said companies are missing a tremendous opportunity "to show that their organizations take this stuff seriously and that it's in the blood of the organization."

Social networkers can help business leaders, HR and ethics professionals improve workplace culture. But companies first need a policy that's "very clear about what's acceptable and not acceptable behavior," Harned stressed.

Not Just Younger Workers

Perhaps not surprisingly, active social networkers (those spending 30 percent or more of their day online) air company linen in public. Six out of 10 said they'd comment on their personal sites about their company if it were in the news; 53 percent share information about work projects at least once a week; and more than a third often comment on personal sites about managers, co-workers and even clients, the study found.

But some findings may come as a surprise. Among them:

- Almost three out of four (72 percent) social networkers spend at least some of their workday on social networking sites, and 28 percent said it's an hour or more. One-third of the 28 percent also admit that none of the activity is work-related.

- Social networking isn't just for the young. Forty-seven percent of active social networkers are under 30, but 40 percent are between the ages of 30 and 44.

- More active social networkers (those who spend 30 percent or more of their day online) are more likely to see and report misconduct (77 percent) than other U.S.

workers (66 percent) and are more likely to experience retaliation when reporting it. The study did not indicate why, but Falcione said it's something compliance and ethics professionals "should consider and continue to monitor."

Training Is Key

Having a solid social media policy and training employees can change behaviors while improving compliance and reducing risk.

CPR (communicate, prepare and respond) is essential, according to Steve Miranda, SPHR, GPHR, managing director of Cornell University's Center for Advanced Human Resource Studies and the Society for Human Resource Management's former chief HR and content integration officer.

Communicate: Have a clearly documented policy. Employees need to know if it's OK to post the company logo on Facebook or whether they're authorized to post something online about the company's downsizing.

Prepare: Train and educate staff. If a contractor offers tickets to a major sporting event, can you accept? Raytheon depicts such scenarios using humorous videos so that "it's not like you're slapping employees on the back of the wrist with a ruler and saying 'Obey!'" Miranda explained.

Review: Use surveys or Internet/security monitoring to gauge whether the policy is working. Is inappropriate or sensitive client information being posted online? Consider highlighting examples of employees (names can be removed) who were dismissed for breaching social media protocol.

Zappos offers Twitter training during new-hire orientation and has hundreds of employees on Twitter, noted Sharlyn Lauby, SPHR, president of ITM Group Inc., a Fort Lauderdale, Fla.-based HR training consulting firm, and a member of SHRM's Ethics and Corporate Social Responsibility special expertise panel.

Even if a company decides not to be active on social media, employees should be trained to use the tools—especially privacy settings, she added.

"Training is an effective way to engage employees and demonstrate commitment to the ethical use of the tool," Lauby said in an e-mail to *SHRM Online*.

Steps Companies Can Take

Generally, Falcione said, companies in the United Kingdom and Europe use social media to communicate compliance and ethics issues more than their U.S. counterparts.

Some organizations offer texting for employees to report actual or potential misconduct. Ultimately, the text might go to the company hotline or a third-party administrator. Others provide Web-based platforms where workers can report misconduct.

Ingrid Fredeen, vice president of NAVEX's ethical leadership group, said companies should think broadly about social media. Setting up a "full-blown" Facebook or LinkedIn page for ethics isn't necessary. She said companies should consider doing the following:

- **Hosting moderated intranet conversation groups.** Compliance professionals can post content, questions and stories in a format that allows employees to comment.
- **Providing video podcasting to share positive stories.** Organizations can invite employees and even business partners to nominate people whose behaviors and actions demonstrate high levels of integrity.
- **Creating a company blog.** The blog can contain commentary about organizational values and ethical performance, like Best Buy's featuring Chief Ethics Officer Kathleen Edmond.
- **Hosting internal webinars.** Through these employees can ask senior leaders ethics compliance questions. It's also good to have an intranet site where managers can download materials to help talk about ethics and compliance with staff, Fredeen said.
- **Using sites like Facebook and YouTube to share positive stories externally.** Many large organizations regularly promote good deeds and their commitment to ethics and compliance.

How Much Is Too Much?

What about the ethics of employees using social media for personal benefit while on the company dime?

Fredeen said many organizations allow "reasonable use" of social media and have found that permitting employees some personal use of networking sites helps keep them engaged and is more realistic from a policy-enforcement perspective.

"Having a policy that bans personal use is really untenable today," and fair and consistent enforcement is virtually impossible, Fredeen wrote in an e-mail to *SHRM Online*. Although the report study said monitoring can help, it's "a thorny legal area," and companies should get legal advice before implementing such a program, she suggested.

"Personal use of social media should not interfere with employees' jobs nor hinder productivity," added Falcione. "As with anything, there is a fine line, and it behooves companies to stay ahead of any negative trends."

Critical Thinking

1. What form of social media usage would encourage you to be more ethical in the workplace? Why?

2. Describe unethical social media practices by employees and companies.

3. Develop a social media policy for employees that encourages ethical behavior.

Internet References

Citadel Information Group

http://citadel-information.com/wp-content/uploads/2010/12/10-social-media-must-haves-for-corporate-compliance-and-ethics-michelle-sherman-2-2012.pdf

Forbes

http://www.forbes.com/sites/davidvinjamuri/2011/11/03/ethics-and-the-5-deadly-sins-of-social-media/

The Network

https://www.tnwinc.com/8665/leverage-social-media-training/

PAMELA BABCOCK is a freelance writer based in the New York City area.

Unit 4

UNIT

Prepared by: Eric Teoro, *Lincoln Christian University*

Ethical Issues and Dilemmas in the Workplace

An ethical issue can be defined as a situation in which a person or group of individuals needs to choose between alternatives, and the need for those alternatives to be assessed as being either morally right or wrong. Typically, ethical issues focus on the conflict between ethical and unethical behavior. An ethical dilemma, on the other hand, refers to a situation in which an individual or group of individuals needs to make a choice between moral requirements. As such, ethical dilemmas pose more complex problems. Regardless of the choice an actor or group of actors makes, they risk violating other ethical principles. Both ethical issues and ethical dilemmas occur within organizational settings. It is imperative, therefore, that managers, employees, and students recognize different courses of actions, and determine the ethicality of those courses.

The articles in this unit represent a variety of ethical issues and dilemmas. Should employees blow the whistle when they are aware of corporate wrongdoing? What if that wrongdoing is not illegal? How should such employees navigate the competing claims of loyalty to an employer and the common good? What if blowing the whistle hurts innocent people? How do multinational companies navigate different ethical systems and cultural norms? What difficulties arise when a company tries to institute ethical practices in a host country when that country's culture is significantly different from the home country's culture? Can they transplant ethical standards from one culture to another? How should one view a multinational corporation that initiates an internal investigation of corruption within a subsidiary? Which should be given greater weight—the self-initiated investigation or the existent corruption? Does a sexually charged workplace constitute sexual harassment? Can a company be considered ethical if it promotes ethical behavior in one area, but apparently fails to do so in another? Is having a diverse workforce an ethical imperative, and does diversity extend to lifestyle choices? What are the rights of employees who engage in behavior such as smoking, when such behavior could result in higher healthcare costs for other employees? What ethical concerns arise when marketing to children? Who is primarily responsible for the marketing messages children receive—companies or parents?

The business use of technology raises ethical questions. Should marketers use developments in neuroscience to influence consumer behavior? What is the role of informed consent in marketing research, especially when such research can be conducted without participant knowledge? Should companies be allowed to track customer computer use? What if such practices resulted in better customer service or desired advertisements? What is the proper use of social media technology by employers and employees? Is it acceptable for companies to consider non-work related postings when making hiring decisions? Is teaching hacking an ethically acceptable practice, especially if one cannot control what alumni do with such knowledge and skills?

Article   Prepared by: Eric Teoro, *Lincoln Christian University*

Overcoming the Fraud Triangle

CURTIS C. VERSCHOOR

Learning Outcomes

After reading this article, you will be able to:

- Describe the three elements that contribute to fraud.

- Describe the role of whistleblowing in combating fraud.

Companies still need to do more to lessen the financial pressures and reduce the rationalizations that lead to fraud.

The Financial Executives Research Foundation (FERF) recently published the results of its surveys of financial executives, managers, and staff. The report, Breaking the Cycle of Fraud, recommends strategies to mitigate wrongdoing in the two areas of the fraud triangle that are most closely connected to ethical matters: financial pressure and rationalization.

The fraud triangle was created by criminology researchers Edwin Sutherland and Donald Cressey to describe the three elements that come together when an individual commits fraud:

- Opportunity (weak internal controls) allows the fraud to occur.
- Financial pressure (motive) is the perceived need for committing the fraud.
- Rationalization (weak ethics) is the mind-set of the fraudster that justifies the crime.

By imposing stronger internal controls and processes, companies can take specific, visible action to reduce the risk of opportunity. But financial pressure and rationalization closely involve individuals' ethical framework and organizational culture, and those are much more difficult to influence overtly and directly.

Financial Pressure

Breaking the Cycle reiterates the widely described importance of a positive tone at the top of the organization in mitigating

financial pressure. The report describes numerous historical examples where a pressured corporate culture brought ruin. In these cases, achieving short-term financial performance targets for bonus purposes was given far higher priority by senior executives than was acting ethically and considering the sustainability of the enterprise.

A resulting ethical culture of failure to "walk the talk" permeates the attitudes of lower-level executives and employees who are likely to do almost anything to please their bosses—even if it violates provisions in the organization's code of conduct as well as their own personal ethical standards.

It doesn't seem like companies are expanding performance goals to avoid this trap. On April 29, 2015, the SEC announced a proposed rule to require companies to disclose "the relationship between executive pay and a company's financial performance." The new rule is intended to help shareholders be better informed when electing directors and voting on executive compensation. The metric chosen to represent company performance is total shareholder return (TSR) calculated on an annual basis and compared to the TSR of a peer group of companies. But this rule will only reinforce the existing focus on short-term financial goals and targets. Performance measurements for rewarding senior executives and others should be expanded to include accomplishment of more ethics-based matter.

Rationalization

The FERF report lists a number of important aspects of an effective ethical culture that strengthen efforts to avoid rationalization of improper behavior. These include useful ethics training tailored to the organization, annual surveys of employee attitudes, and effective whistleblowing programs. The training should involve all levels of the organization. It should contain real-world examples of the negative consequences of unethical behavior, be based on the organization's code of ethics, and include true-to-life applications. Other research has shown that in-person training is likely to be most effective.

The annual surveys of employee attitudes and evaluations of the ethical climate recommended by Breaking the Cycle must be professionally designed to avoid leading questions. Surveys must also be administered anonymously to encourage truthful responses that will be helpful in assessing the ethical climate of the organization and the effectiveness of the ethics program. Otherwise, the effort could backfire.

If administered properly, whistleblower or helpline programs are extremely important in detecting and deterring unethical behavior in an organization. The 2014 biannual survey by the Association of Certified Fraud Examiners (ACFE) reports that the most common method through which occupational fraud and abuse is revealed (40 percent) is tips. This is "more than twice the rate of any other detection method. Employees accounted for nearly half of all tips that led to the discovery of fraud," according to the report.

Encourage Whistleblowing

The Anti-Fraud Collaboration reported in 2014 that many employees are hesitant to report wrongdoing internally using their organization's reporting process. The reasons for hesitating are because they have a significant fear of retaliation or because they believe that senior management is involved or won't take any action to stop unethical behavior. There are some legal protections for whistleblowers in some states and some industries. This is why the IMA Statement of Ethical Professional Practice recommends that individuals having an ethical conflict should consult their own attorney—not someone affiliated with their employer—regarding their legal obligations and rights.

Ethics training should include motivation for everyone in the organization, as well as suppliers, to utilize the helpline when warranted. Some of the features of a well-designed whistleblower helpline include wide access with global language capability and adaptation to local customs, if necessary; a single helpline for all ethics-related issues; protocols for handling any reports professionally, including documented formal processes for timely investigation and procedures for confidential reporting of results; and formal data security and document retention policies.

The IMA Statement requires that all members "shall encourage others within their organization to act in accordance with its overarching principles: Honesty, Fairness, Objectivity, and Responsibility." Have you done your share of encouragement lately?

Critical Thinking

1. Develop concrete steps a company can employ to combat fraud. Defend your recommendations.

2. Describe fraudulent behaviors. How do individuals rationalize them?

Internet References

Business Ethics
   http://business-ethics.com/2014/09/23/1840-business-fraud-culture-is-the-culprit/

EY
   http://www.ey.com/GL/en/Services/Assurance/Fraud-Investigation—Dispute-Services/11th-Global-Fraud-Survey—Driving-ethical-growth—new-markets—new-challenges

Fraud Magazine
   http://www.fraud-magazine.com/article.aspx?id=4294969523

Curtis C. Verschoor, CMA, CPA, is the Emeritus Ledger & Quill Research Professor, School of Accountancy and MIS, and an honorary Senior Wicklander Research Fellow in the Institute for Business and Professional Ethics, both at DePaul University, Chicago. He also is a Research Scholar in the Center for Business Ethics at Bentley University, Waltham, Mass., and chair of IMA's Ethics Committee. He was selected by Trust Across America-Trust Around the World as one of the Top Thought Leaders in Trustworthy Business–2015. His e-mail address is **curtisverschoor@sbcglobal.net**.

Article   Prepared by: Eric Teoro, *Lincoln Christian University*

Opting to Blow the Whistle or Choosing to Walk Away

ALINA TUGEND

Learning Outcomes

After reading this article, you will be able to:

- Describe challenges involved in reporting unethical behavior on the part of managers.

- Discern motives behind whistleblowing.

- Determine when to refrain from making managerial behavior public.

Whistle-blowers have been big news lately—from Chelsea Manning, formerly known as Pfc. Bradley Manning, to Edward J. Snowden. Yet, for most people, the question of whether to expose unethical or illegal activities at work doesn't make headlines or involve state secrets.

But that doesn't make the problem less of a quandary. The question of when to remain quiet and when to speak out—and how to do it—can be extraordinarily difficult no matter what the situation.

And while many think of ethics violations as confined to obviously illegal acts, like financial fraud or safety violations, the line often can be much blurrier and, therefore, more difficult to navigate.

According to the Ethics Resource Center, a nonprofit research organization, the No. 1 misconduct observed—by a third of 4,800 respondents—was misuse of company time. That was closely followed by abusive behavior and lying to employees.

The findings were published in the organization's 2011 National Business Ethics Survey, which interviewed, on the phone or online, employees in the commercial sector who were employed at least 20 hours a week. It has been conducted biannually since 1994.

But offensive behavior that creates a hostile work environment, although often not thought of as unethical behavior, is the leading reason people leave their jobs, said Patricia J. Harned, president of the center. "Abusive and intimidating behavior by supervisors and managers creates a toxic work environment."

So does lying to employees. Lester, who asked that I use only his first name to avoid possible legal issues, worked at a global consulting company for about 3 years, earning high performance ratings. At one point, he said, he accidentally learned that his manager had deliberately lied to deny him a promotion opportunity. Lester spoke to the hiring manager to no avail, and because the company had a strong ethics program—including a specific "no retaliation policy" and a hot line to report ethics complaints—he reported the situation.

An investigation found no wrongdoing, and although Lester appealed the findings, no action was taken against the manager. That is when he says the retaliation began.

"All my direct reports were taken away from me and I was given the most difficult projects with the least resources," he said. "A whole series of things happened, which were unlikely to be a coincidence."

After about 8 months of this, he decided to leave.

Lester's experience may be the reason the misconduct most often seen is not the one most often reported. According to the Ethics Resources Center report, which is sponsored by major corporations like Wal-Mart and Northrop Grumman, less than half of those who observed a boss lying to employees reported it.

On the other hand, while only 12 percent said they had witnessed someone stealing from the company, almost 70 percent of those who saw such activity reported it.

One of the difficulties in cases like Lester's is that no law has been broken. True whistleblowing, according to Stephen M. Kohn, a lawyer and executive director of the National Whistleblowers Center, is when people report seeing or experiencing something at their company that is against the law, rather than cases in which employees feel mistreated, but nothing illegal has occurred.

It appears, however, that an increasing number of employees are willing to come forward in both types of cases. More people are using their companies' ethics procedures to report misconduct, and more people are filing whistle-blower claims.

Mr. Kohn, whose organization refers potential whistle-blowers to lawyers, said there had been a 30 percent increase in the number of people requesting referrals over the last 18 months, which comes to about 1,500 requests a year.

He also said the quality of complaints—with more documentation and from higher-level employees—had increased.

Some of this is because of legislation rewarding whistle-blowers for coming forth and protecting them against retaliation. The most prominent of those is the Dodd-Frank Act, which passed in 2010. Under that act, the Securities and Exchange Commission oversees the Office of the Whistleblower, which in 2012 alone received 3,001 tips.

It may seem counterintuitive that reporting bad behavior would go up during the recession and afterward, when people fear for their jobs. Ms. Harned said, however, that one explanation was that employees were less able to change jobs, so they might be more willing to try to change a negative work culture.

"Historically, when the economy is good, companies take more risks and focus more on the bottom line," Ms. Harned said. "They're not talking about ethics as much."

But, just as reporting is on the rise, so is retaliation. More than one in five employees interviewed said they experienced some sort of reprisal when they reported misconduct, ranging from being excluded from decision-making activities and getting the cold shoulder from other employees to being passed over for promotion.

That is almost double the number who said they were retaliated against in the 2007 study.

Even more alarming, in 2009, 4 percent of those who said they experienced reprisals for reporting wrongdoing cited physical threats to themselves or their property. In 2011, that rose to 31 percent.

"Whistle-blowing does threaten cultures and individuals, even when companies say they want it and think they want it,"

said Kirk O. Hanson, executive director of the Markkula Center for Applied Ethics at Santa Clara University.

And, he said, it's very easy to rationalize that an action—say, denying a promotion—is not actually payback for reporting misconduct, but because the worker isn't a team player.

So, while it's important to expose unethical behavior, it's also necessary to be very clear why you're doing it—and how to do it right.

"A good thing to ask yourself is, 'Why am I doing this? Am I trying to help the company or just get someone in trouble?'" said Stuart Sidle, director of the Industrial-Organizational Psychology program at the University of New Haven.

You need to ensure that you're not talking yourself out of taking an ethical stand, nor talking yourself into reporting something for the wrong reason, Professor Hanson said.

"Have someone you can bounce dilemmas off who has similar values," he said. "To make sure you're not rationalizing not doing anything, and to make sure there's a genuine problem—someone to help you be strong but also to test your realities."

In general, employees should follow the proper channels, like addressing the issue with the person directly supervising the supposed culprit, said John M. Thornton, a professor of accounting ethics at Azusa Pacific University.

Along the same lines, think very hard before going public.

"I question someone trying to report externally before reporting internally," Mr. Sidle said. It's too easy, now, he said, to put up a video of bad behavior on YouTube or lash out on Facebook without ever speaking with the people who might be willing to resolve the problems.

On the other hand, don't shy away from reporting bad behavior because you don't want to be seen as that worst elementary school insult—a tattletale.

"You don't want a culture of tattling, but you do want a culture of telling if something is harming the company and the community," Professor Sidle said.

And companies need to be specific in how they talk about ethics, he added.

"It's useless just to talk about unethical behavior," he said. "Everyone is against fraud. Everyone is against disrespectful behavior, but how is it defined? Leadership has to give examples. If someone asks you to backdate something because the client asked, it's unethical, even if it's commonly done."

And, finally, whistle-blowers should know that most cases are not settled in their favor. "This may be attributable to injustices in the system, or lack of merit or proof of the alleged wrongdoing," Professor Thornton said.

For good or for bad, most of us will never face the decisions that Mr. Manning and Mr. Snowden have. But that doesn't mean our choices—to confront or to ignore—aren't important.

"Some will always cheat on their expense reports," Professor Hanson said. "Some will never cheat. Most of us are in the middle. It's a constant struggle to do the right thing."

Critical Thinking

1. Is reporting unethical behavior ever an unethical act? Why or why not?
2. What are the challenges inherent in whistleblowing?
3. What advice would you give to someone who is considering whistleblowing?

Create Central

www.mhhe.com/createcentral

Internet References

U.S. Department of Labor
http://www.whistleblowers.gov/

U.S. Equal Employment Opportunity Commission
http://www.eeoc.gov/laws/types/facts-retal.cfm

U.S. Securities and Exchange Commission
http://www.sec.gov/whistleblower

Article

Prepared by: Eric Teoro, *Lincoln Christian University*

The Unexpected Cost of Staying Silent

Not blowing the whistle may seem like the easy way out, but those who choose silence pay a price.

AMY FREDIN

Learning Outcomes

After reading this article, you will be able to:

- Recognize that individuals who remain silent about wrongdoing in organizations often regret doing so.

- Recognize various deterrents to whistleblowing, enabling possible reporting improvements.

". . . and another massive fraud was just uncovered today thanks to a whistleblower who came forward with critical information. . ." We've all heard these reports on the news and read about them in the newspapers, but this type of activity wouldn't happen in *my* organization, right? And even if it did, certainly *my* employees would quickly take corrective action, right? Let's take a look at the current landscape for organizational wrongdoing, including fraud, as well as the prevalence of whistleblowing in response to these activities. The findings alone may be surprising.

To bring these topics a little closer to home, additional analysis outlines the situations of wrongdoing some of our fellow IMA members encountered. Many individuals in the survey did blow the whistle in these wrongdoing cases, but others chose not to report the situations. This article looks further at their reasons for staying silent and their subsequent feelings of regret associated with that decision.

What Do the Surveys Say?

PricewaterhouseCoopers (PwC) has conducted several global studies of economic crime over the past decade. Most recently,

its 2011 study reports data from nearly 4,000 companies worldwide, including 156 from the United States. (See www.pwc.com/gx/en/economiccrime-survey/index.jhtml for PwC's 2011, 2009, and 2007 Global Economic Crime Surveys.)

Data from the 2011 study indicates that 34 percent of all companies (45 percent of US companies) reported having uncovered a significant economic crime during the previous 12-month period. The term "significant" means the crime had a definite impact on the business, either from direct, tangible damage or from collateral or psychological damage. These crimes occurred in companies of all sizes and industries. The noted wrongdoings included such instances as cybercrime, bribery and corruption, accounting fraud, and, most frequently, asset misappropriation.

Just 2 years earlier, more than 3,000 companies worldwide (71 US companies) responded to PwC's 2009 survey where 30 percent of companies (35 percent of US companies) reported experiencing a significant economic crime over the previous 12-month period. Considering both of these recent surveys, the prevalence of these crimes is disturbing, to say the least. The loss amounts are staggering as well. In 2011 (and 2009), 54 percent (44 percent) of US companies estimated their fraud losses to be between $100,000 and $5 million, with another 10 percent (8 percent) reporting that their losses amounted to more than $5 million.

PwC also identified detection sources for these crimes. In 2009, 34 percent of the incidences worldwide were initially found because of internal or external "tips," but the largest source of detection during that time frame came from companies' own internal controls, which accounted for 46 percent. In 2011, the global survey reported similar rankings but an even larger disparity between these two detection methods, with only 23 percent of frauds being detected by "tips," while 50 percent were detected from a variety of internal control procedures. Kalaithasan Kuppusamy and David Yong Gun Fie reported similar rankings in their October 2004 article, "Developing Whistleblowing Policies: An Aid to Internal Auditors," in *Accountants Today*. They reported global survey results where auditors ranked first and whistleblowers ranked second in terms of detection sources for economic crime.

Though detail for US detection sources in 2011 wasn't reported, the sources of detection in the US in 2009 looked very different from the global results. "The single most common way that fraud was detected among US survey respondents was through tip-offs," the report notes, where whistleblowers alerted officials to 48 percent of the crimes; internal controls initially detected 28 percent of the crimes during this time period.

With the prevalence of crime and the importance of whistleblowing well documented, it might lead you to believe that more and more individuals are coming forward to report organizational wrongdoing. But what percentage of individuals who either know about or suspect wrongdoing come forward? Going back to 1992, a US federal government survey of its own employees reported that as many as 50 percent of individuals who were aware of a crime chose to remain silent.

A slightly later study, "Whistle-Blower Disclosures and Management Retaliation" by Joyce Rothschild and Terance Miethe, published in the February 1999 issue of *Work and Occupations,* reported a similar level of nonreporting, but does that level still apply today? As we head into a new era where whistleblowers have the potential to be rewarded financially for their information because of the recently instituted Dodd-Frank Wall Street Reform and Consumer Protection Act, it seems appropriate to take an even more current look at the landscape around those who observe organizational wrongdoing.

The IMA Study

In an effort to understand this issue from an insider's perspective, I surveyed attendees at IMA's Annual Conference & Exposition in 2007. Attendees could complete an anonymous survey, which included questions predominantly related to whistleblowing and internal controls, in exchange for a chance to win one of 10 $50 cash prizes. Of the 75 individuals who completed the survey, 45 reported having observed wrongdoing within their organizations, and 27 of these 45 individuals stated that they reported this information to the appropriate authorized party, suggesting a 60 percent report rate.

The 60 percent rate suggests we may be making strides in encouraging whistleblowers to come forward. Yet five of the 27 individuals who blew the whistle on one situation admitted to staying silent on at least one other. The remaining 18 of the 45 individuals who had observed one or more incidences of wrongdoing didn't report any of them. If this last group of 18 nonreporters is analyzed on its own, it suggests that the nonreporter rate is 40 percent. But if the five individuals who both reported and stayed silent on different issues are allowed to be included in both groups, then the nonreporter rate goes up to 51 percent (23 out of 45). At this level, we're back to where we started-the 50 percent range of reporting and nonreporting that previous studies have documented.

In order to better understand the situations behind these reports (and nonreports), the survey asked respondents to describe incidence(s) of wrongdoing that they observed. Table 1

Table 1   Instances of Reported Wrongdoing

Type of Activity Observed	No. of Reports	Examples Noted
Theft of Company Property/Cash	2	Theft of company computer Mishandling of petty cash
Unauthorized/Inappropriate Use of Company Assets	5	Unauthorized use of company vehicle Misappropriation of funds Inappropriate use of grant money Purchase misuse Irrelevant advertising expenditures that weren't approved
Financial Statement Manipulation	5	Misstated product line P&L Aggressive estimates affecting income Income statement misrepresentation Financial statement misstatements Overstatement of inventory value

(conitnued)

Table 1 Instances of Reported Wrongdoing *(continued)*

Type of Activity Observed	No. of Reports	Examples Noted
Claiming Personal Expenses for Reimbursement	4	Airfare for spouse purchased with company credit card
		Inappropriate personal spending on company credit card
		Improper expense submission
		Questionable expense receipts/charges
Sexual Harassment	2	Sexual harassment of a coworker
		Sexual harassment
Inappropriate Human Resources/Payroll Practices	4	Fraud in the selection process
		Hiring spouse of executive
		Back pay being withheld inappropriately
		Inappropriate untaxed bonuses
Other	5	Kickbacks
		Overbilling client
		Employee using counterfeit money in vending machine
		Inappropriate use of cash-basis accounting
		Violation of corporate risk management policy
TOTAL	27	

outlines the situations on which individuals blew the whistle. These reported wrongdoing activities varied greatly from mishandling petty cash to misrepresenting the company's income statement to sexual harassment.

Table 2 describes the other situations—the ones on which individuals remained silent. These unreported situations of wrongdoing also varied greatly—from an employee stealing company supplies to manipulating revenues and expenses to claiming personal expenses for reimbursement. When comparing the situations in Tables 1 and 2, the uncanny crossovers are hard to dismiss. The situations described in both tables are very similar, suggesting that it isn't just the event's nature or the significance that drives an individual to report-or not report-wrongdoing.

Table 3 provides a closer look at the survey respondents to see if there are any key demographic differences between those who reported wrongdoing and those who didn't. This information is provided for the entire group of survey respondents along with comparison detail for the two different reporter groups (reporters, the 27 who reported at least one situation of wrongdoing; nonreporters, the 23 who stayed silent on at least one instance of wrongdoing). There doesn't appear to be much difference in the ages and length of time at current companies of those who blew the whistle as opposed to those who stayed silent. The average age across the board was approximately 47, and average time with their current company was also quite steady at approximately 8 or 9 years.

But there are some gender differences between the groups. Though 55 percent of the entire sample was male, only 48 percent of those blowing the whistle were male. Further, of the individuals who remained silent, 70 percent were male. A meta-analysis by Jessica Mesmer-Magnus and Chockalingam Viswesvaran, "Whistleblowing in Organizations: An Examination of Correlates of Whistleblowing Intentions, Actions, and Retliation," in the Spring 2005 issue of the *Journal of Business Ethics,* looked at four specific studies on actual whistleblowers and noted a similar gender difference across those studies: Women blew the whistle more often than men did.

In addition to a gender difference in my study's respondents, the remainder of the data shows that these individuals come from businesses of all types and sizes and that the whistleblowing reports are spread fairly evenly among all such companies. Further, both the reporter and nonreporter groups appear to be composed of similar individuals in regard to their certifications held and degrees completed: The vast majority are either a CMA® (Certified Management Accountant) or CPA (Certified Public Accountant) or both, and the majority in both groups also have a master's degree. In other words, even these highly educated individuals with valued credentials and experience find it difficult to deal with wrongdoing in the workplace.

Although this detail portrays the background information of all respondents as well as the wrongdoing situations that they observed, the survey asked more probing questions of the silent

Table 2 Instances of Unreported Wrongdoing . . . and Regret Associated with Staying Silent

Type of Activity Observed	No. of Similar Reports	Examples Notes	Level of Regret Experienced*
Theft of Company Property/Cash	2	Employee stealing supplies from the company	no regret
		Unauthorized purchases; incorrect recording of cash	some regret
Inappropriate Use of Company Assets	1	Accessing pornography on work computer	little regret
Financial Statement Manipulation	5	Inappropriate month-end adjustments	great regret
		Accounting estimate adjustments for bad debt	no regret
		Manipulating revenue and expenses	some regret
		Earnings manipulation	some regret
		Income smoothing using accrual manipulation	little regret
Claiming Personal Expenses for Reimbursement	4	Personal travel of children	great regret
		Misclassifying expense reports	little regret
		Personal assets purchased by company	no regret
		Personal expenses purchased on corporate card	little regret
Sexual Harassment	1	Sexist comments	little regret
Inappropriate HR/Payroll Practices	3	Inappropriate time-sheet reporting	little regret
		Profit-sharing calculations unverifiable	little regret
		Reporting payments to employees as travel vs. wages to avoid payroll taxes	little regret
Other	7	Collusion within upper management; sharing inside information	great regret
		Executive cover-up	some regret
		Violation of federal manufacturing law	great regret
		Fraudulent information reported on tax returns	little regret
		Controller cover-up on missing equipment	great regret
		Noncompetitive supplier selected	no regret
		Sabotage of a new process change	great regret
TOTAL	23		

* Subjects were asked if they were currently experiencing (or had in the past experienced) any regret associated with their decision to stay silent. They were asked to respond in one of the following ways: no regret, little regret, some regret, and great regret.

observers. Since the rate of whistleblowing has remained constant at around 50 percent for at least the past 18 years, there must be something more that we can learn from these nonreporters—something that can help us "break through" to future observers that may give them the courage to come forward with their information.

One such survey question asked these individuals to explain why they chose to remain silent. Table 4 reports the reasons they gave. Not surprisingly, the most common reason for not blowing the whistle was fear of retaliation in one form or another, including job loss and difficult working conditions.

Others noted reasons such as the wrongdoing wasn't serious enough to worry about; they didn't feel they had enough proof to bring the allegation forward; and/or they felt somebody else would report the situation. Two individuals further noted that they voluntarily left the company because of what was going on.

. . . the most common reason for not blowing the whistle was fear of retaliation in one form or another . . .

Table 3 Survey Respondents

		All		Reporters		Nonreporters
Age (in years)						
Mean		47.5		46.7		49.1
Range		27 to 71		29 to 67		30 to 71
Tenure with Organization (in years)						
Mean		8.6		9		8.3
Range		0.25 to 31		2 to 20		0.75 to 30
	N	**Percentage**	**N**	**Percentage**	**N**	**Percentage**
Gender						
Male	41	55 percent	13	48 percent	16	70 percent
Female	33	44 percent	14	52 percent	7	30 percent
Missing Data	1	1 percent	0		0	
Total	75		27		23	
Industry Membership						
Manufacturing	27	36 percent	10	37 percent	7	30 percent
Professional Services	17	23 percent	7	26 percent	6	26 percent
Education	7	9 percent	2	7 percent	5	22 percent
Government	5	7 percent	1	4 percent	1	4 percent
Pharmaceuticals/Healthcare	4	5 percent	1	4 percent	0	0 percent
Other/Missing	15	20 percent	6	22 percent	4	17 percent
Total	75		27		23	
# of Employees in Company						
Less than 100	20	27 percent	11	41 percent	6	26 percent
101 to 500	19	25 percent	5	19 percent	6	26 percent
501 to 2,000	10	13 percent	5	19 percent	5	22 percent
2,001 to 10,000	11	15 percent	1	4 percent	3	13 percent
More than 10,000	13	17 percent	4	15 percent	3	13 percent
Missing	2	3 percent	1	4 percent	0	0 percent
Total	75		27		23	
Certifications Held						
CMA (w/o CPA)	22	29 percent	8	30 percent	7	30 percent
CPA (w/o CMA)	16	21 percent	6	22 percent	3	13 percent
CMA & CPA	20	27 percent	8	30 percent	5	22 percent
Others (no CMA or CPA)	3	4 percent	1	4 percent	1	4 percent
None/Missing	14	19 percent	4	15 percent	7	30 percent
Total	75		27		23	
Highest Degree Completed						
Associate's	1	1 percent	1	4 percent	1	4 percent
Bachelor's	29	39 percent	10	37 percent	7	30 percent
Master's	41	55 percent	16	59 percent	14	61 percent
Doctorate	3	4 percent	0	0 percent	1	4 percent
Missing	1	1 percent	0	0 percent	0	0 percent
Total	75		27		23	

Table 4 Reasons for Not Reporting the Wrongdoing

Reason Given	Number of Similar Reports
Fear of job loss and/or other retaliation	10
Not that big of a deal	4
Didn't have enough proof	3
Thought somebody else would report it	2
Chose to leave the company instead	2
Other	5
Total*	**26**

* Three individuals each gave two reasons for staying silent, thus the total adds up to 23 + 3 = 26.

Regret from Not Blowing the Whistle

But what have these individuals experienced since their decision to remain silent? Did they avoid the retaliation they were hoping to avoid, or were there other negative consequences associated with staying silent, too? One question asked these silent observers whether they were currently experiencing (or had in the past) any regret associated with their decision to remain silent. This data speaks for itself. Presented alongside the unreported situations in the last column of Table 2, the vast majority of silent observers, 19 of the 23 individuals who chose not to report the wrongdoings, acknowledge having experienced at least some regret (rated as either little, some, or great) associated with their decision to remain silent.

It further appears that these individuals have experienced regret-to varying degrees-for many different types of wrongdoing situations. Not only did some experience regret for the "bigger" issues, such as "fixing" the numbers or theft of property, but individuals also experienced regret for letting "smaller" issues go unreported, including such things as bypassing proper procedures in order to justify a purchase or letting some personal expenses count for reimbursement.

Tone at the Top

It's clear that there's no easy way to deal with wrongdoing in the workplace. Once an individual becomes aware of illegal and/or unethical activity, there are ramifications for reporting and not reporting it. Unfortunately, organizational wrongdoing occurs in companies of all sizes and in all industries. Further,

Once an individual becomes aware of illegal and/or unethical activity, there are ramifications for reporting and not reporting it.

given that many businesses today find themselves in fragile financial positions with lower-than-desired headcounts, there are fewer resources to allocate toward enhanced internal controls and ethics training.

But there's still something companies can do, at relatively no cost to them, to combat and prevent fraud and wrongdoing. Businesses can espouse an ethical culture, one that truly is motivated from the top tiers of the organizational chart, to show their employees that they mean business. The importance of a company's "tone at the top" certainly it isn't a new phenomenon (see "Tone at the Top: Insights from Section 404" by Dana Hermanson, Daniel Ivancevich, and Susan Ivancevich in the November 2008 *Strategic Finance*). And this is getting even more pronounced attention as a fraud prevention factor in today's fast-paced, risk-laden marketplace. PwC captured this message loud and clear when it concluded its 2011 global economic crime survey with the following statement: "Establishing the right 'tone at the top' is key in the fight against economic crime."

No Easy Way Out

The data in this article suggests that the level of whistleblowing has stayed relatively constant over the past two decades at around 50 percent and gives reasons as to why the remaining 50 percent chose to remain silent on these issues. Yet through this analysis it becomes clear that these silent observers don't come out unscathed because they have to live with their decision, knowing that some individuals are benefitting at the expense of others. They have to live with their regret-knowing that their silence may be perpetuating fraud, harassment, law violations, and the like, within that company. The stress associated with this regret may be a cost that they didn't anticipate, but it's a cost nonetheless. Perhaps the potential for financial rewards will now give some of these otherwise silent observers enough incentive to come forward with their information. And perhaps these and other reward opportunities will eventually give all whistleblowers the compensation they desire and deserve to help offset the personal costs that come with whistleblowing.

One thing is certain, though. We can all learn something from the survey respondents. Blowing the whistle on organizational wrongdoing isn't an easy thing to do, but staying silent on these issues may not be an easy way out, either.

Critical Thinking

1. Comment on the methodology used in the IMA Study reported in the article. Are the results of the study generalizable given its methodology? Why or why not?

2. Examine Table 4 in the article. Of the reasons given for not reporting wrongdoing (i.e., not blowing the whistle), which of the reasons do you find most compelling? Why? Which the least compelling? Why?

3. Examine Table 2 in the article. What might be the reasons for a finding of great regret versus a finding of no regret? Make a list of possible reasons for feeling or not feeling of regret for use in class discussion.

4. Examine Table 1—Instance of Reported Wrongdoing. Develop a table or a chart in which you analyze the seriousness of the reported wrongdoing. Then, relate your analysis of Table 1 to the results reported in Table 2. What conclusion might you draw from Tables 1 and 2?

Create Central

www.mhhe.com/createcentral

Internet References

New York Times

http://www.nytimes.com/1987/02/22/us/survey-of-whistle-blowers-finds-retaliation-but-few-regrets.html

Reuters

http://www.reuters.com/article/2012/02/17/us-citigroup-whistleblower-idUSTRE81G06Y20120217

The Guardian

http://www.theguardian.com/money/2014/sep/23/whistleblower-bank-personal-cost-sec

AMY FREDIN, PhD, is an assistant professor of accounting at St. Cloud State University in St. Cloud, Minn. She also is a member of IMA's Central Minnesota Chapter. You can reach her at (320) 308-3287 or ajfredin@stcloudstate.edu.

Article   Prepared by: Eric Teoro, *Lincoln Christian University*

Challenges of Governing Globally

A strong understanding of the three distinct corporate governance systems around the world will help managers conduct business more effectively in other countries.

MARC J. EPSTEIN

Learning Outcomes

After reading this article, you will be able to:

- Describe different governance systems.

- Understand factors that affect Board performance.

Shortly after New Year's Day in 2009, just 6 months after Satyam and its politically influential chairman, Ramalinga Raju, were honored by the World Council for Corporate Governance, the company and its senior leadership became the subject of the largest corporate fraud investigation in India's history. Raju admitted to fabricating 70 billion rupees ($1.5 billion) of Satyam's assets and 95 percent of the previous year's revenue. Despite its record for good governance, this large, respected outsourcing firm saw its market value fall more than 80 percent in 24 hours. Long before the confession, shareholders had expressed dissatisfaction with Raju's leadership. Many charged that the board of directors and its members failed to meet their basic responsibilities.

Senior executives aren't the only perpetrators of corporate fraud. A scandal at Volkswagen (VW), Germany's largest carmaker, erupted in 2005 when it was discovered that managers and labor representatives had received improper benefits from the company and its suppliers. A quid-pro-quo agreement had developed between managers and labor that centered around the important role that union representatives play on German boards (workers' representatives have 50 percent of the seats on the supervisory boards of companies with 2,000 or more employees). In return, the local government, which was the controlling shareholder of the corporation with only 18 percent ownership (the voting rights of any single share-holder are limited to 20 percent), was satisfied with the ability to guarantee regional job security. Yet it seemed that the other shareholders may not have been receiving equal benefits, and the VW board found itself unable or unwilling to protect its minority owners from actions that didn't maximize the returns to everyone.

Not all corporate governance failures involve financial fraud. In 2010, BP, one of the world's largest oil and gas companies, saw its market value fall by more than 50 percent in less than 60 days after the infamous explosion at a deepwater drilling rig off the US Gulf Coast. The incident killed 11 employees and resulted in the largest marine oil spill in history, costing BP billions of dollars in compensation for victims and cleanup costs. The government investigation of the explosion revealed numerous causes and guilty parties. Many people have suggested that BP's board failed to put the right processes in place to ensure that reasonable safety measures were taken to prevent such a disaster.

These stories occur far too often in corporations all over the world. Enron, WorldCom, and Tyco in the US and Parmalat in Italy immediately come to mind. Sometimes these failures are fraud, and sometimes they're the result of poor oversight. Nevertheless, they have caused us to reexamine the structures, systems, and processes of corporate governance.

As you know, corporate governance is the system by which corporations are directed, controlled, and made accountable to shareholders and other stakeholders. Failures such as those outlined above occur in a wide variety of companies and industries and in different countries around the world. Understanding corporate governance practices globally should be a priority for managers who work in multinational corporations or with international clients.

Table 1   General Characteristics of Global Corporate Governance Systems

General Characteristics	Anglo-American	Communitarian	Emerging Markets
Examples of Countries/Regions	United States, United Kingdom, Australia, Canada, South Africa	Japan, Germany, Belgium, Scandinavia	China, Eastern Europe, India, Brazil, Mexico, Russia
General Characteristics	• Shareholder-centric • Market centered • Unitary board structure • Boards primarily composed of nonexecutive directors (and independent directors) • Common law legal system • High levels of disclosure and more rules on disclosure • Large pay incentives for managers, including pay for performance	• Stakeholder-centric • Bank centered • Two-tier board structure (supervisory & management) • Labor, founding family, and bank are common members—interlocking common • Civil law legal system • Moderate levels of disclosure • Pay incentives moderate	• Stakeholder-centric • Government/Family centered • Board structure varies • Few independent board members • Legal systems relatively weak • Low levels of disclosure • Pay incentives smaller

Understanding corporate governance practices globally should be a priority for managers who work in multinational corporations or with international clients.

Here I'll describe three corporate governance systems—Anglo-American, Communitarian, and Emerging Markets—and provide a comparison that you can use to recognize and evaluate differences in practice. This is a summary of extensive work that I recently completed in response to many inquiries from senior managers who want to better understand how to evaluate corporate and board performance in other countries.

Table 1 summarizes some of the major differences in the general characteristics of each system.

Global Corporate Governance Systems

Corporate governance practices vary globally as a result of significant country differences, such as culture, history, regulatory systems, and economic and financial development. All of you who interact with corporate managers in other countries or have affiliates or subsidiaries throughout the world must understand these differences because it's critical to the evaluation of

corporate board performance and to corporate success. It also has important implications for corporate governance, corporate financial and operational transactions, and global relationships.

Let's look at some of the basic differences.

Anglo-American Corporate Governance System

The Anglo-American system of governance evolved in countries to which the United Kingdom exported its common law legal system during its colonial period, such as the United States, Australia, New Zealand, Canada, and South Africa. Originally developed to protect private landholders from nobility, the common law legal system sets a broad legal precedent that protects shareholders and tries to prevent a company's leaders from acting against shareholder interests.

In the Anglo-American system, corporations focus primarily on the shareholder and aim to maximize shareholder wealth. Directors usually are elected by shareholders and can be replaced if shareholders aren't satisfied with the company's financial results. The system emphasizes transparency and disclosure about a company's audited financial status, board composition, and corporate strategy.

Since well-developed financial markets heavily influence corporate governance practices, the Anglo-American system is considered market based with a large share of corporate ownership traded frequently on large, public exchanges. Under this system, corporate boards are structured as unitary boards and are composed primarily of nonexecutive directors (directors who aren't company employees) who represent the interests of large shareholders. These boards also have independent directors with little financial interest in the future performance of the firm. Critics of this system have argued that boards are frequently too large (with as many as 20 members) and that directors have often failed to dedicate enough time to their roles.

Communitarian Corporate Governance System

A Communitarian corporate governance system has evolved in much of continental Europe and in Japan. This system has its origins in the Romano-Germanic civil law codes developed more than a millennium ago. Instead of relying on strong legal protections for investors, performance is regulated through statutes, codes, and relationships with stakeholders.

The Communitarian system is relationship based, which provides for a stakeholder-centric approach to governance and focuses on a broader set of stakeholders that often includes lenders, members of supply chains, customers, employees, and the community. These relationships allow stakeholders to wield strong control over corporations and hold them accountable. In Germany and Japan, for example, it's common for companies and banks to cross-invest in their suppliers and customers, creating associations of corporations that play an active role in deciding corporate governance standards. Boards often include representatives from various stakeholders who are representing their own interests. A banking representative may be interested in a decision's impact on the corporation but also on the bank he or she works for. Similarly, a union representative on the board is interested in the impact of a decision on the corporation and its shareholders but particularly on the workers that the union represents. This stakeholder orientation provides for a broader set of interests and representation on the board.

Corporate governance under the Communitarian system relies heavily on banks instead of capital markets for financing, and representatives from these banks often sit on the board of directors of a company that they finance. This system generally uses a two-tier board structure, dividing board functions between a supervisory board and a management board.

Critics of the system have argued that it fails to protect minority shareholders and lacks representation for outside investors.

Emerging Markets Corporate Governance System

Emerging Markets countries—such as China, Brazil, India, Mexico, Russia, and much of Eastern Europe—still have relatively young legal systems that haven't fully developed the legal framework necessary to classify their corporate governance systems into the other categories. In China, for example, the first corporations were founded centuries after countries with more defined corporate governance systems began their corporate history. These countries also differ in legal traditions, language, and culture, so it's still uncertain how corporate governance will likely evolve there.

Yet there are some recognizable patterns. The lack of defined legal systems means that shareholders often have few credible legal protections, so boards are expected to vigorously monitor and protect shareholder interests. Also, low levels of disclosure and a lack of transparency often make it difficult for shareholders to exercise informed control over the company.

Corporate governance in Emerging Markets countries tends to be stakeholder-centric and centered around family or government relationships. In addition, large corporate shareholders dominate boards and are well-known worldwide. For example, about 30 Korean family groups that are organized as chaebols (business conglomerates) control almost 40 percent of that country's economy. There's also a large amount of state participation. Even in countries where the government has privatized its corporate holdings, it often retains significant control over corporations by regulating equity markets or influencing board members. For example, often the government retains a regulatory interest in supervising large transactions that have an impact on the state. (All governments do this to some extent, but it's far more common in the Emerging Markets countries.)

Roles of the Board Globally

Though significant differences in corporate governance practices exist, some general principles are present globally that are critical for effective corporate governance. Boards of directors are usually expected to fulfill three separate but related roles: accountability, senior-level staffing and evaluation, and strategic oversight. (For more details on roles and responsibilities of corporate boards, see Marc J. Epstein and Marie-Josée Roy, "Corporate Governance Is Changing: Are You a Leader or a Laggard?" *Strategic Finance*, October 2010, pp. 31–37.)

Accountability

In Anglo-American countries, boards of directors traditionally have been responsible for holding managers accountable to shareholders. In the Communitarian system, it's common for the corporation, management, and board to also be accountable to other stakeholders, such as employees, suppliers, and customers. In the Emerging Markets system, boards are typically accountable to the controlling shareholders in the corporation, which can be the state, a family group, or a corporate conglomerate. Thus, it's common to have representatives of these other stakeholders on boards in non-Anglo-American countries.

Senior-Level Staffing and Evaluation

Evaluating senior management, determining their compensation, and having important input to senior staffing decisions are important roles for the board in all three governance systems. But there are important application differences. In the Anglo-American system, many corporations pay managers a huge amount of compensation for their performance in exchange for relentless attention to financial returns. In the Communitarian and the Emerging Markets systems, pay levels, performance-based pay, and the role of the board in determining pay are considerably smaller.

Strategic Oversight

In all three governance systems, strategic oversight is an important board role. In the Anglo-American system, managers focus on strategy formulation, and the board, though providing some oversight, often plays a more passive role in approving important strategic moves. In the Communitarian system, the management board is more assertive in its strategic oversight role and is often more involved in the formulation of strategy than in oversight only. And in the Emerging Markets system, many board members view the formulation and oversight of strategy as the primary role of the board.

Though these specific roles manifest themselves differently in different settings, they greatly impact the mechanisms that ensure managers fulfill shareholder expectations regarding corporate performance.

Strategic oversight is an important board role in all three governance systems.

Internal Determinants of Corporate Boards

How successfully a board performs its duties depends on several internal factors that differ substantially among the three global governance systems (see Table 2). These factors may affect managers' roles and interactions with the board, as well as their compensation. They include:

1. Board composition,
2. Board systems and structure, and
3. Performance evaluation and compensation systems.

Board Composition

Board composition choices determine board competencies, skills, and power structures. Many corporate governance experts and international guidelines advocate increased board member independence and increased numbers of nonexecutive directors on boards, yet the role of nonexecutive and independent directors is markedly different in each corporate governance system.

In the Anglo-American system, boards are composed primarily of nonexecutive directors who represent the interests of large shareholders, as well as independent directors with no significant financial interest in the future performance of the firm. Usually, there are stringent requirements for board independence since these board members often have a significant amount of power. In Canada, for example, 70 percent of companies have independent directors serving as their board chair.

In the Communitarian system, independent directors are less common but still hold a considerable amount of power. Since national codes and companies typically don't stress the independence of board directors, most corporation board members in Japan, Italy, and much of continental Europe are internal.

Table 2   Internal Determinants of Corporate Governance Systems

Corporate Governance Mechanism	Anglo-American	Communitarian	Emerging Markets
Board Composition, Systems, & Structure			
Board composition	• Balance between internal and independent directors	• Few independent directors	• Independent directors rare
Board structure	• Unitary	• Two-tier	• Varies
Board accountability	• Shareholders	• Stakeholders (including entire value chain and employees)	• Stakeholders and government or founding family
Executive compensation	• Large performance pay	• Moderate performance pay	• Little performance pay

This is partly because of codetermination laws that mandate high levels of employee participation on the supervisory board.

The Emerging Markets system features many of the regulatory requirements of the Anglo-American system with regard to independent directors, but truly independent directors are uncommon and wield little power relative to controlling interests on the board. In China, for example, listed companies are required to have two independent directors. Despite these requirements, many believe that Chinese directors show few signs of true independence and are still strongly influenced by the government.

Board Systems and Structure

Board systems and structure are the mechanisms typically used to translate board roles, responsibilities, and composition into decisions. They also vary significantly across governance systems.

Again, in the Anglo-American system, a unitary board typically combines executive directors (company executives who are on the corporate board) and nonexecutive directors. Boards usually are organized into committees—such as audit, nomination, and compensation—that perform much of the board's functions.

In the Communitarian system, the executive directors and nonexecutive directors are divided into two separate entities. The management board, composed mainly of senior-level management, is primarily responsible for managerial decisions, such as strategy, marketing, and product development. The supervisory board, composed of company insiders, such as employees, as well as company outsiders, such as independent accountants, is primarily responsible for overseeing executive management, accounting, senior-level staffing, and evaluation. Employees also can play a significant role in determining the composition of the supervisory board. Shareholders elect the supervisory board, and the supervisory board appoints members of the management board. In Germany, employees elect a third to a half of the members of the supervisory board. In addition, representatives from founding families or national banks may also serve on this board.

In the Emerging Markets system, the board structure varies between countries and even among corporations in the same country. Some corporations have adopted the two-tier board structure of Communitarian countries, and others utilize the unitary board structure of the Anglo-American system. The largest shareholders, usually the state or family groups, often are permitted to control the boards.

Performance Evaluation and Compensation Systems

Performance evaluation and compensation systems also differ among governance systems. In the Anglo-American system, boards are expected to perform rigorous evaluations of senior manager and corporate performance. It's common to structure executive compensation so that a large percentage of that pay is tied to the financial performance of the corporation. Evaluation procedures only recently have become part of corporate governance in the Communitarian system, and most companies in the Emerging Markets system lack explicit evaluation mechanisms. In the two latter systems, large performance-based pay is significantly less common and accounts for a much smaller percentage of overall executive compensation than in Anglo-American countries.

External Determinants of Corporate Board Systems

External factors also affect how boards of directors perform their roles and responsibilities. Three that determine key components of corporate governance are:

1. Markets,
2. Legal systems, and
3. Ownership and control structures.

These mechanisms (see Table 3) ensure that corporations act according to national expectations regarding corporate governance. An understanding of these external factors will provide managers with insight into board regulation, objectives, operations, and decisions.

Markets

The existence of markets for ownership and control of corporations is an important aspect of corporate governance since the threat of takeovers increases when mechanisms for governance fail. Takeovers are most common in the Anglo-American system, particularly in the United States while the existence of a controlling shareholder in the Communitarian and Emerging Markets systems lessens the likelihood of a takeover.

Beyond corporate control, stock markets determine the returns available to stockholders in a corporation and diversify ownership. In the Anglo-American system, these markets are quite active. More than 6,000 domestic companies are listed publicly in the United States, and more than 1,000 are listed in the United Kingdom. But only a relatively small number of firms are listed in Communitarian countries. In Germany, for example, there are fewer than 500 listed companies. In Emerging Markets, stock exchanges are developing rapidly, although there is a great deal of variation across countries. China, for example, has become a "dominant force" in the initial public offering (IPO) market in the last 2 years with its large exchange in Hong Kong. Yet in Mexico, only a small percentage of transfers occurs through the public markets.

Market listing requirements play another important role in corporate governance. In the Anglo-American system, these

Table 3 External Determinants of Corporate Governance Systems

Corporate Governance Mechanism	Anglo-American	Communitarian	Emerging Markets
Markets			
Financial markets	• Strong and active	• Weak and not commonly used	• Volatile
Investment purpose	• Short-term return	• Long-term return	• Policy and political goals
Methods of finance	• Financial markets	• Bank credit and retained earnings	• Private and state-owned banks
Legal Systems			
Legal history	• Common law system	• Civil law system	• Combined systems that are still rapidly evolving
Transactional methods	• Contracts	• Relationship-based transactions	• Relationship-based transactions
Ownership & Control Structures			
Ownership structure	• Diverse individual and institutional ownership	• Concentrated family and corporate ownership	• Concentrated family, corporate, and government ownership
Minority shareholder protections	• Strong	• Moderate	• Weak
Dominant control	• Voting and board representation	• Cross-holding, pyramidal groups, lending relationships	• Internal mechanisms and external mechanisms

regulations have become a dominant mechanism for implementing corporate governance reforms. Several large stock exchanges in Anglo-American countries have adopted mandatory listing requirements that include more stringent corporate governance measures, such as the qualification and roles of board members, having a majority of independent directors, and having a requirement for certain committees such as audit and compensation for publicly traded companies. Many Communitarian and Emerging Markets stock exchanges have followed suit more recently.

Legal Systems

Legal systems affect other aspects of corporate governance, including investor protection for minority shareholders, ownership structure, and financial markets. They also are an important aspect of how investors are protected. The Anglo-American corporate governance system, developed from the common law tradition, often exhibits the best legal protection for investors and tends to provide better enforcement of these laws. The Communitarian corporate governance system, derived from the civil law system, has developed other mechanisms to ensure that capital is allocated efficiently. These include concentrated ownership and control, mandatory dividends, and limited equity markets. Countries in the Emerging Markets system have even fewer shareholder protections than in civil law countries and

have evolved a severely concentrated ownership structure to compensate for these weak protections. In addition, the state often plays a much more active role as a corporate owner.

Ownership and Control Structures

Concentrated ownership and minority control mechanisms can be viewed as corporate governance mechanisms that evolve in the absence of basic shareholder protections. As a result, the most concentrated ownership structures are usually in Emerging Markets economies. One of the most glaring examples of this concentration is in China, where the state still owns majority holdings in most of the large firms, and Hong Kong, where a small group of business tycoons controls most large companies through concentrated shareholdings.

There's considerable ownership concentration in Communitarian countries as well. In Germany and Japan, for example, large banks, corporate groups, or families can control large portfolios of companies. Although these groups don't always hold majority stakes, they use a variety of tactics to steer the company in the direction that they prefer. These tactics include cross-shareholding, where two or more companies controlled by the same family group or government invest in each other, and pyramidal shareholding, where a company owns a sizable minority stake in a holding company that owns smaller stakes in more companies.

In Anglo-American countries, financial institutions, including pension funds, own more than 60 percent of all equity capital, yet ownership is quite dispersed. In this system, countries typically lack a controlling shareholder, so officers and directors have more control over decisions. This means that boards are responsible for ensuring that these decisions are in the best interests of the shareholders.

Closely related to ownership and control of corporations are the existence and enforcement of minority shareholder rights. These rights deal with voting privileges, corporate meetings, and dividends. For example, can major shareholders control corporate decisions, and must these decisions be for the benefit of the entire corporation, for all of its shareholders, for all of its stakeholders, or for only the small limited set of controlling shareholders? For an individual small owner of stock, the Anglo-American system provides far more protection both by regulation and through the legal system. In other systems, small shareholders must often just go along with what a major shareholder wants whether it is in their best interests or not.

In Emerging Markets economies, the state is frequently the controlling owner and can use its political power to derive wide control over corporations. In China, for example, rules surrounding the boards of directors of major corporations and financial markets are structured to give the state control over corporations. Even in countries where the state has started to turn control of corporations over to the private sector—such as in India, Brazil, and Russia—governments continue to wield significant power because of their ability to control the legal framework and market environment.

Understanding the Systems Is Critical

As corporations become more global, senior financial executives constantly deal with international contractors, licensees, affiliates, suppliers, and subsidiaries. Since these global associations and entities are often subject to different regulatory regimes and corporate governance systems, their decision-making processes can provide surprises. They may choose to ignore that your bid is the lowest and choose a higher-cost bid from a controlling shareholder, but it may be that the decision is to choose a contract from a controlling shareholder that benefits their relationship and benefits the other corporation—who is a common shareholder on multiple entities. Also, it may seem strange to a US manager that a corporation might decide to make decisions that benefit the environment or the labor union over shareholders since the US model is shareholder focused. Remember: The other systems aren't better or worse, but they *are* different—and it's important for managers to understand this as they are doing

business in other countries. To better understand decisions and constraints and to conduct business around the world more effectively, executives must understand the context, regulations, and processes of corporate governance in other countries. Without this understanding, evaluating and/or improving performance globally is difficult.

Note

1. This article draws heavily from Marc J. Epstein, "Governing Globally: Convergence, Differentiation, or Bridging," in Eds. Antiono Davila, Marc J. Epstein, and Jean-François Manzoni, *Performance Measurement and Management Control: Global Issues,* Emerald: UK, 2012.

Critical Thinking

1. What are the salient characteristics of the three different global corporate governance systems presented in the article? List the characteristics and be prepared to discuss them during class.

2. What are the implications for placing a firm's code of ethics in a host country plant given different governance systems in the host country than in the home country?

3. What are the internal determinants of corporate boards?

4. What are the external determinants of corporate boards?

5. How do differing legal systems in various countries affect corporate governance?

6. How do differing legal systems in various countries affect implementation of a firm's ethics programs?

Create Central

www.mhhe.com/createcentral

Internet References

Emerging Markets ESG
http://www.emergingmarketsesg.net/esg/wp-content/uploads/2011/01/Three-Models-of-Corporate-Governance-January-2009.pdf

Finnbay
http://www.finnbay.com/media/news/insider-versus-outsider-convergence-governance-systems/

Social Science Research Network
http://papers.ssrn.com/sol3/papers.cfm?abstract_id=2049764

MARC J. EPSTEIN is Distinguished Research Professor of Management at the Jesse H. Jones Graduate School of Business at Rice University in Houston, Texas. He also is a member of IMA®. You can reach Marc at (713) 348-6140 or epstein@rice.edu.

Article Prepared by: Eric Teoro, *Lincoln Christian University*

Conceptualizing a Framework for Global Business Ethics

WILLIAM J. KEHOE

Learning Outcomes

After reading this article, you will be able to:

- Trace the history of business ethics literature.

- Describe unethical business practices being conducted in a global market.

- Develop a system that promotes global business ethics.

The imperative of globalization arguably is one of the more significant changes experienced by business in the past several decades (Levitt, 1983; Kehoe and Whitten, 1999; Hill, 2001; Cateora and Graham, 2002; Czinkota, Ronkainen, and Moffett, 2002; Keegan, 2002; Griffin and Pustay, 2003; Hill, 2003; Lascu, 2003; Yip, 2003). In pursuing globalization, firms analyze, and debate various entry strategies to host-country markets; carefully consider the appropriateness of sourcing equipment, financing, materials, personnel, and other factors of production across the global arena; argue the merits of operating in a home-country currency versus host-country currencies; and study the cultures of host countries. However, the challenges of implementing an ethical system globally sometimes are addressed only as an afterthought, particularly when an ethical problem occurs.

This manuscript addresses the importance of developing and implementing an ethical framework to facilitate the application of ethics across the expanse of a global firm's operating arena. Prior to presenting the framework, the field of global business ethics is summarized, and the more interesting, well-conceptualized, and significant literature in the field is reviewed. Then, unethical business practices in global business are identified and discussed, so as to present a platform for the development of a framework for global business ethics. The framework is conceptualized and discussed and implementation suggestions for management are presented.

Global Business Ethics as a Field of Study

Almost a decade ago, DeGeorge (1994) opined, "business ethics is still a young field, and its international dimensions have scarcely been raised, much less adequately addressed." While still relatively a young field, the literature base of global business ethics is developing rapidly and has a richness of content.

Literature of 1960s and 1970s

Among the more interesting and well-conceptualized literature in the field during the 1960s and 1970s is the work of such scholars as Baumhart (1961) introducing the concept of ethics in business and exploring the ethics of business practitioners. Raths, Harmin, and Simon (1966) provided important underpinnings on values and teaching for the new field of business ethics; Smith (1966) advanced a theory of moral sentiments; Boulding (1967) provided important underpinnings to business ethics in his scholarly examination of value judgments in economics; and Perlmutter (1969) reflected on the difficult evolution of a multinational corporation. Other notable literature of the period includes work by Kohlberg (1971) conceptualizing stages of moral development, by Bowie (1978) developing an early taxonomy of ethics for multinational corporations, and by Carroll (1979) presenting a model of corporate social performance.

Literature of the 1980s

Moving to the 1980s, significant scholarship included such literature as Engelbourg (1980) in a significant examination of the early history of business ethics and Drucker (1981) examining the concept of business ethics. Nash (1981), enlivening Bowie's (1978) taxonomy, posited 12 questions for managers to ask when considering the ethical aspects of a business decision and offered a taxonomy of shared conditions for successful ethical inquiries. Berleant (1982) explored problems of ethical consistency in multinational firms, raising questions relevant to this day.

Laczniak (1983) developed one of the first primers in ethics for managers. McCoy (1983), in a classic article, presented a parable that is used to differentiate corporate and individual ethics. Donaldson (1985) reconciled international norms with ethical business decision-making, Kehoe (1985) examined ethics, price fixing, and the management of price strategy, and Lacaznik and Murphy (1985) published a book of ethical guidelines for marketing managers. Ferrell and Gresham (1985) conceptualized a contingency framework for understanding ethical decision-making, Hoffman, Lange, and Fedo (1986) examined ethics in multinational corporations, and Murphy (1988) focused on processes for implementing business ethics. The literature period of the 1960s/1970s/1980s closed with a comprehensive work by Donaldson (1989) examining the ethics of international business.

Overall, the literature of the 1960s/1970s/1980s tended to be descriptive in methodology, nature, and tone. Of course, a descriptive nature is to be expected, as business ethics was an embryonic field at that time then. The literature introduced ethical concepts and theories to academics and practitioners in business. It anchored the field of business ethics, conceptualized its early content, developed taxonomies, and established the importance and the validity of the concept of ethics in business with both academics and practitioners.

Literature of the Early 1990s

The period of the early 1990s saw the field of business ethics begin to flourish conceptually, empirically, and operationally. Bowie's (1990) article on business ethics and cultural relativism signaled a movement from the field's descriptive tone toward higher levels of abstraction and inquiry. DeGeorge (1990) authored a book chapter examining international business systems and morality, while Donaldson (1992) presented a classic article on the language of international corporate ethics. Koehn (1992) examined the ethic of exchange, an important article in that the concept of exchange is a central underpinning of business. Velasquez (1992) explored questions of morality and the common good in international business. DeGeorge (1993) addressed the concept of competing with integrity. Green (1993) placed business ethics in a wider global context, while Kehoe (1993) examined theory and application in business ethics.

The Business Ethics Quarterly heralded a defining moment in the scholarship of business ethics by publishing an entire issue (January 1994) devoted to international business ethics. Nicholson (1994) presented a framework for inquiry in organizational ethics, the first such framework in the literature. Fraedrich, Thorne, and

Ferrell (1994) assessed the application of cognitive moral development theory to business ethics. Rossouw (1994) addressed the ethics of business in developing countries, an important article given that many ethical abuses occur in developing countries.

Delener (1995) advanced earlier scholarship on ethical issues in international marketing, Smith (1995) described marketing strategies for an ethics era, while Rogers, Ogbuehi, and Kochunny (1995) raised troubling questions of the ethics of transnational corporations in developing countries. Perhaps fittingly, given the emerging questions about ethics of transnational corporations, the Caux Roundtable's Principles for Business (1995) were published at this time, believed to be the first international code of ethics created through collaboration of business leaders in Europe, Japan, and the United States (Skelly, 1995; Davids, 1999).

Literature of the Later 1990s

Donaldson (1996), perhaps building from the troubling questions about ethics in the early 1990s, examined values in tension when home-country ethics are employed in host-country markets away from a home country. Bowie (1997) posited the moral obligations of multinational corporations, while Johnson (1997) foreshadowed ethics during turbulent times as he examined ethics in brutal markets. Kung (1997) reminded scholars that globalization calls for a global ethic. Becker (1998) applied the philosophy of objectivism to integrity in organizations. Costa (1998) argued that moral business leadership is an ethical imperative, and Dunfee (1998), in an article based on a 1996 speech, explored the marketplace of morality from the focus of a theory of moral choice. Hasnas (1998), in an article subtitled "a guide for the perplexed," attempted to clarify the field of business ethics in an interesting article examining three leading normative theories of business ethics—the stockholder theory, the stakeholder theory, and the social contract theory.

A more scholarly tone in business ethics is found particularly in works by Brock (1998), questioning whether corporations are morally defensible and by Collier (1998), theorizing the ethical organization. Other significant literature includes Ferrell (1998) examining business ethics in a global economy, Bowie (1999) reaffirming the place of a Kantian perspective in business ethics, and Buller and McEvoy (1999) examining how to create and to sustain an ethical capability in a multinational corporation. Lantos (1999) considered how to motivate moral corporate behavior, Mackenzie and Lewis (1999) focused on the case of ethical investing, and Weaver, Trevino, and Cochran (1999) posited corporate ethics programs as control systems.

In each of these articles of the later 1990s, a more scholarly, more theoretical, and less descriptive approach is manifest than in many earlier articles in the field, particularly in the literature of the 1960s, 1970s, and early 1980s.

A New Century's Literature

Continuing the scholarly tone of the later 1990s, Chonko and Hunt (2000) presented an important retrospective analysis and prospective commentary on ethics and marketing management, while Freeman (2000) examined business ethics at the millennium. Robin (2000) developed a hierarchical framework of ethical missions and a model of corporate moral development. Velasquez (2000) considered globalization and the failure of ethics. Werhane (2000) authored a seminal work on global capitalism in the 21st century—a work that foreshadows the level of analysis and depth of scholarship to which business ethics aspires and which it must attain.

A question for consideration is whether business ethics is moving toward a postmodern phase (Carroll, 2000; Gustafson, 2000), in which it is not the rules of ethics but rather the "questions that raise issues of responsibility" that will guide business ethics to its tomorrows beyond. Is the field moving toward an interesting future for scholarship in ethics in which content and issues about ethical issues not envisioned in the early 1980s will emerge for serious reflection and scholarship? Contents and issues such as a cross-cultural comparison of ethical sensitivity (Blodgett, Lu, Rose, and Vitell, 2001); myth and ethics (Geva, 2001); an examination of questions at the intersection of ethics and economics (Hosmer and Chen, 2001); ethics and perceived risk (Cherry, 2002); ethics and privacy (Connolly, 2000; McMaster, 2001); ethics and stakeholder theory (Cragg, 2002; Jensen 2002; Kaufman, 2002; Orts and Strudler, 2002); religiosity and ethical behavior (Weaver and Agle, 2002), and multinationality and corporate ethics (van Tulder and Kolk, 2001; Singer, 2002). All of these emergent areas of reflection and scholarship are areas of inquiry important in a home country, but exponentially more critical for examination as organizations move increasingly to host-country markets throughout the world.

From Literature Emerges Imperatives for Research

As the tomorrows emerge for the field of business ethics, several imperatives flow from an examination of the extant literature. One, the field of business ethics, over the past several decades, has been descriptive in nature and tone. It is imperative that business ethics rises above its descriptive beginning. Second, is the necessity to develop a replication tradition. It is troubling that the field of business ethics is somewhat lacking of a replication tradition, possibly due to being an emergent field of inquiry. There is little replication in the field, even into the 1990s or so it seems. A third imperative, possibly related to the lack of a replication tradition or perhaps causative of a lack of replication, concerns a low heuristic power of much of extant research. It is imperative that scholars in the field replicate research and build from and upon the research of others.

Diversity in Understanding of Ethics

Just as there is diversity in research in business ethics, so, too, is there diversity in the understanding of systems of ethics in the conduct of global business, a diversity of understanding that is a function of a host of economic, political, religious, and social variables that define the differences between peoples, nations, and cultures. As an example, Donaldson and Dunfee (1994), postulated that "Muslim managers may wish to participate in systems of economic ethics compatible with the teachings of the Prophet Muhammad, European and American managers may wish to participate in systems of economic ethics giving due respect to individual liberty, and Japanese managers may prefer systems showing respect for the value of the collective." In each of these situations and in similar situations within the many countries of the world, a given system of ethics, particularly a system of ethics that is home-country specific, may not be accepted, respected, understood, or practiced by host-country nationals.

While the ethics of individuals differ around the world and while a system of ethics from a home country may not be embraced by host-country nationals, managers of global firms nevertheless must raise ethics in the consciousness of their employees regardless of where employees are assigned in the world or whatever their national origins. In raising ethical consciousness, it is insufficient to do so simply by establishing a code of ethics in an organization. Rather, management must develop an ethical culture across an organization (O'Mally, 1995) and put in place an organizational structure or framework for ethics, perhaps a framework such as is advocated in this manuscript.

By advocating an ethical culture as well as having an ethical framework, Paine (1994) argued that the reputation of a firm is enhanced and its relationships with its constituencies are strengthened. Sonnenberg and Goldberg (1992) found that employees feel better about a firm and perform at higher levels when they sense ethics as part of its culture. As a result, it is posited in this research that a firm will realize higher-level results when a concern for ethics pervades the organization and is a part of its culture.

A concern for ethics and ethical values must be developed for a global firm to be holistic, to be greater than the sum of its many parts, whether a firm and its operating units are located in the home country and/or in host countries. Global holism is a necessity for success in global business and requires that "the organization has shared beliefs, attitudes, and values," including a system of ethics, which, when taken together, "creates a consistency in the way the firm treats customers, vendors, other business partners, and each other, wherever business is being done" (Daniels and Daniels, 1994). A concern for ethics in global business is a major responsibility of management, is an integral aspect (Roddick, 1994) of international trade, contributes to global holism, and is an imperative for success in global business (Trevino, Butterfield, and McCabe, 1998).

Unethical Practices in Global Business

There are many ways in which a firm might engage in unethical business practices in the global business arena, hopefully inadvertently rather than deliberately. Unethical corporate behavior may have genesis in a lack of understanding of, or an appreciation for, the culture of a host country in which a firm is operating. Many examples of unethical practices are reported in the literature. Presented below are examples developed by Kehoe (1998) and selected by a panel of executives as being among the most egregious. Since being developed as 12 examples in 1998, the research has been updated to include 15 examples reported in the following paragraphs in no particular order of significance.

- The first egregious example is an unethical practice of making of payments, often unrecorded, to officials in a host country in the form of bribes, kickbacks, gifts, and/or other forms of inducement (Landauer, 1979; Kimelman, 1994; Rossouw, 2000; Sidorov, Alexeyeva, and Shklyarik, 2000; Economist Reporter, 2002c; Hanafin, 2002). These payments often are made in spite of prohibitions of the US Foreign Corrupt Practices Act (1977) against such practices.
- A second egregious example is management representing a firm as financially healthier than its actual condition. This allegedly occurred by managers requiring employees to alter forecasts, plans, and budgets in order to mirror market expectations (Fuller and Jensen, 2002), to report sales or business activity at inflated levels (Leopold, 2002), or to inflate pro forma earnings (Roman, 2002). Additionally, some managers allegedly established complex and off-balance-sheet financial structures (Colvin, 2002; Economist Editorial, 2002; Elins, 2002; McLean, 2002; Zellner and Arndt, 2002; Zellner, France, and Weber, 2002) with assets of dubious quality designed to cause an organization to appear financially healthier than was actually its true condition.
- A third egregious example is for an individual to use a position within a firm to advance one's personal wealth at the expense of others, as is alleged to have occurred in Enron (Colvin, 2002; Elins, 2002; McLean, 2002; Nussbaum, 2002; Schmidt, 2002; Schwartz, 2002; Zellner, Anderson, and Cohn, 2002) and Nortel Networks Corporation (Crenshaw, 2002).

- A fourth egregious example, related to the first, second, and third examples and as equally egregious, and is a situation of management punishing those employees who come forward to report or blow a whistle about an unethical practice or practices (Alford, 2001; Economist Reporter, 2002a, 2002b; Mayer and Joyce, 2002). Posited as perhaps even more egregious is to ignore or to marginalize a whistleblower, alleged to have occurred in the Enron bankruptcy situation (Arndt and Scherreik, 2002; Krugman, 2002; Mayer and Joyce, 2002; Morgenson, 2002; Sloan and Isikoff, 2002; WSJ Editorial, 2002; Zellner, Anderson, and Cohn, 2002).
- A fifth example is the marketing of products abroad that have been removed from a home-country market due to health or environmental concerns. Examples given by Hinds (1982) include chemical, pharmaceutical, and pesticide products, as well as contraceptive devices, which were removed from the US market allegedly for being unsafe to the environment and/or to health, but for which marketing in other countries was continued, and, in some cases, was accelerated.
- Marketing products in host countries that are in questionable need or which are detrimental to the health, welfare, and/or economic well-being of consumers is a sixth egregious unethical practice. An often-cited example (Willatt, 1970; Post, 1985; French and Granrose, 1995; Ferrell, Fraedrich, and Ferrell, 2002) is the marketing of infant formula in developing countries by Nestle S.A. (www.nestle.com). Parents in developing countries are alleged to have been unable to afford the formula, unable to read directions to use the formula appropriately, unable to find sanitary sources of water for preparing the formula, and not to have needed the formula until Nestle convinced them that its use was necessary. Another example (White, 1997; Ferrell, Fraedrich, and Ferrell, 2002) is marketing of cigarettes in developing countries by advertising that implies that most people in the United States smoke and that smoking is "an American thing to do."
- A seventh example is a firm operating in countries that are known to violate human rights and/or failing to be an advocate for human rights in such countries. During the apartheid era in South Africa, US firms were criticized for doing business in the country and for failing to advocate human rights by publicly opposing the discrimination, oppression, and segregation of apartheid (Deresky, 1994; Sethi and Williams, 2001).
- An eight example is a firm moving jobs from a home country to low-wage host countries. When this occurs, workers in the home country are hurt because of loss of jobs (Kehoe, 1995), while workers in a host country are

exploited by low wages. For example, Ballinger (1992) argued that Nike's (www.nike.com) profits increased due, in part, to the lower wages paid to workers in Nike-contracted plants outside the United States. Employees in these plants allegedly worked in excess of 10 hours per day, six days a week, for a weekly salary of less than US $50 for their efforts. The Associated Press (1997) reported that employees in Nike-contracted plants in Vietnam were paid US 20 ¢ per hour for working a 12-hour day. Encouragingly, reports in *The New York Times* (Staff Report, 1997), *Time* (Saporito, 1998), and *Fortune* (Boyle, 2002) imply that Nike is correcting the alleged abuses of employees in contracted plants in Vietnam.

- Utilizing child labor (Nichols et.al., 1993) in host countries when the law in a firm's home country prohibits such use is the ninth example of an unethical practice. While the use of child labor in a host country may be a necessity to support a child and her/his family, be preferable to unemployment, and not be of a concern to the host government, is it ethical to use children as laborers? In the past several years, a group of firms, including Nike, Reebok, L.L. Bean, Liz Claiborne, and Toys R Us, committed to a policy of prohibiting the employment of children younger than 15 years of age in factories in host countries (Headden, 1997; Bernstein, 1999; Singer, 2000). Additionally, Toys R Us has requested suppliers to seek SA 8000 certification, an international standard certifying working conditions (Singer, 2000).

- Tenth is a practice of operating in countries whose environmental standards are lax, or, the converse, being lax in respect for a host country's environment. In the Amazon, global corporations are reported (Thomson and Dudley, 1989) to have ignored their own and the host country's environmental guidelines in extracting oil. In Ireland, global firms are suspected (Keohane, 1989) of ignoring environmental regulations and to be illegally dumping hazardous waste throughout the country. In several countries, large agriculture conglomerates are bioengineering and genetically modifying crops, perhaps to the determent of the environment, animals, and people (Comstock, 2000). Finally, an emerging issue under the tenth example is the dumping of waste materials in less-developed host countries, sometimes waste of a hazardous nature that would require special handling in a home country but which is dumped carelessly in host countries (Ferrell, Fraedrich, and Ferrell, 2002).

- Eleventh is operating in a host country with a lower regard for workers' health and well-being than in the home country. Japanese companies are alleged (Itoh, 1991) to have over worked their employees both in Japan and in host countries and to have been indifferent to their health. Union Carbide is alleged (Daniels and Radebaugh, 1993) to have operated a plant in Bhopal, India with lower safety standards than its plants in more developed countries.

- Conducting business in a developing nation in such a manner as to dominate the nation's economy is a 12th example of an unethical practice. Several rubber companies have been accused of dominating the economies of the developing nations in which they operated rubber plantations. Such domination has been called *dependencia* (Turner, 1984), and has been shown to be damaging to a host country's economy, demoralizing to its people, and of questionable ethics.

- A 13th example is intervening in the affairs of a host country through such activities as influence peddling or other efforts to affect local political activity. In Italy, for example (Anonymous, 1993a), an investigation was undertaken into the alleged illegal financing of political parties by Italian business firms, as well as by foreign business entities operating in the country.

- Taking actions abroad that would be unpopular, controversial, unethical, or illegal in the home country is a 14th example. For instance, MacKenzie (1992) raised the controversial issue of whether, given advances in DNA research, a business firm has a right to patent a life form? Officials at the European Parliament in Brussels debated the legal and moral issues of this question. While a conclusion has not been reached, assuming an affirmative conclusion, may a non-European firm, operating in a European market, patent life forms in Europe if such patenting activity is unethical or illegal in the firm's home country?

- A 15th and final example is an egregious practice of a firm reinvesting little of the profit realized in a host country back in that country due to a restrictive covenant in corporate policy requiring that a majority of profit earned in a host country be repatriated back to the home country. This means that a global firm may reinvest very little back in a host country, and the citizens of the country may be exploited as a result.

Conceptualizing a Framework for Global Business Ethics

It is posited in this research that a framework for ethics is needed for firms engaged in global business across the many cultures that are encountered. A framework that points a firm safely along the global road—a code for the road, as in the lyrics of Crosby, Stills and Nash (1970), "you, who are on the road, must have a code that you can live by. . . ." Is it possible to design such a framework and to develop a code by which global businesses might live? Where do managers begin the process?

The framework for global business ethics presented here has eight stages. A firm ideally should progress through all eight stages in designing and implementing a global ethical system. The framework begins with the stage of understanding the orientation of a firm, and concludes with recommendations for promulgating and using a framework of global business ethics.

Step One—Orientation of a Firm

The first step in a framework for global business ethics is to define a firm's orientation in the global business arena. A firm may participate in global business as an exporter, a multinational firm, a multilocal multinational firm, a global firm, or some combination of these methods. Each of these methods of participation moves a firm further from being a domestic firm and gives it an increasing array of experiences in world markets. The orientation of a firm may be ethnocentric—home-country oriented; polycentric—adaptive to host countries; or geocentric—open to using the best resources wherever they are available in the world. Each of these orientation positions has implications for ethics.

As an exporter, the orientation of a firm may be generalized as primarily ethnocentric. The logic-in-use of an exporter may be generalized as being that home-country approaches should be applied wherever in the world the firm may operate. This ethnocentric logic means that home-country approaches to ethics are considered to be superior to those elsewhere in the world and may be applied whenever possible.

When a firm moves toward multinational operations, management's orientation will evolve, as the result of the experiences in host countries, from an ethnocentric viewpoint of an exporter toward a polycentric orientation as its managerial logic-in-use. This orientation recognizes that a firm must adapt to the unique aspects of each national market in which it operates. The logic-in-use is broadened by a willingness to adapt the home-country's ethical system in the various host countries in which the firm operates. This willingness to adapt its home-country ethical system is strengthened as a firm focus astutely on each host country, develops a multilocal approach to its multinational operations, brings host-country national into management positions, and grants greater autonomy from the home-country parent. All of these things heighten a firm's willingness to adapt and/or to customize its ethical system to fit the culture of a host country.

When a firm evolves to being a global firm, management's orientation becomes geocentric, with an acceptance of and openness to concepts, ideas, processes, and people from throughout the world, including approaches to ethics. The implication of a geocentric orientation is that a firm will be more amenable to addressing values that are inherent in the culture of a host country as a system of ethics is developed.

In developing a framework for global business ethics, a global firm, with a geocentric orientation of its management, is posited to be more open to using a system of global ethics than is an exporter, whose orientation tends to be ethnocentric. In terms of orientation, a global firm generally exhibits a greater readiness to develop ethical systems that appreciate and include the diversity of culture differences found in the world. An exporter, by contrast, is a domestic firm and is posited generally to prefer home-country ethical systems.

Step Two—Differences and Similarities Between Countries

The second step toward a framework for global business ethics is to appreciate and understand the differences and similarities between countries. In global business, there obviously are significant differences between peoples, countries, and cultures. This diversity adds richness to the experience of living on the earth, but may be problematic in establishing an ethical culture in a firm.

Comparing any two countries in regard to ethics in business would find striking differences as well as similarities. For example, consider a comparison of Japan and the United States.

Japan's business culture is characterized (Shimada, 1991) as having excessive corporate competition and a focus on rationality in decision making, based on economic factors at the expense of human factors. Itoh (1991) reported that Japanese managers are criticized for being indifferent to the health of their employees. Hammer, Bradley, and Lewis (1989) found cases of influence-peddling scandals involving leading business executives and Japanese politicians. In fact, breaches in business ethics was suggested by Whenmouth (1992) to be part of the system of doing business in Japan, with unethical behavior having origins deep in the country's cultural tradition.

In comparison, business in the United States has experienced some of the same ethical lapses as in Japan. For example, Labich (1992) presented evidence showing that for some US managers, ethics had an economic basis. These managers became lax in regard for ethics during difficult economic times, but returned to a stronger appreciation of ethics when business conditions improved. The increasing number of whistleblowing cases in the United States argues that something may be remiss in corporate ethics programs (Driscoll, 1992; Dworkin and Near, 1997; Mayer and Joyce, 2002). Research by Sandroff

(1990) and others found such ethical abuses as lying to employees and clients, expense account padding, favoritism, nepotism, sexual harassment, discrimination, and taking credit for the work of others are part of US business culture. All of which has led to an increasing number of business firms offering in-house training in ethics (Hager, 1991), developing games and simulations in ethics (Ireland, 1991), establishing permanent ethics committees (Labrecque, 1990), publishing codes of ethics (Court, 1988), and contracting with ethics' consulting firms for advice and programs, in what Cordtz (1994) has called an *ethicsplosion*. One consulting firm, Transparency International, is reported (Anonymous, 1993b) to have programs to improve ethics and standards of conduct, and to have worked with companies to prevent bribe paying in the conduct of global business.

Step Three—Identify Things of Broad Agreement

While there are differences and similarities in the appreciation for ethics among countries of the world, and while there are differences and similarities in lapses of ethics among businesses from various countries, there are things about ethics to which peoples across the world may agree. This is the third step in the framework. To identify those things, or values, in which there may be common agreement around the world.

Valasquez (1992, p. 30) identified the *global common good* as an area of worldwide agreement. He argued that individuals in international business have a responsibility to contribute to the global common good, including "maintaining a congenial global climate, . . . maintaining safe transportation routes for the international flow of goods, . . . maintaining clean oceans, . . . and the avoidance of global nuclear war. The global common good is that set of conditions that are necessary for the citizens of all or of most nations to achieve their individual fulfillment. . . . "

Beyond the aspects of a global common good to which people in international business might agree, there are certain attributes of life in any society to which a majority might agree (Kehoe, 1994). These include such values and principles (Goodpaster, Note 383-007) as, obeying the law; not harming others; respecting the rights and property of others; never lying, cheating, or stealing; keeping promises and contracts; being fair to others; helping those in need; and encouraging and reinforcing these values in others, all of which Goodpaster called *moral common sense*. These moral values are reaffirmed and enlarged by Scott (2002) in identifying honest communications, respect for property, respect for life, respect for religion, and justice as important organizational moral values.

Another example of attributes to which people throughout the world agree is found in a code of ethics of Rotary International. The attributes to which some 1.2 million Rotarians in 162 countries (Rotary, 2002) agree are: truth telling, fairness to others, goodwill toward others, and acting in ways beneficial to others. These concepts are embodied in a code called the 4-Way Test of Rotary International. The code, consisting of 24 words, is as follows: 1. Is it the truth? 2. Is it fair to all concerned? 3. Will it build goodwill and better friendships? 4. Will it be beneficial to all concerned?

Step Four—Find Voice to Express Agreement

Having identified the things of broad agreement, the fourth step of the framework is to identify a voice or way of expressing those things. Understanding voice is important because it is arguably likely that there are different voices used by people in different countries to express the same value or ethical concept. In fact, within the same country, an ethical concept may be voiced differently (Gilligan, 1982) by men than by women. The challenge is to find a voice or moral language appropriate for each culture wherein a global firm may operate. The challenge further is to recognize when a change in voice is required in order to express an ethical concept in a different culture.

In order to find a voice appropriate for situations in global business ethics, an underpinning of ethical theory is an initial step. In brief, ethical theory might be presented from a teleological or a deontological frame.

Teleological theory is concerned with the *consequences* of an action or business decision. The teleological principle of utilitarianism requires that an individual act in a way to produce the greatest good for the greatest number. In acting in this manner, an individual considers not only self in a decision or action, but the impact of the act on others. An individual applying utilitarianism in decision-making "would determine the effects of each alternative and would select the alternative that optimizes the satisfactions of the greatest number of people." (Kehoe, 1993, p. 16).

Deontological theory is concerned with the *rules* used to arrive at an action or a decision rather than the consequences of the action; that is, deontological theory is rule based, whereas teleological theory is consequences based. The deontological principle of the categorical imperative (Kant, 1785) is: "Act only according to that maxim by which you can at the same time will that it should be a universal law." In other words, the categorical imperative proscribes that individuals only do those things that they can recommend to others. That is, there are certain things that must be done in order to maintain basic humanity in a society, just as there certain things that must be practiced by individuals to maintain order in an organization. These things make up the shared moral values of an organization and are a part of its ethical culture. For example, a manager who does not participate in bribery because he or she could not admit or recommend it to others may be said to be adhering to the categorical imperative. Likewise, as other individuals in a firm adhere to the categorical imperative, it becomes a shared moral value and a part of the ethical culture of a firm.

Kidder (1994) conceptualized an example of shared moral values. He surveyed "ethical thinkers" from around the world and identified eight shared moral values that have broad application across cultures. These included love, truthfulness, fairness, freedom, unity, tolerance, responsibility, and respect for life.

A second example of shared moral values is by DeGeorge (1994). He suggested that there are moral norms that cross cultures that may be used to develop ethical standards for global business. Examples of such shared moral norms are truthfulness, respect for property, fairness, and trust.

Research by Scott (2002) elevated a third example of shared moral values. Arguing that the most important organizational value for analysis is an organization's moral values, she identified five moral values for organizations—justice, honest communication, respect for property, respect for life, and respect for religion.

Perhaps the most useful example of shared moral values is by Donaldson (1992). He analyzed six moral languages for their appropriateness in global business ethics. The languages were: virtue and vice; self-perfection through self control; maximization of human welfare; avoidance of human harm; rights and duties; and social contract. He argues (Donaldson, 1992, p. 280) that "the former three (virtue and vice; self perfection through self control; maximization of human welfare) are inappropriate for establishing a system of ethics in global business," while the "latter three (avoidance of human harm; rights and duties; social contract) are deontological ethical languages with the capacity to establish minimum rather than perfectionist standards of behavior" and are, therefore, better suited for addressing ethical issues in global business. These moral languages give voice to ethics in global business.

Step Five—Use Voice to Develop Ethical Statements

Generalizing from the conclusions concerning the appropriateness of moral languages for global business ethics, the fifth step of the framework emerges. That step is to use voice to develop ethical statements or codes of ethics.

It is posited that the voice used in a framework for global business ethics should be deontological rather than teleological, and minimum rather than perfectionist. This means that the statements developed in a framework for global business ethics should be rule based and be minimum in standard. Said another way, simpler and shorter statements are more appropriate in developing a framework for global business ethics. Parsimony must be the guiding principle in using voice to develop ethical statements.

Step Six—Separate Core and Peripheral Values

Being guided by voice to use rule based, minimum in standard, simple, and short statements, a global business organization, as a sixth step, should determine the core values to be included in its ethical framework and in its global code of ethics. Then identify the peripheral values that may be altered or even deleted from its global code of ethics according to the culture of a host country. This means, for example, if a global firm's home country is the United States, and if it operates also in China, India, Mexico, and Russia, its global code of ethics should contain core-value statements of the home country as well as statements common across all the countries, but may contain different peripheral-value statements in each of the host countries.

It is an imperative that individuals in a global firm understand its core values and its peripheral values. Collins (1995) defined a core value as something a firm would hold even if it became a competitive disadvantage. Donaldson (1996) identified three core values that have basis in Western and non-Western culture and religious traditions—respect for human dignity, respect for basic rights, and good citizenship through support of community institutions. He postulated (Donaldson, 1996, p. 53) that core values "establish a moral compass for business practice. They can help identify practices that are acceptable and those that are intolerable—even if the practices are compatible with a host country's norms and laws. Dumping pollutants near people's homes and accepting inadequate standards for handling hazardous materials are two examples of actions that violate core values. Similarly, if employing children prevents them from receiving a basic education, the practice is intolerable" and violates core values.

To separate core and peripheral values, consider this situation. If the core values of a firm include acknowledging human equality, promoting human welfare, providing high-quality products, having fair prices, contributing to the community, and compliance with national laws, these values should be reflected in a firm's global code of ethics and promulgated to all host-country subsidiaries. If, however, a firm believes that relationships among employees, with customers, and with suppliers are best addressed at the country level, these are peripheral values to be addressed in ethical statements developed by employees in each operating location. In brief, a firm, as noted by Laczniak and Murphy (1993), should strive to have a single worldwide policy on ethics to address its core values, those values never to be compromised, but may allow addenda to its worldwide core-value policy on ethics to address peripheral values that are inherent in the culture of a host country.

Step Seven—Writing a Global Code of Ethics

The seventh step of the framework concerns writing a global code of business ethics that will be a central part of a firm's framework for global business ethics. A global code cannot and should not be written at the home-country headquarters. Rather, contributions to the code must be sought from around the world. Individuals from throughout a firm's global expanse must be involved in developing the code. This means that a committee or task force that is charged with developing the code should have representation from each geographic region in which a firm operates, or even, if possible, from each host country. Likewise, individuals from across functions and levels of hierarchy should be included, so that the result is a multifunctional, multilevel, and multinational task force. The goal must be to be as inclusive as possible in developing a global code of ethics.

Global inclusiveness is important so that a code does not contain only the concepts, ideas, prejudices theories, values, and words of a firm's home country. This is part of using voice to develop a global code. A firm's values that are reflected in a code must be stated in a globally inclusive manner. This is not easily accomplished. It can only be accomplished by being as globally inclusive in voice as possible in writing the code. This implies that those charged with developing a global code of ethics must be empowered to be in close and regular contact wherever located in the world. This may mean that a firm regularly uses teleconferencing while developing the code. It also may mean that meetings of the task force are held regularly in various host countries while the code is being developed. Put simply, a global code of ethics cannot and should not be developed solely in a home-country venue.

Step Eight—Promulgating and Using a Global Code of Ethics

The final step of a framework for global business ethics is to promulgate and use the code of ethics. This means that the code must be translated effectively to the language of each host country. In each host country, some process for ethics representation should be arranged. It may be that a manager is assigned responsibility for ethics in addition to other duties, or preferably an ethics officer is designated formally in each country. That individual should be charged with promulgating the code of ethics, encouraging its use, and managing and refining the firm's framework for global business ethics. The posited result of having a framework of global business ethics is that there should be higher levels of ethical behavior across a global firm when a framework is in place, as was reported by Ferrell and Skinner (1988) with codes of ethics in domestic firms. Simply put, ethics must be made "salient and be part of an ongoing conversation" within an organization (Freeman, 2001). The goal of developing a framework for global business ethics is to have ethics often considered, rather than seldom or never considered in the conduct of global business (Kehoe, 1998).

Conclusion

A mosaic of diversity continues to shine brilliantly across the landscape of global business. It is a landscape of business firms, large and small, operating in various ways in an increasing number of the countries of the world. It is a landscape of diverse cultures, with differing appreciations for and understandings of ethics. It is a landscape of individual managers encountering choices that reflect all the ambiguities, differences, and subtleties of a global mosaic of diversity. It is a landscape of people unified by shared moral values and of global firms in which ethics must be an imperative.

More than 40 years ago, Berle (1954) made a statement that is relevant for today's global corporations. The statement addressed ethics and the responsibilities of management. "The really great corporation management must consider the kind of community in which they have faith and which they will serve and which they intend to help construct and maintain. In a word, they must consider the ancient problems of the good life and how their operations in the community can be adapted to affording or fostering it."

The framework conceptualized in this research is anchored in a concept of shared moral values and developed by using moral languages to give meaning to ethics across cultures. The framework allows for a firm to remain loyal to its core values in situations involving questions of ethics, but allows different peripheral-value statements in host countries. When developing a framework for global business ethics, contributions must be sought from throughout the world. This means that individuals from throughout a firm's global expanse must be involved in developing the framework. Such a global corporate community developed framework will contribute to a concept of ethics being embraced throughout a firm, and to ethics being a word often spoken by employees throughout a firm, rather than a word seldom spoken or never spoken.

A report of the Center for Business Ethics (Hoffman, 2000) noted "business ethics is no longer a set of national initiatives, if it ever was. It is now a global affair." Anywhere a firm operates in the world, its activities must be ethical and adapted to affording or fostering the good life. This is an ethical imperative. Simply yet profoundly stated (Freeman, 2002), "ethics is about the most important parts of our lives and must be center stage" in any activity whether of a business or a personal nature. The practice of ethics in global business is posited to enhance a global corporation, uplift it and its stakeholders, and ensure that its actions foster the good life.

References

Alford, C. Fred (2001). *Whistleblowers: Broken Lives and Organizational Power.* Ithaca, NY: Cornell University Press.

Anonymous (1993a). "The Purging of Italy, Inc.," *Economist,* March 20, pp. 69–70.

Anonymous (1993b). "Clean, Not Laundered," *Economist,* May 8, p. 78.

Arndt, Michael and Susan Scherreik (2002). "Five Ways to Avoid More Enrons," *Business Week,* February 18, pp. 36–37.

Associate Press Report (1997). "Conditions Deplorable at Nike's Vietnamese Plants," *The Daily Progress,* March 28, p. A2.

Ballinger, Jeffrey (1992). "The New Free-Trade Hall," *Harper's,* August, pp. 45–47.

Baumhart, Raymond C. (1961). "How Ethical Are Businessmen?" *Harvard Business Review,* July/August, pp. 6–12.

Becker, Thomas E. (1998). "Integrity in Organizations," *Academy of Management Review,* Volume 23 (1), pp. 154–161.

Berle, A. A. (1954). *The 20th Century Capitalist Revolution.* New York, NY: Harcourt, Brace and World, pp. 166–176.

Berleant, Arnold (1982). "Multinationals and the Problem of Ethical Consistency," *Journal of Business Ethics,* 3, August, pp. 185–195.

Bernstein, Aaron (1999). "Sweatshops: No More Excuses," *Business Week,* November 8, pp. 104–106.

Blodgett, Jeffrey G., Long-Chaun Lu, G. M. Rose and S. J. Vitell (2001). "Ethical Sensitivity to Stakeholder Interests: A Cross-Cultural Comparison," *Journal of the Academy of Marketing Science,* Volume 29 (2), pp. 190–202.

Boulding, Kenneth (1967). "The Basis of Value Judgments in Economics," in Sidney Hook, ed., *Human Values and Economic Policy.* New York, NY: New York University Press.

Bowie, Norman E. (1978). "A Taxonomy for Discussing the Conflicting Responsibilities of a Multinational Corporation," in Norman E. Bowie, *Responsibilities of Multinational Corporations to Society.* Arlington, VA: Council of Better Business Bureaus, pp. 21–43.

Bowie, Norman E. (1990). "Business Ethics and Cultural Relativism," in Peter Madsen and Jay M. Shafritz, eds., *Essentials of Business Ethics.* New York, NY: Penguin Books, pp. 366–382.

Bowie, Norman E. (1997). "The Moral Obligations of Multinational Corporations," in Norman E. Bowie, ed., *Ethical Theory and Business.* Upper Saddle River, NJ: Prentice-Hall, pp. 522–534.

Bowie, Norman E. (1999). *Business Ethics: A Kantian Perspective.* New York, NY: Blackwell Publishers.

Boyle, Matthew (2002). "How Nike Got Its Swoosh Back," *Fortune,* Volume 145, June 11, p. 31.

Brock, Gillian (1998). "Are Corporations Morally Defensible?" *Business Ethics Quarterly,* Volume 8, October, pp. 703–721.

Buller, Paul F. and Glen M. McEvoy (1999). "Creating and Sustaining Ethical Capability in the Multinational Corporation," *Journal of World Business,* 34 (4), pp. 326–343.

Business Ethics Quarterly (1994, Volume 4, January). Issue devoted entirely to international business ethics, pp. 1–110.

Carroll, Archie B. (1979). "A Three-Dimensional Conceptual Model of Corporate Social Performance," *Academy of Management Review,* Volume 4, pp. 497–505.

Carroll, Archie B. (2000). "Ethical Challenges for Business in the New Millennium," *Business Ethics Quarterly,* Volume 10, Number 1, pp. 33–42.

Cateora, Philip R. and John L. Graham (2002). *International Marketing.* New York, NY: McGraw-Hill Companies, Inc.

Caux Roundtable, Principles for Business. (1995). *Society for Business Ethics Newsletter,* May, pp. 14–15.

Cherry, John (2002). "Perceived Risk and Moral Philosophy." *Marketing Management Journal,* Volume 12, Issue 1, pp. 49–58.

Chonko, Lawrence B. and Shelby D. Hunt (2000). "Ethics and Marketing Management: A retrospective and Prospective Commentary," *Journal of Business Research,* 50, pp. 235–244.

Collier, Jane (1998). "Theorising the Ethical Organization," *Business Ethics Quarterly,* Volume 8, October, pp. 621–654.

Collins, James M. (1995). "Change Is Good—But First, Know What Should Never Change," *Fortune,* May 29, p. 141.

Colvin, Geoffrey (2002). "Wonder Women of Whistleblowing," *Fortune,* August 12, p. 56.

Comstock, Gary L. (2000). *Vexing Nature? On the Ethical Case Against Agricultural Biotechnology.* Boston, MA: Kluwer Academic Publishers.

Connolly, P. J. (2000). "Privacy as Global Policy," *InfoWorld,* September 11, pp. 49–50.

Cordtz, Dan (1994). "Ethicsplosion," *Financial World,* August 16, pp. 58–60.

Costa, John Dalla (1998). The Ethical Imperative: *Why Moral Leadership Is Good Business.* Reading, MA: Addison-Wesley.

Court, James (1988). "A Question of Corporate Ethics," *Personnel Journal,* September, pp. 37–39.

Cragg, Wesley (2002). "Business Ethics and Stakeholder Theory," *Business Ethics Quarterly,* Volume 12, Number 2, April, pp. 113–142.

Crenshaw, Albert B. (2002). "Nortel Executive Quits Amid Accusations," *The Washington Post,* February 12, pp. E1 and E4.

Crosby, Stills and Nash. (1970).

Czinkota, Michael R., Ilkka A. Ronkainen and Michael H. Moffett (2002). *International Business.* Fort Worth, TX: Harcourt College Publishers.

Daniels John D. and L. H. Radebaugh (1993). *International Dimensions of Contemporary Business.* Boston, MA: PWS-Kent Publishing Company, pp. 79–80.

Daniels John L. and N. Caroline Daniels (1994). *Global Vision: Building New Models for the Corporation of the Future.* New York, NY: McGraw-Hill, Inc., p. 12.

Davids, Meryl (1999). "Global Standards, Local Problems," *Journal of Business Strategy,* January/February, pp. 38–43.

DeGeorge, Richard T. (1990). "The International Business System, Multinationals, and Morality," in Richard T. DeGeorge, *Business Ethics.* New York, NY: Macmillan Publishing Company.

DeGeorge, Richard T. (1993). *Competing With Integrity in International Business.* New York, NY: Oxford University Press.

DeGeorge, Richard T. (1994). "International Business Ethics," *Business Ethics Quarterly,* Volume 4, January, pp. 1–9.

Delener, Nejdet, ed. (1995). *Ethical Issues in International Marketing.* New York, NY: International Business Press.

Deresky, Helen (1994). *International Management.* New York, NY: Harper Collins College Publishers, pp. 516–519.

Donaldson, Thomas (1985). "Multinational Decision Making: Reconciling International Norms," *Journal of Business Ethics,* December, pp. 357–366.

Donaldson, Thomas (1989). *The Ethics of International Business.* New York, NY: Oxford University Press.

Donaldson, Thomas (1992). "The Language of International Corporate Ethics," *Business Ethics Quarterly,* Volume 2, July, pp. 271–281.

Donaldson, Thomas (1996). "Values in Tension: Ethics Away From Home," *Harvard Business Review,* September–October, p. 53.

Donaldson, Thomas and T. W. Dunfee (1994). "Toward a Unified Conception of Business Ethics: Integrative Social Contracts Theory," *Academy of Management Review,* April, p. 261.

Driscoll, Lisa (1992). "A Better Way to Handle Whistle Blowers: Let Them Speak," *Business Week,* July 27, p. 36.

Drucker, Peter (1981). "What is Business Ethics?" *The Public Interest,* Spring, pp. 18–37.

Dunfee, Thomas W. (1998). "The Marketplace of Morality: Small Steps Toward a Theory of Moral Choice," *Business Ethics Quarterly,* Volume 8, January, pp. 127–145.

Dworkin, Terry M. and J.P. Near (1997). "A Better Statutory Approach To Whistle Blowing," *Business Ethics Quarterly,* Volume 7, January, pp. 1–16.

Economist Reporter (2002a). "In Praise of Whistleblowers," *The Economist,* January 12, pp. 13–14.

Economist Reporter (2002b). "As Companies Cut Costs They Cut Corners Too. Time to Blow the Whistle?" *The Economist,* January 12, pp. 55–56.

Economist Reporter (2002c). Special Report: Bribery and Business," *The Economist,* March 2, pp. 63–65.

Elins, Michael (2002). "Year of the Whistleblower," *Business Week,* December 16, pp. 106–110.

Engelbourg, Saul (1980). *Power and Morality: American Business Ethics, 1840–1914.* Westport, CT: Greenwood Press.

Ferrell, O. C. (1998). "Business Ethics in a Global Economy," *Journal of Marketing Management,* Volume 9 (1), pp. 65–71.

Ferrell, O. C. and L. G. Gresham (1985). "A Contingency Framework for Understanding Ethical Decision Making," *Journal of Marketing,* 49 (Summer), pp. 87–96.

Ferrell, O. C. and S. J. Skinner (1988). "Ethical Behavior and Bureaucratic Structure in Marketing Research Organizations," *Journal of Marketing Research,* 25 (February), pp. 103–109.

Ferrell, O. C., John Fraedrich and Linda Ferrell (2002). *Business Ethics.* Boston, MA: Houghton Mifflin.

File: Framework for Global Business Ethics, RR&R, 2003.

Fraedrich, John, Debbie M. Thorne and O. C. Ferrell (1994). "Assessing the Application of Cognitive Moral Development Theory to Business Ethics," *Journal of Business Ethics,* 13, pp. 829–838.

Freeman, R. Edward (2000). "Business Ethics at the Millennium," *Business Ethics Quarterly,* Volume 10, January, pp. 169–180.

Freeman, R. Edward (2001). Presentation to the FBI/UVA Annual Meeting, University of Virginia, December 12, 2001.

Freeman, R. Edward (2002). Presentation to Beta Gamma Sigma Ethics Symposium, University of Virginia, February 1, 2002.

French, Warren A. and John Granrose (1995). *Practical Business Ethics.* Englewood Cliffs, NJ: Prentice-Hall, Inc.

Fuller, Joseph and Michael C. Jensen (2002). "Just Say No to Wall Street," *Working Paper 02-01,* Tuck School of Business, Dartmouth College and Harvard Business School.

Geva, Aviva (2001). "Myth and Ethics in Business," *Business Ethics Quarterly,* Volume 11, October, pp. 575–597.

Gilligan, Carol (1982). *In a Different Voice: Psychological Theory and Women's Development.* Cambridge, MA: Harvard University Press.

Goodpaster, Kenneth E. (Note 383-007). "Some Avenues for Ethical Analysis in General Management," *Harvard Business School Note 383-007,* p. 6.

Green, Ronald M. (1993). "Business Ethics in a Global Context," in Ronald M. Green, *The Ethical Manager.* New York, NY: Macmillan Publishing Company.

Griffin, Ricky W. and Michael W. Pustay (2003). *International Business.* Upper Saddle River, NJ: Prentice Hall.

Gustafson, Andrew (2000). "Making Sense of Postmodern Business Ethics," *Business Ethics Quarterly,* Volume 10, July, pp. 645–658.

Hager, Bruce (1991). "What's Behind Business' Sudden Fervor for Ethics?," *Business Week,* September 23, p. 65.

Hammer, Joshua, Bradley Martin and David Lewis (1989). "The Dark Side of Japan, Inc.," *Newsweek,* January 9, p. 41.

Hanafin, John J. (2002). "Morality and Markets in China," *Business Ethics Quarterly,* Volume 12 (January), 1–18.

Hasnas, John (1998). "The Normative Theories of Business Ethics: A Guide for the Perplexed," *Business Ethics Quarterly,* Volume 8, January, pp. 19–42.

Headden, Susan (1997). "A Modest Attack on Sweatshops," *U. S. News and World Report,* April 28, p. 39.

Hinds, M. (1982). "Products Unsafe at Home Are Still Unloaded Abroad," *The New York Times,* August 22, p. 56.

Hill, Charles W. L. (2001). *International Business.* New York, NY: McGraw-Hill.

Hill, Charles W. L. (2003). *Global Business Today.* New York, NY: McGraw-Hill.

Hoffman, W. Michael (2000). *Business Ethics: Reflections for the Center.* Waltham, MA: Center for Business Ethics, p. 6.

Hoffman, W. Michael, A.E. Lange, and D. A. Fedo, eds. (1986). *Ethics and the Multinational Enterprise.* Lanham, MD: University Press of America.

Hosmer, LaRue T. and Feng Chen (2001). "Ethics and Economics: Growing Opportunities for Research," *Business Ethics Quarterly,* Volume 11, October, pp. 599–622.

Ireland, Karin (1991). "The Ethics Game," *Personnel Journal,* March, pp. 72–75.

Itoh, Yoshiaki (1991). "Worked to Death in Japan," *World Press Review,* March, p. 50.

Jensen, Michael C. (2002). "Value Maximization, Stakeholder Theory and the Corporate Objective Function," *Business Ethics Quarterly,* Volume 12, Number 2, April, pp. 235–256.

Johnson, Elmer W. (1997). "Corporate Soulcraft in the Age of Brutal Markets," *Business Ethics Quarterly,* Volume 7, October, pp. 109–124.

Kant, Immanuel (1785). *Foundations of the Metaphysic of Morals,* L. W. Beck, translator. New York, NY: Bobbs-Merrill, 1959, p. 39.

Kaufman, Allen (2002). "Managers' Double Fiduciary Duty: To Stakeholders and To Freedom," *Business Ethics Quarterly,* Volume 12, Number 2, April, pp. 189–214.

Keegan, Warren J. (2002). *Global Marketing Management.* Upper Saddle River, NJ: Prentice Hall.

Kehoe, William J. (1985). "Ethics, Price Fixing, and the Management of Price Strategy," in Gene R. Laczniak and Patrick E. Murphy, eds., *Marketing Ethics: Guidelines for Managers.* Lexington, MA: D. C. Heath and Company, pp. 71–83.

Kehoe, William J. (1993). "Ethics in Business: Theory and Application," *Journal of Professional Services Marketing,* Volume 9, Number 1, pp. 13–25.

Kehoe, William J. (1994). "Ethics and Employee Theft," in John E. Richardson, ed., *Annual Editions: Business Ethics.* Guilford, CT: The Dushkin Publishing Group.

Kehoe, William J. (1995). "NAFTA: Concept, Problems, Promise," in B. T. Engelland and D. T. Smart, eds., *Marketing: Foundations For A Changing World.* Evansville, IN: Society for Marketing Advances, pp. 363–367.

Kehoe, William J. (1998). "The Environment of Ethics in Global Business," *Journal of Business and Behavioral Sciences,* Volume 4, Fall, pp. 47–56.

Kehoe, William J. and Linda K. Whitten (1999). "Structuring Host-Country Operations: Framing a Research Study," *Proceedings of the American Society of Business and Behavioral Sciences,* Volume 5, pp. 1–9.

Keohane, K. (1989). "Toxic Trade Off: The Price Ireland Pays for Industrial Development," *The Ecologist,* 19, pp. 144–146.

Kidder, R.M. (1994). *Shared Values for a Troubled World: Conversations with Men and Women of Conscience.* San Francisco, CA: Jossey-Bass, pp. 18–19.

Kimelman, John (1994). "The Lonely Boy Scout," *Financial World,* August 16, pp. 50–51.

Koehn, Daryl (1992). "Toward an Ethic of Exchange," *Business Ethics Quarterly,* Volume 2, July, pp. 341–355.

Kohlberg, Lawrence (1971). "Stages of Moral Development as a Basis for Moral Education," in C. M. Beck, B. S. Crittenden and E. V. Sullivan, eds., *Moral Education.* Toronto, Canada: University of Toronto Press.

Krugman, Paul (2002). "A System Corrupted," *The Wall Street Journal,* January 18, p. C1.

Kung, Hans (1997). "A Global Ethic in An Age of Globalization," *Business Ethics Quarterly,* Volume 7, July, pp. 17–32.

Labich, Kenneth (1992). "The New Crisis in Business Ethics," *Fortune,* April 20, pp. 167–176.

Labrecque, Thomas G. (1990). "Good Ethics Is Good Business," *USA Today: The Magazine of The American Scene,* May, pp. 20–21.

Laczniak, Gene R. (1983). "Business Ethics: A Manager's Primer," *Business,* January–March, pp. 23–29.

Laczniak, Gene R. and Patrick E. Murphy (1985). *Marketing Ethics: Guidelines for Managers.* Lexington, MA: D. C. Heath and Company.

Laczniak, Gene R. and Patrick E. Murphy (1993). *Ethical Marketing Decisions: The Higher Road.* Boston, MA: Allyn and Bacon.

Landauer, J. (1979). "Agency Will Define Corrupt Acts Abroad by U. S. Businesses," *The Wall Street Journal,* September 21, p. 23.

Lantos, Geoffrey P. (1999). "Motivating Moral Corporate Behavior," *Journal of Consumer Marketing,* Volume 16 (3), pp. 222–233.

Lascu, Dana-Nicoleta (2003). *International Marketing.* Cincinnati, OH: Atomic Dog Publishing.

Leopold, Jason (2002). "En-Ruse? Workers at Enron Sat They Posed as Busy Traders to Impress Visiting Analysts," *The Wall Street Journal,* February 7, pp. C1 and C13.

Levitt, Theodore. (1983). "The Globalization of Markets," *Harvard Business Review,* May–June, pp. 92–93.

Mackenzie, Craig and Alan Lewis (1999). "Morals and Markets: The Case for Ethical Investing," *Business Ethics Quarterly,* Volume 9, July, pp. 439–452.

MacKenzie, Debora (1992). "Europe Debates the Ownership of Life," *New Scientist,* January 4, pp. 9–10.

Mayer, Caroline E. and Amy Joyce (2002). "Blowing the Whistle," *The Washington Post,* February 10, pp. H1 and H4–H5.

McCoy, Bowen H. (1983). "The Parable of the Sadhu," *Harvard Business Review,* September/October, pp. 103–108.

McLean, Bethany (2002). "Monster Mess: The Enron Fallout has Just Begun," *Fortune,* February 4, pp. 93–96.

McMaster, Mark (2001). "Too Close for Comfort," *Sales & Marketing Management,* July, pp. 42–48.

Morgenson, Gretchen (2002). "Enron Letter Suggests $1.3 Billion More Down the Drain," *The New York Times,* January 17, pp. C1 & C10.

Murphy, Patrick E. (1988). "Implementing Business Ethics," *Journal of Business Ethics,* Volume 7, pp. 907–915.

Nash, Laura L. (1981). "Ethics Without the Sermon," *Harvard Business Review,* November/December, pp. 79–90.

Nichols, Martha, P. A. Jacobi, J. T. Dunlop and D. L. Lindauer (1993). "Third World Families at Work: Child Labor or Child Care?," *Harvard Business Review,* January–February, pp. 12–23.

Nicholson, Nigel (1994). "Ethics in Organizations: A Framework for Theory and Research," *Journal of Business Ethics,* 13, pp. 581–596.

Nussbaum, Bruce (2002). "Can You Trust Anybody Anymore?" *Business Week,* January 28, pp. 31–32.

O'Mally, Shaun F. (1995). "Ethical Cultures—Corporate and Personal," *Ethics Journal,* Winter, p. 9.

Orts, Eric W. and Alan Strudler (2002). "The Ethical and Environmental Limits of Stakeholder Theory," *Business Ethics Quarterly,* Volume 12, Number 2, April, pp. 215–233.

Paine, Lynn S. (1994). "Managing for Organizational Integrity," *Harvard Business Review,* March–April, pp. 106–117.

Perlmutter, Howard W. (1969). "The Tortuous Evolution of the Multinational Corporation," *Columbia Journal of World Business,* January–February, pp. 11–14.

Post, James M. (1985). "Assessing the Nestle Boycott," *California Management Review,* Winter, pp. 113–131.

Raths, Louis E., Merrill Harmin and Sidney Simon (1966*). Values and Teaching.* Columbus, OH: Merrill Publishing.

Robin, Donald P. (2000). *Questions and Answers About Business Ethics: Running an Ethical and Successful Business.* Cincinnati, OH: Dame, Thompson Learning.

Roddick, Anita (1994). "Corporate Responsibility," *Vital Speeches of the Day,* January 15, pp. 196–199.

Rogers, Hudson P., Alponso O. Ogbuehi, and C. M. Kochunny (1995). "Ethics and Transnational Corporations in Developing Countries: A Social Contract Perspective" in Nejdet Delener, ed., *Ethical Issues in International Marketing.* New York, NY: International Business Press, pp. 11–38.

Roman, Monica (2002). "Deflating those Pro Forma Figures," *Business Week,* January 28, p. 50.

Rossouw, G. J. (1994). "Business Ethics in Developing Countries," *Business Ethics Quarterly,* Volume 4, January, pp. 43–51.

Rotary (2002). "Rotary at a Glance," *The Rotarian,* January, p. 44. See also the Rotary International website at www.rotary.org/aboutrotary/4way.html.

Sandroff, Ronni (1990). "How Ethical Is American Business? The Working Woman Report," *Working Woman,* September, pp. 113–129.

Saporito, Bill (1998). "Taking a Look Inside Nike's Factories," *Time,* Volume 151, Issue 12, pp. 52–53.

Schmidt, Susan (2002). "Lawmaker Challenges Skilling's Denials," *The Washington Post,* February 12, pp. E1 and E5.

Schwartz, John (2002). "An Enron Unit Chief Warned and Was Rebuffed," *The New York Times,* February 20, pp. C1 and C4.

Scott, Elizabeth D. (2002). "Organizational Moral Values," *Business Ethics Quarterly,* Volume 12, Number 1, January, pp. 33–55.

Sethi, S. Prskash and Oliver F. Williams (2001). *Economic Imperatives and Ethical Values in Global Business: The South African Experience and International Codes Today.* South Bend, IN: University of Notre Dame Press.

Shimada, Hauro (1991). "The Desperate Need for New Values in Japanese Corporate Behavior," *Journal of Japanese Studies,* Winter, pp. 107–125.

Sidorov, Alexey, Irina Alexeyeva and Elena Shklyarik (2000). "The Ethical Environment of Russian Business," *Business Ethics Quarterly,* Volume 10, October, pp. 911–924.

Singer, Andrew W. (2000). "When it Comes to Child Labor, Toys R Us Isn't Playing Around," *Ethikos,* May/June, pp. 4–14.

Singer, Peter (2002). "Navigating the Ethics of Globalization," *The Chronicle of Higher Education,* October 11, pp. B7–B10.

Skelly, Joe (1995). "The Rise of International Ethics," *Business Ethics,* March/April, pp. 2–5.

Sloan, Allen and Michael Isikoff (2002). "The Enron Effect," *Newsweek,* January 28, pp. 34–35.

Smith, Adam (1966). *The Theory of Moral Sentiments.* New York, NY: Kelley Publishers.

Smith, N. Craig (1995). "Marketing Strategies for the Ethics Era," *Sloan Management Review,* Summer, pp. 85–97.

Sonnenberg, Frank K. and Beverly Goldberg (1992). "Business Integrity: An Oxymoron?," *Industry Week,* April 6, pp. 53–56.

Staff Report (1997). "Nike Suspends a Vietnam Boss," *The New York Times,* p. C3.

Thomson, Roy and Nigel Dudley (1989). "Transnationals and Oil in Amazonia," *The Ecologist,* November, pp. 219–224.

Trevino, Linda K., K. D. Butterfield and D. L. McCabe (1998). "The Ethical Context of Organizations: Influences on Employee Attitudes and Behaviors," *Business Ethics Quarterly,* Volume 8, July, pp. 447–476.

Turner, Louis (1984). "There's No love Lost Between Multinational Companies and the Third World," in W. M. Hoffman and J. M. Moore, eds., *Business Ethics.* New York, NY: McGraw-Hill Book Company, pp. 394–400.

U. S. Foreign Corrupt Practices Act (1977). www.usdoj.gov/criminal/fraud/fcpa/dojdocb.htm

van Tulder, Rob and Ans Kolk (2001). "Multinationality and Corporate Ethics," *Journal of International Business Studies,* Volume 32 (2), pp. 267–283.

Velasquez, Manual (1992). "International Business, Morality, and the Common Good," *Business Ethics Quarterly,* Volume 2, January, p. 30.

Velasquez, Manual (2000). "Globalization and the Failure of Ethics," *Business Ethics Quarterly,* Volume 10, January, pp. 343–352.

WSJ Editorial (2002). "Enron's Sins," *The Wall Street Journal,* January 18, p. A10.

Weaver, Gary R., Linda K. Trevino and Philip L. Cochran (1999). "Corporate Ethics Programs as Control Systems," *Academy of Management Journal,* Volume 42 (1), pp. 41–57.

Weaver Gary R. and Bradley R. Agle (2002). "Religiosity and Ethical Behavior In Organizations," *Academy of Management Review,* Volume 27, Number 1, pp. 77–97.

Werhane, Patricia H. (2000). "Exporting Mental Models: Global Capitalism in the 21st Century," *Business Ethics Quarterly,* Volume 10, January, pp. 353–362.

Whenmouth, Edwin (1992). "A Matter of Ethics," *Industry Week,* March 16, pp. 57–62.

White, Anna (1997). "Joe Camel's World Tour," *The New York Times,* April 23, p. A31.

Willatt, Norris (1970). "How Nestle Adapts Products to Its Markets," *Business Abroad,* June, pp. 31–33.

Yip, George S. (2003). *Total Global Strategy II.* Upper Saddle River, NJ: Prentice Hall/Pearson Education, Inc.

Zellner, Wendy and Michael Arndt (2002). "The Perfect Sales Pitch: No Debt, No Worries," *Business Week,* January 28, p. 35.

Zellner, Wendy, Stephanie F. Anderson and Laura Cohn (2002). "The Whistle Blower: A Hero and a Smoking-Gun Letter," *Business Week,* January 28, pp. 34–35.

Zellner, Wendy, Michael France and Joseph Weber (2002). "The Man Behind the Deal Machine," *Business Week,* February 4, pp. 40–41.

Critical Thinking

1. What are important considerations in developing a global code of ethics?

2. Should a firm change its home-country code of ethics when operating in another country? Why or why not?

3. Of the eight-stage framework for developing a global code of ethics presented in the article, what stage do you believe is most critical for a firm operating in the global business arena? Why is it a critical stage?

4. How should a firm promulgate its code of ethics in countries in which it operates?

Create Central

www.mhhe.com/createcentral

Internet References

Association of Corporate Council
http://www.acc.com/legalresources/quickcounsel/daiagcoc.cfm

Ethics Resource Center
http://www.ethics.org/files/u5/LRNGlobalIntegrity.pdf

Article   Prepared by: Eric Teoro, *Lincoln Christian University*

Taking Your Code to China

KIRK O. HANSON AND STEPHAN ROTHLIN

Learning Outcomes

After reading this article, you will be able to:

- Recognize the difficulty of developing a global standard for ethical behavior in business.

- Describe the unique challenges in conducting business in China.

- Develop a schema for promoting ethical business practices in China.

Introduction

The proliferation of codes of conduct and ethical standards among American and European companies has been dramatic over the past 20 years. It is rare today to find a large publicly held company in the West that does not have some type of ethics code and is not involved in the growing dialog over global standards of conduct. But one of the most difficult challenges facing these companies is how to apply these codes and these ethical standards to the companies' operations in developing countries, particularly in Africa, the Middle East, and Asia. Among these cases, perhaps the most urgent challenge is for each company to decide how to adapt and apply its code to operations in China. Companies such as Rio Tinto, Google, and Foxconn are recent case studies in ethical conflicts arising from doing business in China.

With pressures for human rights, environmental sensitivity, and fighting corruption rising in their domestic homelands and in global commerce, nothing is more critical to these companies' reputation and success than learning how to "take their code to China."

This article presents the learning of the two authors and companies they have consulted and worked with over the last 10 years in China. Our experience is that Western companies have generally progressed very slowly in applying their codes to their operations in China. This article summarizes why it is so difficult to do so, and what the most successful companies are doing to make it work.

Pressures for a Global Standard of Company Behavior

The fundamental problem any company faces in creating a global commitment to ethical behavior in its own organization is that cultural, competitive, economic, and political conditions vary significantly from country to country. It is often said that ethical values themselves differ significantly between countries. From our experience, however, we believe values do not differ as much as common practice—or how companies typically behave. Actual behavior, of course, depends on historical patterns, government regulation and enforcement, social pressures and acceptance, and the moral resolve of the actors. While corruption is common in many countries of the world, one cannot really say that corruption is welcomed or valued anywhere. There are anticorruption coalitions among domestic companies in almost every national setting. Even in those countries with the most corruption, there is an awareness of the corrosive effects it brings to the country, and the drag corruption creates for economic development.

Nonetheless, there are some value and cultural differences of significance, and different countries that are at different stages of development often have different priorities for social and economic progress. Further, the national and local governments in host countries present different challenges depending on their history and leadership.

Western companies really have little choice whether to "take their code to China" and to the other countries they operate in. They are facing four key developments which make "taking their codes" to wherever they operate more important and often more difficult. The first is that global companies are under increasingly insistent demands, both legal and from key constituencies in their home countries to adopt and implement standards of behavior abroad that match those at home. The United States' Foreign Corrupt Practices Act (FCPA), which was passed in 1977, makes some forms of corruption abroad crimes in the United States; in 1999 almost all OECD countries signed similar laws.

Because home country constituencies will not tolerate different (i.e. lower) ethical standards abroad, most large Western companies adopt and implement "global codes of conduct" which are expected to guide company behavior to be the same across all countries in which the firm operates. Many companies have commented that, from a purely practical point of view, adherence to a single global standard of behavior reduces the incidence of rogue local behavior, and rationalizations that the firm's conduct must be "adapted" to local conditions.

The second development is a growing global movement, reflected in an increasing number of developing countries, to deal seriously with bribery and corruption. Thirty-eight countries have now signed up to the OECD's 1997 anticorruption convention, leading to a spatter of cross-border prosecutions. Local constituencies in host countries then pressure companies from developed Western countries to join the reform coalitions to counter corruption. Local affiliates of Transparency International are most significant in this development.

The third development is a growing global dialog on "global standards" for business behavior. The United Nations Global Compact is an initiative launched in 1999 at the World Economic Forum in Davos by former Secretary General Kofi Anan but enthusiastically continued under his successor Ban Kee Moon. Companies and NGOs in over 80 countries have pledged to follow the 10 principles of the Global Compact in the crucial area of human rights, labor conditions, environmental protection and anticorruption. Similar efforts are being pursued in specific industries and in specific dimensions of corporate behavior such as employment policies and environmental behavior. Efforts such as these to promote a global standard of behavior are making it more difficult to operate under different practices in different countries. Such pressure requires companies to commit publicly to various global standards, which are then reinforced in their own company codes.

Finally, the explosive growth of the global media in all its forms has led to an increasing scrutiny of corporate behavior, even in the most distant and remote areas of the developing world. It has become difficult for a company to behave differently abroad without it coming to the attention of its home and host country constituencies. Corporate sweatshops, or environmental practices, can be documented by amateur reporters with cellphone cameras, even in the most restricted societies. Such disclosure dramatically increases pressures on Western companies to behave by a single global standard.

The Realities of Operating in Developing Countries

In each country where a company operates, it must confront a set of unique realities in applying its code of corporate behavior. Among the most important are the following:

Cultural expectations and standards—Each country has a set of cultural standards, or more informal expectations, that may conflict with the ethical standards the company operates by elsewhere. While some cultural expectations are benign—modes of greeting and signs of respect—others can be more problematic. In some societies, vendors are often selected primarily because they are a "related company" or are operated by a local employee's family or by a relative of a government official. In other societies, it is expected that potential business partners will develop a deep and reciprocal relationship before a contract is signed. In discussing China, the cultural tradition of gift giving to support such relationships can be a particularly problematic issue to manage.

Social and business community pressure to conform—Foreign companies operating in any society can be very disruptive, whether it is their pay scales or their insistence on arms-length contracting practices. When the foreign company operates by standards that challenge or constitute implied criticisms of local practices, there will be significant pressure on the foreign firm to conform to local practices, lest their presence create greater costs for indigenous firms, or create dissatisfaction in the local firm's workforce. The Western firm may find itself frozen out of business opportunities or subjected to selective regulatory enforcement if it is considered to be "disruptive."

Local management's comfort and loyalty to local standards—Foreign companies seek to hire local managers as quickly as possible and for as many positions as possible. Often local managers, particularly more senior managers already experienced in local companies, have adopted the local values and ways of doing things. Changing these managers' ways of operating can be particularly difficult.

Priorities of economic and political development—The national and local governments of host countries have many priorities and needs, and often choose to focus on issues unimportant to foreign firms while ignoring issues central to these newcomers. Chinese government decisions about how to deal with copyright violations, liberty issues such as access to the internet, and expressions of dissent may create significant difficulties for Western firms.

Western companies as targets of opportunity—Finally, any firm entering a developing country is a target for opportunistic individuals who seek to take advantage of the firm, particularly the substantial investment capital it plans to commit. They may negotiate deals overly favorable to the local partner, and may enmesh the firm in ethically questionable activities before it knows the local situation well enough to avoid such entanglements. Any firm must exercise particular caution until it develops an understanding of the local culture and acquires trusted business partners.

Special Reasons Why Operating in China Is Harder

China, as the "Middle Kingdom," is acutely proud of its long and complex history and culture. There is a widespread conviction that everything which comes from outside China needs a profound process of adaptation and inculturation in order to become accepted and relevant in the Chinese context. Companies seeking to implement "global standards" are sometimes met with distrust and disdain.

A second consideration is that there is a respect for local hierarchies that appears to be all-pervasive in Chinese society. There is a perceived need to give face to influential officials and individuals, which reflects the history of Chinese dynasties and has become distinctly different than the democratic traditions of other countries. A number of behavior patterns reflect this Imperial style. There are rituals and cultural patterns designed primarily to maintain social stability through these hierarchical relationships. On the level of companies and institutions this means that company leaders tend to be given the status of benevolent dictators who are accountable to no one. The way up to the top positions in many organizations may be paved more by one's ability to flatter a senior person at the right moment than by one's competency.

A third consideration, drawn from the long and revered Confucian tradition is the focus of the morally refined person, a "qunzi," who is expected to inspire much more moral behavior than the mere observance of the law. It is felt that the law cannot quite be trusted to ensure that the rights of every individual to be safeguarded. In its place, family bonds remain the strongest social reference, as also reflected strongly in the Confucian tradition. Thus, doing business with family members is often preferred to conducting arms-length transactions.

Finally, it is also true that the recent history of foreign aggression toward China, such as during the Opium wars or the Japanese invasion and massacres in the 1930s and 1940s, are featured frequently in the media and emerge frequently in the memory of the Chinese. These concerns erupt periodically, and affect attitudes toward all Western companies, not just those from the United Kingdom or Japan. There is a particular sensitivity to the perceived aggression of US support for Taiwan, for example. Eruptions of such feelings can delay or derail deal making and normal operations at unexpected moments.

The Chinese Context in 2010

After the end of the so-called "Cultural Revolution" from 1966 until 1976 and the turmoil of the "Gang of Four," China has witnessed the strongest economic growth in history due to the policies the paramount leader Deng Xiaoping introduced in 1978. Special economic zones have been opened in Shenzhen and other cities in China and foreign companies from the United States and Europe now have substantial investments, as well as substantial manufacturing and outsourcing operations to China.

Not surprisingly, the prospect of getting their teeth into a new huge market created the illusion for many foreign firms that enormous and immediate profits would be theirs for the taking. This has been almost always proven to be an illusion from the very beginning. It has been an extremely difficult challenge to be able to compete in China where the web of relationships—"guanxi" in Chinese—especially with government officials—seems to be crucial for one's success. It took the Swiss Multinational firm Nestle, which settled into Mainland China in 1983, 20 years in order to reach profitability. Many joint ventures—such as Pepsi Cola with its partner in Sichuan, Danone with Wahaha—were arranged in haste and have experienced a long and dreadful divorce and seemingly endless litigation. The Chinese companies involved, mostly state owned enterprises, seemed able to appeal to some government body or appeal publicly to nationalistic pride and xenophobic resentment in order to justify an opportunistic escape from their foreign partnership obligations. Despite a still wide spread "Gold Rush Mentality" to make the big deal quickly, a large majority of foreign business ventures have ended in failure or only limited success.

A major element of discomfort of Western companies in 2010 stems from the ambiguous role of the Chinese government dealing with the phenomenon of wide spread corruption which seems to be deeply engrained in the society. On one side, there have been serious attempts from the Central Government since the 1990s to curb corruption with various anticorruption campaigns. This has been more than lip service. Several actions have shown how steps have been taken. After the appointment of Zhu Rongji as Prime Minister in 1998 a whole empire of corruption, smuggling, and prostitution collapsed in the Eastern province of Fujian as bold actions were taken. The year 2006 sticks out as a year when a number of prominent multinationals such as Whirlpool, McKinsey, and ABB were punished by the Chinese government due to their kickback payments to the local government in Shanghai. In the same year the mayor, Mr. Cheng Liangyu, was sacked. During the last National Parliament Congress, blunt statements denouncing wide spread corruption stunned the public.

However, the same government—especially on lower levels—seems to represent a culture of deeply engrained patterns of soliciting favors and the rampant abuse of power. According to a survey among prominent business schools in China, including Hong Kong and Macau, a record number of 49 percent of the respondents thought that interacting with lower level government officials would most likely bring them into conflict with their personal value system.

There is a noticeable rise of public concern in China regarding business and government misbehavior. A number of recent incidents have had a significant impact on the Chinese public. When news broke out in 2007 that more than a thousand people, including children and disabled people, were being abused in kiln mines in the Shanxi province, it became surprising news coverage and a national tragedy. The link between the most brutal abuse of human beings and corrupt officials (and also local media) who have been paid to keep their mouth shut became obvious to everyone. An indigenous consumer movement, already strong in Hong Kong and Macau, has grown stronger in the wake of the lead paint scandals in the toy industry, the tainted milk scandals in Anhui Province (2001) and Hebei Province (2008), and the gas explosion in Northern China on the Songhua River in November 2005. This explosion stands out as the most devastating ecological disaster in recent history. The clean up will take at least 10 more years under the best circumstances.

It is said the Chinese citizen is also awakening to personal responsibility. The earthquake, which occurred in Wenchuan in the Sichuan province on May 12, 2009, provoked such a surprising outpouring of help and mutual assistance that even critical newspapers were hailing the birth of a civil society in China. Public philanthropy and public scrutiny of powerful companies and government officials are both evidence of a growing civil society.

While stories in the West emphasize limitations on the media in China, and there is the tight control from government censorship, it also seems that the so called "New Media"—a term for aggressive investigative journalism—with newspapers like Southern Weekly, Caijing, and China Newsweek—has had a significant impact in featuring stories of the abuse of power by some local officials. This new media has presented stories about both exemplary and shoddy behavior by Western companies operating in China.

There is even an emerging study of ethics and responsibility for the next generation of Chinese leaders. The Central Party School has not only been engaged in integrating Business Ethics and Corporate Social Responsibilities program within their curriculum, but also invited law professors and other experts from other countries to their school in order to engage in a serious debate about the rule of law and how civil society may be implemented in China. And according to a survey conducted by Jiaotong University, Shanghai, 39 percent of the business schools in China do actually include CSR and business ethics in their program.

Background Issues in Implementing a Code in China

There is much debate in China on several major issues which influence how a code is implemented. The first is the question whether the values of a company's Chinese employees are similar to those of their Western counterparts. Some Party ideologues are strongly arguing that Chinese values are divergent from the rest of the world. If there were no common ground, it would indeed be hard to implement in China the same code used in the West. By contrast, when China joined the World Trade Organization (WTO), in July 2001 it was presumed that the internationally accepted standards of the WTO could be implemented in China, that there were enough common values.

Another debate has been developed regarding the term of "Dignity," a term commonly used in recent Chinese government statements. What in Western terminology might be termed as "human rights" appears quite similar to the Chinese term of "Dignity" (zuiyan). Some suggest this represents a commitment to common values and may provide a language to address concerns important to Western companies.

Many Western executives operating in China have come to believe the goal to achieve in implementing a code must be far more than the formal agreement and legal compliance sought in the West. We believe implementing global standards in China will only work if they are formally agreed to AND take into account several aspects of the exceeding complex Chinese organizational culture.

For example, it is a good rule in China to assume that at the beginning of a project or implementation that "Nothing Is Clear." A common source of irritation is that partnerships and projects are formally agreed to, but too hastily arranged. Western companies assume all important details have been taken care of, when they have not. Often, a kind of very brief honeymoon is celebrated, followed by a long and painful divorce due to neglect of informal relationships and agreements, which must also be developed. Countless case studies document this pattern. In the most notorious cases, such as the breakdown of the joint venture between the French company, Danone, with its Chinese partner Wahaha, the relationship deteriorated so badly that the respective governments felt compelled to step in and impose a truce. It is, therefore, wise to understand that any successful cooperation with Chinese partners, or even one's own employees, takes much more time. It is frequently a necessary strategy to adopt stronger methods of control if common agreements are to be properly understood and honored. It is unfortunately common that a Western company's first partnership ends up in failure.

When a misunderstanding arises, one should adopt the Confucian self-critical attitude in figuring out the reasons for such a failure rather than putting the blame on the Chinese side. Most often, it will be the neglect of informal agreements and relationships. Only in a deeper relationship and through much more informal and formal communication can the true meaning of agreements in China be clarified.

Another area of general concern in implementing codes is that Western companies often do not appreciate the strong divide between the city and the countryside in China. Implementing agreements and employee and partner standards can be harder in some rural conditions. Roughly two-thirds of the Chinese still live in the countryside where carefully orchestrated rituals are even more important to the successful implementation of agreements. For example, in some circumstances a host may insist on offering hospitality with excessive drinking. While in the cities the foreign guest may be able to politely refuse at some point to continue with the drinking games, in the countryside it may be considered rude to stop the dynamics of getting drunk together.[1] Clearly, a company must find ways of limiting participation in the most objectionable practices. Besides excessive drinking games, there are some banquets and karaoke sessions where women are hired to act as prostitutes. Such objectionable practices can create significant legal exposure for a company as well.

Codes must be written and implemented with an understanding of extensive new legislation in China addressing labor conditions, corruption, whistleblowing, sexual harassment, consumer, and environmental issues. Despite the difficulties of introducing a global ethics code in China, there are opportunities for Western companies to contribute significantly to the implementation and success of these new laws, all of which will make the companies' task easier in the future. There is an interest in growing segments of the government and the Chinese business community to see these laws made effective.

Finally, Western companies must keep abreast of developments in a growing commitment to the rule of law. In many ways, Hong Kong represents a model of the implementation of the Rule of Law in the Chinese context. Hong Kong, which reverted to China in 1997, continues its role as a beacon of clean government. Forty years ago rampant cases of corruption were common in Hong Kong. However, due to the establishment of the Independent Commission against Corruption (ICAC), significant headway has been made in diminishing corruption so that now Hong Kong ranks besides Singapore as the cleanest country in Asia. This has encouraged greater transparency concerning corruption in other parts of China.

The conclusion of the recent publication of the Anticorruption report of Mr. Xiao Yang (2009) who served as Supreme Judge in the PRC has been very clear. He argued that corruption on Mainland China has strongly increased in the last 15 years and has involved more and more Ministries. He argued for the implementation of an institution modeled on ICAC designed to investigate and prosecute cases of abuse cases of public.

Shaping Your Code to Fit China

The first choice every company faces is whether to operate by global standards or to adjust and adapt to local norms. Our experience suggests there is always some adherence to local norms, though not always by changing the actual words in the code, and hopefully, this adherence is within the framework of global standards a company claims to follow wherever it operates. However, in some settings, more adjustments and more recognition of the ethical traditions of the host country may be necessary. We think this is true of China.

We have observed the most successful Western firms in China following these steps to "take their codes to China":

Inculturate Your Code

The term "inculturation" represents a compromise between unchanging global standards and complete local accommodation. "Inculturation" in China has a long history. The Roman Catholic Church has sought, since the time of Matteo Ricci, a Jesuit priest who came to China in 1583, of "inculturating" the Christian message to Chinese conditions. For Ricci and even for Catholics today, religious "inculturation" indicates the dynamic process when key values enshrined in the Gospel such as truth, honesty, and charity are not just imposed from outside, but get truly integrated within a given culture. This process makes possible global consistency with local sensitivity. This is most important in countries like China that have a history of foreign domination and a sensitivity to imperialistic behavior.

For the company choosing to operate in China, inculturation means adhering to global principles that have specific local meanings and therefore, local rules. The most obvious example is gift giving. In a gift giving culture like China, a company would find it hard to adhere to an absolute "no gift" policy as some companies adopt elsewhere in the world. An inculturated gift policy would permit gift giving, albeit tightly limited, but also scaled so that larger gifts, again within a firmly established upper limit, would be permitted to higher executives or officials. An inculturated Chinese policy would also even permit small but scaled gifts to government officials, as this is in China a show of respect. A top value of $75 or $100 for the highest corporate or government official visited is viable and allows the Western company to respect and adhere to local cultural gift-giving practice, but not to engage in bribery. The company also must make it absolutely clear that gifts of any greater value are forbidden.

Inculturation would also recognize the cultural tradition of relationship building and the necessary entertainment to that purpose. However, a Western company should very explicitly and clearly communicate the limits on the value and frequency of such entertainment. Inculturation in China should also recognize the particular context of ethics hotlines and of whistle blowing. With particular adjustments, even this Western concept can be made to work in China, as noted below.

Make the Company Code Consistent with Chinese Laws

China is proud of the progress made in recent years in promulgating and adopting regulatory standards and laws that protect the interests of employees, consumers, and shareholders. It is a necessary step in taking ones's code to China to assess the alignment of these local laws (many very recently adopted) and the company's code of conduct. This process must, of course, be an ongoing one, making future adjustments to the company's code as new laws are adopted in China.

Align Your Code with Chinese Concepts and Slogans of Key Government Officials

In addition to the laws adopted by the National Congress and Communist Party rules adopted by the every 5-year Central Party Congress, Chinese party and government leaders introduce key phrases or slogans which are meant to organize and direct the path of Chinese economic and social development.

Under Jiang Zemin the former President of the PRC, there was considerable attention to the "Three Represents," a doctrine by which the all-powerful Communist Party of China represented the masses of people, the productive forces of society, and the culture. The key message was the preeminence of the Party, but the detailed message gave room to cast corporate codes and decisions as advocating the masses, the development of productive capacity, and even the proper cultural development of China. Under the first 5-year term of Hu Jintao, the current President of China, the concept of "Harmonious Society" was adopted as a preeminent national goal. Later, Hu promoted the concept of "a Scientific Society" wherein, among other things, empirical data and facts should drive decisions more than bias or entrenched interests.

Tying corporate norms and standards of conduct to that objective can strengthen corporate efforts, both because employees understand the alignment of corporate objectives, but also because the company could occasionally secure government help in enforcing its code that it would not otherwise receive.

Incorporate References to Global Standards Embraced by the Chinese

Over the past 10 years, the Chinese government has participated in the formulation of, and conferences on, many international codes and standards. The United Nations Global Compact has 195 signatories in China. The WTO code was widely publicized to Chinese industries in 2001 when China officially joined the WTO. References to these documents and standards strengthen acceptance of a company's global code.

Publish the Code in Bilingual Format

A company code should be published in both English and in Chinese language versions, perhaps side by side. Any Chinese company and every Western company operating in China will have English speakers, and they or other employees will be eager to *compare* the actual English words with the Chinese characters chosen as direct translations. And of course, any company will have Chinese speakers who do not read English. Translation into Chinese demonstrates a seriousness of purpose and a commitment to enforce the code, which must be addressed in the published document.

Introduce the Code in the Chinese Way

Too often, ethics codes are introduced in the United States and in Western Europe by email or by distribution of a printed booklet, perhaps with a card to return acknowledging receipt of the code. This approach will simply not work in China.

Chinese employees will expect that any code or standard they are actually expected to follow will be introduced with considerable time available for discussion, objection, and clarification, and in a workshop conducted in their own dialect. At minimum, they will expect to be able to argue about adaptations to the Chinese context, and the particular Chinese characters used to translate the English or European language concepts. Rather than interpret this as dissent and obfuscation, those introducing the code should consider it a productive opportunity to explain the code and get good feedback on the application of the code to the Chinese context.

Other aspects of the introduction should proceed much as they do in the West. The code must be introduced by line officers of the company with a seriousness that convinces employees that these are actually to be the desired standards. Training must address the most common dilemmas employees will face to give clear and understandable signals about the type of behavior expected. Specific examples are more important in the Chinese context because employees will have generally experienced the rollout of multiple initiatives that have had little impact and less staying power.

Education regarding the code must be given to all new hires. Education in the code must be tailored to the several hierarchical levels within the firm, including senior executives, middle managers, and hourly employees.

Do Whistleblowing the Chinese Way

Without giving up the principle of reporting violations, a Chinese hotline can be positioned and promoted as a "Help line" designed to advise employees on how a particular action should be taken. This approach has been used by many companies in the

West. Further, because of the sensitivity to reporting on a senior, there must be greater opportunity for an employee to have his or her complaint treated as genuinely confidential and anonymous. There is a greater sensitivity to cases where the complaint, by its very nature, might be traced back to an individual employee. A Chinese help line will require more promotion and explanation, and may be more effective if it is structured to have complaints dealt with by the highest authority in a company—for example, by the board of directors. Because of deference to hierarchy, only the board can effectively address wrongdoing by senior level officials.

Extending the Code to Business Partners

There is a growing understanding among Chinese businesses that American and European companies must extend their standards and codes to their business partners, and have a right to expect their partners to adhere to the same standards. In the past, too many Western companies have thrown up their hands and despaired of actually influencing the behavior of business partners, accepting signed assurances of compliance but not really expecting adherence. Today, more Western companies are vetting their partners for their capacity and willingness to conform to codes, and then are monitoring and assessing compliance over time.

The first step in the process must be the selection of partners who have the basic capacity to be in alignment with the values and code of the Western firm. This requires due diligence, either by the company's own managers, or by a firm hired explicitly to evaluate potential partners. Such due diligence is usually hard to accomplish, and virtually every firm reports one or more disasters trying to integrate business partners into the business's activities. Nonetheless, Chinese firms, particularly those with experience operating in an international business environment, and firms with experience in previous partnerships with Western companies, can be effective and ethical local partners. In China, there has developed a language often used to describe projects and companies capable of operating by such standards. This is known as operating by "international standards" as opposed to Chinese or local standards. Projects are said to be built to or operating by international standards. Chinese businesses are said to be "international standards companies." Such firms are more likely to be effective partners.

Preparing Local Leadership to Enforce Your Code in China

As in virtually all settings where a company seeks to infuse a code and its standards into actual behavior, local leadership will exercise the strongest influence in China. Chinese executives

and managers will be anxious to adopt the latest developments in leadership. It is important to position the code as a key part of cutting edge and modern management.

An extended dialog with the chief local official regarding the code before it is introduced is essential. Only a local executive can identify the unavoidable points of stress in the implementation of a code. A local executive will expect to be consulted on the "inculturation" process, and may be the best source of ideas for doing this successfully without abandoning the firm's global standards. And only a local executive can highlight where enforcement must be emphasized.

Much has been made regarding the wisdom of having a Chinese national or a foreign passport holder as a Western company's top officer in China. Both have risks for the implementation of a corporate code of conduct. The foreign executive enforcing the code may make the code seem more foreign and less practical in the local context. On the other hand, some Chinese executives may not believe in the code as fully, or may go through the motions without truly requiring adherence within the organization. A Chinese executive who genuinely believes in the code may be more effective in getting compliance from the organization, or recognizing lip service when it is being given.

Company leaders, both at the Western headquarters and in China, need to create a system of accountability—of monitoring and auditing compliance with the code. This is even more important in China than it is in the West. There are so many initiatives and slogans thrown at Chinese managers, that they are looking for signals that this one is not merely lip service. Too often they conclude that ethics codes are not serious because they are introduced in ineffective ways and without the accountability and follow-up.

It is absolutely essential to the success of any code that the offending employee or manager must be subject to firing, and that occasionally an employee does get fired for violating the code. Even more so than in the West, it is critical all understand that the behavior of senior managers and executives be subject to the code, and risk dismissal if they violate the code. There is a predisposition to believe the code is both lip service and/or applied selectively on lower level employees, and not to those higher in the hierarchy.

In summary, we believe Western companies following the preceding principles can and are making genuine progress "taking their codes to China" and establishing a truly global standard of behavior in their firms.

Note

1. Obviously, such games may seriously harm the health of those who are unable to put a timely end to this ritual. Recently, there have again been reports of death of government officials due to excessive drinking.

References

Organization for Economic Co-operation and Development. (2009). *Ratification Status as of March 2009.*

Retrieved from www.oecd.org/dataoecd/59/13/40272933.pdf The Foreign Corrupt Practices Act of 1977 § 15 U.S.C. § 78dd-1(1977).

United Nations Global Compact Office. (2005). *The ten principles.* Retrieved from www.unglobalcompact.org/AboutTheGC/TheTenPrinciples/index.html

United Nations Global Compact Office. (2010). *Participant search* [Data File]. Retrieved from www.unglobalcompact.org/participants/search?business_type=all&commit=Search&cop_status=all&country[]=38&joined_after=&joined_before=&keyword=&organization_type_id=& page=1&per_page=100&sector_id=all

Yang, X. (2009). Fantan baogao (Anti-Corruption Report). Beijing: Law Press.

Critical Thinking

1. What are the realities facing a firm when applying its code of ethics in other countries?

2. What are the reasons why operating in China with a code of ethics is harder than elsewhere in the world?

3. How should a code of ethics be shaped to fit China's marketplace?

4. How should a firm prepare its local managers to enforce a code of ethics in China?

Create Central

www.mhhe.com/createcentral

Internet References

Forbes
http://www.forbes.com/sites/russellflannery/2010/08/17/on-the-front-line-in-china-challenging-business-ethics/

Institute of Business Ethics
http://www.ibe.org.uk/userfiles/chinaop.pdf

Markula Center for Applied Ethics
http://www.scu.edu/ethics/publications/ethicalperspectives/business-china.html

---

Article   Prepared by: Eric Teoro, *Lincoln Christian University*

Wal-Mart Inquiry Reflects Alarm on Corruption

Stephanie Clifford and David Barstow

Learning Outcomes

After reading this article, you will be able to:

- Describe Wal-Mart's challenges with bribery and compliance issues in international markets.

- Describe Wal-Mart's response to bribery allegations and the extent of the company's internal investigation.

- Recognize the difficulty large companies have in sustaining consistent ethical practices.

Wal-Mart on Thursday reported that its investigation into violations of a federal antibribery law had extended beyond Mexico to China, India, and Brazil, some of the retailer's most important international markets.

The disclosure, made in a regulatory filing, suggests Wal-Mart has uncovered evidence into potential violations of the Foreign Corrupt Practices Act, as the fallout continues from a bribery scheme involving the opening of stores in Mexico that was the subject of a *New York Times* investigation in April.

The announcement underscores the degree to which Wal-Mart recognizes that corruption may have infected its international operations, and reflects a growing alarm among the company's internal investigators. People with knowledge of the matter described how a relatively routine compliance audit rapidly transformed into a full-blown investigation late last year—involving hundreds of lawyers and three former federal prosecutors—when the company learned that *The Times* was examining problems with its operations in Mexico.

A person with direct knowledge of the company's internal investigation cautioned that Thursday's disclosure did not mean Wal-Mart had concluded it had paid bribes in China, India, and

Brazil. But it did indicate that the company had found enough evidence to justify concern about its business practices in the three countries—concerns that go beyond initial inquiries and that are serious enough that shareholders needed to be told.

Wal-Mart issued a statement confirming the new disclosures, and said it would be inappropriate to comment further on the new allegations until it had concluded the investigations.

The Justice Department and the Securities and Exchange Commission, with Wal-Mart's cooperation, are also looking into the company's compliance with the antibribery law.

The Times reported in April that 7 years ago, Wal-Mart had found credible evidence that its Mexican subsidiary had paid bribes in its effort to build more stores, a violation of the corrupt practices act, and that an internal investigation had been suppressed by executives at the company's Arkansas headquarters.

Wal-Mart has so far spent $35 million on a compliance program that began in spring 2011, and has more than 300 outside lawyers and accountants working on it, the company said. It has spent $99 million in 9 months on the current investigation.

Consequences of the expanding investigation could include slower expansion overseas and the identification of even more problems. The company said in the filing on Thursday that new inquiries had begun in countries "including but not limited to" China, India, and Brazil.

While the disclosure did not specify the nature of the possible bribery problems in the three countries, it "clearly will cause more scrutiny on every real estate project being considered, and one would think at the minimum it will slow down the process as more controls need to be passed through," said Colin McGranahan, an analyst with Sanford C. Bernstein.

International growth is critical to Wal-Mart, the world's largest retailer, and Brazil, India, China, and Mexico together make up the largest portion of the company's foreign locations.

Wal-Mart's international division had been on a growth binge, though that has been slowing lately. In third-quarter results reported Thursday, the company said international sales rose 2.4 percent to $33.2 billion, making up about 29 percent of the company's overall sales.

More than half of Wal-Mart's 10,524 stores are international. Mexico has 2,230 stores. Brazil has 534, China, 384.

C. Douglas McMillon, chief executive of Walmart International, said in June that he did not expect the investigation to hinder international growth. "Only time will tell," he said.

Wal-Mart's expanding investigation began in spring 2011 as a relatively routine audit of how well its foreign subsidiaries were complying with its anticorruption policies. It is keeping the Justice Department and the S.E.C. apprised of the investigation.

The review was initiated by Jeffrey J. Gearhart, Wal-Mart's general counsel, who had seen news reports about how Tyson Foods had been charged with relatively minor violations of the Foreign Corrupt Practices Act. He decided it made sense to test Wal-Mart's internal defenses against corruption.

The audit began in Mexico, China, and Brazil, the countries Wal-Mart executives considered the most likely source of problems. Wal-Mart hired the accounting firm KPMG and the law firm Greenberg Traurig to conduct the audit. The firms conducted interviews and spot checks of record systems to check whether Wal-Mart's subsidiaries were carrying out required compliance procedures.

For example, Wal-Mart's anticorruption policy requires background checks on all third-party agents—lawyers, lobbyists—who represent the company before government agencies. The firms checked whether background checks were in fact being done. By July 2011, the firms had identified significant weaknesses in all three subsidiaries.

"It was clear they were not executing," a Wal-Mart official with knowledge of the audits said.

The problems were enough to persuade Wal-Mart to expand the audit to all 26 of its foreign subsidiaries. This work began in Autumn 2011. The outside firms dispatched "compliance teams" of lawyers and accountants all over the world. The teams attributed many of the problems they identified to a lack of training.

Senior Wal-Mart executives were concerned by the findings, but not overly alarmed. The audit was uncovering the kinds of problems and oversights that plague many global corporations.

But in late 2011, Wal-Mart learned that *The Times* was examining Wal-Mart's response in 2005 to serious and specific accusations of widespread bribery by Wal-Mart de Mexico, the company's largest foreign subsidiary.

In October 2005, a former lawyer for Wal-Mart de Mexico had spent hours telling company investigators how Wal-Mart de Mexico's leadership had orchestrated a vast campaign of bribery to accelerate expansion. Hundreds of bribes, he said, were paid to obtain construction permits and other licenses needed to open new stores. The lawyer's accusations were especially powerful because he had been in charge of getting permits for Wal-Mart de Mexico's new stores.

Wal-Mart rapidly escalated its internal investigation. It hired new outside lawyers, this time from the firm Jones Day. They began to investigate whether top executives had quashed the company's investigation into the lawyer's claims. In December 2011, Wal-Mart sent Jones Day lawyers to Mexico to interview the lawyer and other crucial players. The company began to look into other specific accusations of wrongdoing, both in Mexico and it its other subsidiaries.

It effectively created two lines of inquiry—the first being the global compliance review begun by Greenberg Traurig and KPMG. The second was the internal inquiry into specific accusations of bribery and corruption.

Some changes at Wal-Mart have already resulted. General counsels for each country used to report in to the chief executives of that country—which could create conflicts of interest if the chief executive was involved in corruption—and now they report to the general counsel of Walmart International. The company recently hired several compliance executives, and a vice president for global investigations who had previously worked at the F.B.I. It has also changed its protocol on investigations, including asking international subsidiaries to alert the global ethics office in Bentonville before any inquiry into wrongdoing begins.

The new disclosure by Wal-Mart on Thursday "does support their effort to be transparent," said Matthew J. Feeley, a lawyer with Buchanan Ingersoll & Rooney who focuses on foreign bribery cases. In cases like these, a company will regularly update the S.E.C. and the Justice Department with "very detailed presentations about the results of the internal investigation" in the hope of receiving lesser punishment from the agencies.

Though the government issued new compliance guidelines for the law on Wednesday, largely aimed at lawyers handling such cases, the Wal-Mart disclosure was not a result of those new guidelines. It was included in the company's third-quarter earnings announcement.

It was not clear Thursday whether authorities in China, India, and Brazil were conducting investigations of their own into Wal-Mart's practices, as the authorities in Mexico have done in response to the bribery accusations in that country.

Last month, Indian regulators started looking into whether Wal-Mart violated an Indian foreign investment rule.

Charlie Savage, Vikas Bajaj and Andrew Downie contributed reporting.

This article has been revised to reflect the following correction:

Correction: November 17, 2012

An article on Friday about Wal-Mart's broadening of an internal investigation into possible violations of a federal antibribery law described incorrectly, in some editions, a foreign investment rule that the company may have violated in India. The initialism F.D.I. stands for "foreign direct investment," but the Indian rule is not "known as" F.D.I.

Critical Thinking

1. Do you think Wal-Mart's response to the bribery allegations is commendable? Why or why not?

2. What practices could Wal-Mart implement to lower the probability of continued bribery in international markets?

3. How can multinational companies develop consistent compliance to ethical standards?

Create Central

www.mhhe.com/createcentral

Internet References

Business Insider
   http://www.businessinsider.com/new-details-in-walmart-bribery-scandal-2012-12

The New York Times
   http://www.nytimes.com/2014/06/05/business/after-walmart-bribery-scandals-a-pattern-of-quiet-departures.html

Wal-Mart Hushed Up a Vast Mexican Bribery Case by David Barstow, Alejandra Xanic, and James C. McKinley Jr.

139

Article

Prepared by: Eric Teoro, *Lincoln Christian University*

Wal-Mart Hushed Up a Vast Mexican Bribery Case

DAVID BARSTOW, ALEJANDRA XANIC, AND JAMES C. MCKINLEY JR.

Learning Outcomes

After reading this article, you will be able to:

- Describe the facts related to Wal-Mart's Mexican bribery case.

- Recognize the need for strong internal controls to promote ethical behavior.

- Recognize that ethical breaches of omission can be as serious as ethical breaches of commission.

In September 2005, a senior Wal-Mart lawyer received an alarming e-mail from a former executive at the company's largest foreign subsidiary, Wal-Mart de Mexico. In the e-mail and follow-up conversations, the former executive described how Wal-Mart de Mexico had orchestrated a campaign of bribery to win market dominance. In its rush to build stores, he said, the company had paid bribes to obtain permits in virtually every corner of the country.

The former executive gave names, dates and bribe amounts. He knew so much, he explained, because for years he had been the lawyer in charge of obtaining construction permits for Wal-Mart de Mexico.

Wal-Mart dispatched investigators to Mexico City, and within days they unearthed evidence of widespread bribery. They found a paper trail of hundreds of suspect payments totaling more than $24 million. They also found documents showing that Wal-Mart de Mexico's top executives not only knew about the payments, but had taken steps to conceal them from Wal-Mart's headquarters in Bentonville, Ark. In a confidential report to his superiors, Wal-Mart's lead investigator, a former F.B.I. special agent, summed up their initial findings this way: "There is reasonable suspicion to believe that Mexican and USA laws have been violated."

The lead investigator recommended that Wal-Mart expand the investigation.

Instead, an examination by The *New York Times* found, Wal-Mart's leaders shut it down.

Neither American nor Mexican law enforcement officials were notified. None of Wal-Mart de Mexico's leaders were disciplined. Indeed, its chief executive, Eduardo Castro-Wright, identified by the former executive as the driving force behind years of bribery, was promoted to vice chairman of Wal-Mart in 2008. Until this article, the allegations and Wal-Mart's investigation had never been publicly disclosed.

But The *Times*'s examination uncovered a prolonged struggle at the highest levels of Wal-Mart, a struggle that pitted the company's much publicized commitment to the highest moral and ethical standards against its relentless pursuit of growth.

Under fire from labor critics, worried about press leaks and facing a sagging stock price, Wal-Mart's leaders recognized that the allegations could have devastating consequences, documents and interviews show. Wal-Mart de Mexico was the company's brightest success story, pitched to investors as a model for future growth. (Today, one in five Wal-Mart stores is in Mexico.) Confronted with evidence of corruption in Mexico, top Wal-Mart executives focused more on damage control than on rooting out wrongdoing.

In one meeting where the bribery case was discussed, H. Lee Scott Jr., then Wal-Mart's chief executive, rebuked internal investigators for being overly aggressive. Days later, records show, Wal-Mart's top lawyer arranged to ship the internal investigators' files on the case to Mexico City. Primary responsibility for the investigation was then given to the general counsel of Wal-Mart de Mexico—a remarkable choice since the same general counsel was alleged to have authorized bribes.

The general counsel promptly exonerated his fellow Wal-Mart de Mexico executives.

When Wal-Mart's director of corporate investigations—a former top F.B.I. official—read the general counsel's report, his appraisal was scathing. "Truly lacking," he wrote in an e-mail to his boss.

The report was nonetheless accepted by Wal-Mart's leaders as the last word on the matter.

In December, after learning of *The Times*'s reporting in Mexico, Wal-Mart informed the Justice Department that it had begun an internal investigation into possible violations of the Foreign Corrupt Practices Act, a federal law that makes it a crime for American corporations and their subsidiaries to bribe foreign officials. Wal-Mart said the company had learned of possible problems with how it obtained permits, but stressed that the issues were limited to "discrete" cases.

"We do not believe that these matters will have a material adverse effect on our business," the company said in a filing with the Securities and Exchange Commission.

But *The Times*'s examination found credible evidence that bribery played a persistent and significant role in Wal-Mart's rapid growth in Mexico, where Wal-Mart now employs 209,000 people, making it the country's largest private employer.

A Wal-Mart spokesman confirmed that the company's Mexico operations—and its handling of the 2005 case—were now a major focus of its inquiry.

"If these allegations are true, it is not a reflection of who we are or what we stand for," the spokesman, David W. Tovar, said. "We are deeply concerned by these allegations and are working aggressively to determine what happened."

In the meantime, Mr. Tovar said, Wal-Mart is taking steps in Mexico to strengthen compliance with the Foreign Corrupt Practices Act. "We do not and will not tolerate noncompliance with F.C.P.A. anywhere or at any level of the company," he said.

The Times laid out this article's findings to Wal-Mart weeks ago. The company said it shared the findings with many of the executives named here, including Mr. Scott, now on Wal-Mart's board, and Mr. Castro-Wright, who is retiring in July. Both men declined to comment, Mr. Tovar said.

The Times obtained hundreds of internal company documents tracing the evolution of Wal-Mart's 2005 Mexico investigation. The documents show Wal-Mart's leadership immediately recognized the seriousness of the allegations. Working in secrecy, a small group of executives, including several current members of Wal-Mart's senior management, kept close tabs on the inquiry.

Michael T. Duke, Wal-Mart's current chief executive, was also kept informed. At the time, Mr. Duke had just been put in charge of Wal-Mart International, making him responsible for all foreign subsidiaries. "You'll want to read this," a top Wal-Mart lawyer wrote in an Oct. 15, 2005, e-mail to Mr. Duke that gave a detailed description of the former executive's allegations.

The Times examination included more than 15 hours of interviews with the former executive, Sergio Cicero Zapata, who resigned from Wal-Mart de Mexico in 2004 after nearly a decade in the company's real estate department.

In the interviews, Mr. Cicero recounted how he had helped organize years of payoffs. He described personally dispatching two trusted outside lawyers to deliver envelopes of cash to government officials. They targeted mayors and city council members, obscure urban planners, low-level bureaucrats who issued permits—anyone with the power to thwart Wal-Mart's growth. The bribes, he said, bought zoning approvals, reductions in environmental impact fees and the allegiance of neighborhood leaders.

He called it working "the dark side of the moon."

The Times also reviewed thousands of government documents related to permit requests for stores across Mexico. The examination found many instances where permits were given within weeks or even days of Wal-Mart de Mexico's payments to the two lawyers. Again and again, *The Times* found, legal and bureaucratic obstacles melted away after payments were made.

The Times conducted extensive interviews with participants in Wal-Mart's investigation. They spoke on the condition that they not be identified discussing matters Wal-Mart has long shielded. These people said the investigation left little doubt Mr. Cicero's allegations were credible. ("Not even a close call," one person said.)

But, they said, the more investigators corroborated his assertions, the more resistance they encountered inside Wal-Mart. Some of it came from powerful executives implicated in the corruption, records, and interviews show. Other top executives voiced concern about the possible legal and reputational harm.

In the end, people involved in the investigation said, Wal-Mart's leaders found a bloodlessly bureaucratic way to bury the matter. But in handing the investigation off to one of its main targets, they disregarded the advice of one of Wal-Mart's top lawyers, the same lawyer first contacted by Mr. Cicero.

"The wisdom of assigning any investigative role to management of the business unit being investigated escapes me," Maritza I. Munich, then general counsel of Wal-Mart International, wrote in an e-mail to top Wal-Mart executives.

The investigation, she urged, should be completed using "professional, independent investigative resources."

The Allegations Emerge

On Sept. 21, 2005, Mr. Cicero sent an e-mail to Ms. Munich telling her he had information about "irregularities" authorized "by the highest levels" at Wal-Mart de Mexico. "I hope to meet you soon," he wrote.

Ms. Munich was familiar with the challenges of avoiding corruption in Latin America. Before joining Wal-Mart in 2003, she had spent 12 years in Mexico and elsewhere in Latin America as a lawyer for Procter & Gamble.

At Wal-Mart in 2004, she pushed the board to adopt a strict anticorruption policy that prohibited all employees from "offering anything of value to a government official on behalf of Wal-Mart." It required every employee to report the first sign of corruption, and it bound Wal-Mart's agents to the same exacting standards.

Ms. Munich reacted quickly to Mr. Cicero's e-mail. Within days, she hired Juan Francisco Torres-Landa, a prominent Harvard-trained lawyer in Mexico City, to debrief Mr. Cicero. The two men met three times in October 2005, with Ms. Munich flying in from Bentonville for the third debriefing.

During hours of questioning, Mr. Torres-Landa's notes show, Mr. Cicero described how Wal-Mart de Mexico had perfected the art of bribery, then hidden it all with fraudulent accounting. Mr. Cicero implicated many of Wal-Mart de Mexico's leaders, including its board chairman, its general counsel, its chief auditor and its top real estate executive.

But the person most responsible, he told Mr. Torres-Landa, was the company's ambitious chief executive, Eduardo Castro-Wright, a native of Ecuador who was recruited from Honeywell in 2001 to become Wal-Mart's chief operating officer in Mexico.

Mr. Cicero said that while bribes were occasionally paid before Mr. Castro-Wright's arrival, their use soared after Mr. Castro-Wright ascended to the top job in 2002. Mr. Cicero described how Wal-Mart de Mexico's leaders had set "very aggressive growth goals," which required opening new stores "in record times." Wal-Mart de Mexico executives, he said, were under pressure to do "whatever was necessary" to obtain permits.

In an interview with *The Times*, Mr. Cicero said Mr. Castro-Wright had encouraged the payments for a specific strategic purpose. The idea, he said, was to build hundreds of new stores so fast that competitors would not have time to react. Bribes, he explained, accelerated growth. They got zoning maps changed. They made environmental objections vanish. Permits that typically took months to process magically materialized in days. "What we were buying was time," he said.

Wal-Mart de Mexico's stunning growth made Mr. Castro-Wright a rising star in Bentonville. In early 2005, when he was promoted to a senior position in the United States, Mr. Duke would cite his "outstanding results" in Mexico.

Mr. Cicero's allegations were all the more startling because he implicated himself. He spent hours explaining to Mr. Torres-Landa the mechanics of how he had helped funnel bribes through trusted fixers, known as "gestores."

Gestores (pronounced hes-TORE-ehs) are a fixture in Mexico's byzantine bureaucracies, and some are entirely legitimate. Ordinary citizens routinely pay gestores to stand in line for them at the driver's license office. Companies hire them as quasi-lobbyists to get things done as painlessly as possible.

But often gestores play starring roles in Mexico's endless loop of public corruption scandals. They operate in the shadows, dangling payoffs to officials of every rank. It was this type of gestor that Wal-Mart de Mexico deployed, Mr. Cicero said.

Mr. Cicero told Mr. Torres-Landa it was his job to recruit the gestores. He worked closely with them, sharing strategies on whom to bribe. He also approved Wal-Mart de Mexico's payments to the gestores. Each payment covered the bribe and the gestor's fee, typically 6 percent of the bribe.

It was all carefully monitored through a system of secret codes known only to a handful of Wal-Mart de Mexico executives.

The gestores submitted invoices with brief, vaguely worded descriptions of their services. But the real story, Mr. Cicero said, was told in codes written on the invoices. The codes identified the specific "irregular act" performed, Mr. Cicero explained to Mr. Torres-Landa. One code, for example, indicated a bribe to speed up a permit. Others described bribes to obtain confidential information or eliminate fines.

Each month, Mr. Castro-Wright and other top Wal-Mart de Mexico executives "received a detailed schedule of all of the payments performed," he said, according to the lawyer's notes. Wal-Mart de Mexico then "purified" the bribes in accounting records as simple legal fees.

They also took care to keep Bentonville in the dark. "Dirty clothes are washed at home," Mr. Cicero said.

Mr. Torres-Landa explored Mr. Cicero's motives for coming forward.

Mr. Cicero said he resigned in September 2004 because he felt underappreciated. He described the "pressure and stress" of participating in years of corruption, of contending with "greedy" officials who jacked up bribe demands.

As he told *The Times*, "I thought I deserved a medal at least."

The breaking point came in early 2004, when he was passed over for the job of general counsel of Wal-Mart de Mexico. This snub, Mr. Torres-Landa wrote, "generated significant anger with respect to the lack of recognition for his work." Mr. Cicero said he began to assemble a record of bribes he had helped orchestrate to "protect him in case of any complaint or investigation," Mr. Torres-Landa wrote.

"We did not detect on his part any express statement about wishing to sell the information," the lawyer added.

According to people involved in Wal-Mart's investigation, Mr. Cicero's account of criminality at the top of Wal-Mart's most important foreign subsidiary was impossible to dismiss. He had clearly been in a position to witness the events he described. Nor was this the first indication of corruption at Wal-Mart de Mexico under Mr. Castro-Wright. A confidential investigation, conducted for Wal-Mart in 2003 by Kroll Inc., a leading investigation firm, discovered that Wal-Mart de Mexico had systematically increased its sales by helping favored high-volume customers evade sales taxes.

A draft of Kroll's report, obtained by *The Times*, concluded that top Wal-Mart de Mexico executives had failed to enforce their own anticorruption policies, ignored internal audits that raised red flags and even disregarded local press accounts asserting that Wal-Mart de Mexico was "carrying out a tax fraud." (The company ultimately paid $34.3 million in back taxes.)

Wal-Mart then asked Kroll to evaluate Wal-Mart de Mexico's internal audit and antifraud units. Kroll wrote another report that branded the units "ineffective." Many employees accused of wrongdoing were not even questioned; some "received a promotion shortly after the suspicions of fraudulent activities had surfaced."

None of these findings, though, had slowed Mr. Castro-Wright's rise.

Just days before Mr. Cicero's first debriefing, Mr. Castro-Wright was promoted again. He was put in charge of all Wal-Mart stores in the United States, one of the most prominent jobs in the company. He also joined Wal-Mart's executive committee, the company's inner sanctum of leadership.

The Initial Response

Ms. Munich sent detailed memos describing Mr. Cicero's debriefings to Wal-Mart's senior management. These executives, records show, included Thomas A. Mars, Wal-Mart's general counsel and a former director of the Arkansas State Police; Thomas D. Hyde, Wal-Mart's executive vice president and corporate secretary; Michael Fung, Wal-Mart's top internal auditor; Craig Herkert, the chief executive for Wal-Mart's operations in Latin America; and Lee Stucky, a confidant of Lee Scott's and chief administrative officer of Wal-Mart International.

Wal-Mart typically hired outside law firms to lead internal investigations into allegations of significant wrongdoing. It did so earlier in 2005, for example, when Thomas M. Coughlin, then vice chairman of Wal-Mart, was accused of padding his expense accounts and misappropriating Wal-Mart gift cards.

At first, Wal-Mart took the same approach with Mr. Cicero's allegations. It turned to Willkie Farr & Gallagher, a law firm with extensive experience in Foreign Corrupt Practices Act cases.

The firm's "investigation work plan" called for tracing all payments to anyone who had helped Wal-Mart de Mexico obtain permits for the previous 5 years. The firm said it would scrutinize "any and all payments" to government officials and interview every person who might know about payoffs, including "implicated members" of Wal-Mart de Mexico's board.

In short, Willkie Farr recommended the kind of independent, spare-no-expense investigation major corporations routinely undertake when confronted with allegations of serious wrongdoing by top executives.

Wal-Mart's leaders rejected this approach. Instead, records show, they decided Wal-Mart's lawyers would supervise a far more limited "preliminary inquiry" by in-house investigators.

The inquiry, a confidential memo explained, would take two weeks, not the 4 months Willkie Farr proposed. Rather than examining years of permits, the team would look at a few specific stores. Interviews would be done "only when absolutely essential to establishing the bona fides" of Mr. Cicero. However, if the inquiry found a "likelihood" that laws had been violated, the company would then consider conducting a "full investigation."

The decision gave Wal-Mart's senior management direct control over the investigation. It also meant new responsibility for the company's tiny and troubled Corporate Investigations unit.

The unit was ill-equipped to take on a major corruption investigation, let alone one in Mexico. It had fewer than 70 employees, and most were assigned to chasing shoplifting rings and corrupt vendors. Just four people were specifically dedicated to investigating corporate fraud, a number Joseph R. Lewis, Wal-Mart's director of corporate investigations, described in a confidential memo as "wholly inadequate for an organization the size of Wal-Mart."

But Mr. Lewis and his boss, Kenneth H. Senser, vice president for global security, aviation and travel, were working to strengthen the unit. Months before Mr. Cicero surfaced, they won approval to hire four "special investigators" who, according to their job descriptions, would be assigned the "most significant and complex fraud matters." Mr. Scott, the chief executive, also agreed that Corporate Investigations would handle all allegations of misconduct by senior executives.

And yet in the fall of 2005, as Wal-Mart began to grapple with Mr. Cicero's allegations, two cases called into question Corporate Investigations' independence and role.

In October, Wal-Mart's vice chairman, John B. Menzer, intervened in an internal investigation into a senior vice president who reported to him. According to internal records, Mr. Menzer told Mr. Senser he did not want Corporate Investigations to handle the case "due to concerns about the impact such an investigation would have." One of the senior vice president's subordinates, he said, "would be better suited to conduct this inquiry." Soon after, records show, the subordinate cleared his boss.

The other case involved the president of Wal-Mart Puerto Rico. A whistle-blower had accused the president and other executives of mistreating employees. Although Corporate Investigations was supposed to investigate all allegations against senior executives, the president had instead assigned an underling to look into the complaints—but to steer clear of those against him.

Ms. Munich objected. In an e-mail to Wal-Mart executives, she complained that the investigation was "at the direction of the same company officer who is the target of several of the allegations."

"We are in need of clear guidelines about how to handle these issues going forward," she warned.

The Inquiry Begins

Ronald Halter, one of Wal-Mart's new "special investigators," was assigned to lead the preliminary inquiry into Mr. Cicero's allegations. Mr. Halter had been with Wal-Mart only a few months, but he was a seasoned criminal investigator. He had spent 21 years in the F.B.I., and he spoke Spanish.

He also had help. Bob Ainley, a senior auditor, was sent to Mexico along with several Spanish-speaking auditors.

On Nov. 12, 2005, Mr. Halter's team got to work at Wal-Mart de Mexico's corporate headquarters in Mexico City. The team gained access to a database of Wal-Mart de Mexico payments and began searching the payment description field for the word "gestoria."

By day's end, they had found 441 gestor payments. Each was a potential bribe, and yet they had searched back only to 2003.

Mr. Cicero had said his main gestores were Pablo Alegria Con Alonso and Jose Manuel Aguirre Juarez, obscure Mexico City lawyers with small practices who were friends of his from law school.

Sure enough, Mr. Halter's team found that nearly half the payments were to Mr. Alegria and Mr. Aguirre. These two lawyers alone, records showed, had received $8.5 million in payments. Records showed Wal-Mart de Mexico routinely paid its gestores tens of thousands of dollars per permit. (In interviews, both lawyers declined to discuss the corruption allegations, citing confidentiality agreements with Wal-Mart.)

"One very interesting postscript," Mr. Halter wrote in an e-mail to his boss, Mr. Lewis. "All payments to these individuals and all large sums of $ paid out of this account stopped abruptly in 2005." Mr. Halter said the "only thing we can find" that changed was that Mr. Castro-Wright left Wal-Mart de Mexico for the United States.

Mr. Halter's team confirmed detail after detail from Mr. Cicero's debriefings. Mr. Cicero had given specifics—names, dates, bribe amounts—for several new stores. In almost every case, investigators found documents confirming major elements of his account. And just as Mr. Cicero had described, investigators found mysterious codes at the bottom of invoices from the gestores.

"The documentation didn't look anything like what you would find in legitimate billing records from a legitimate law firm," a person involved in the investigation said in an interview.

Mr. Lewis sent a terse progress report to his boss, Mr. Senser: "FYI. It is not looking good."

Hours later, Mr. Halter's team found clear confirmation that Mr. Castro-Wright and other top executives at Wal-Mart de Mexico were well aware of the gestor payments.

In March 2004, the team discovered, the executives had been sent an internal Wal-Mart de Mexico audit that raised red flags about the gestor payments. The audit documented how Wal-Mart de Mexico's two primary gestores had been paid millions to make "facilitating payments" for new store permits all over Mexico.

The audit did not delve into how the money had been used to "facilitate" permits. But it showed the payments rising rapidly, roughly in line with Wal-Mart de Mexico's accelerating growth. The audit recommended notifying Bentonville of the payments.

The recommendation, records showed, was removed by Wal-Mart de Mexico's chief auditor, whom Mr. Cicero had identified as one of the executives who knew about the bribes. The author of the gestor audit, meanwhile, "was fired not long after the audit was completed," Mr. Halter wrote.

Mr. Ainley arranged to meet the fired auditor at his hotel. The auditor described other examples of Wal-Mart de Mexico's leaders withholding from Bentonville information about suspect payments to government officials.

The auditor singled out Jose Luis Rodriguezmacedo Rivera, the general counsel of Wal-Mart de Mexico.

Mr. Rodriguezmacedo, he said, took "significant information out" of an audit of Wal-Mart de Mexico's compliance with the Foreign Corrupt Practices Act. The original audit had described how Wal-Mart de Mexico gave gift cards to government officials in towns where it was building stores. "These were only given out until the construction was complete," Mr. Ainley wrote. "At which time the payments ceased."

These details were scrubbed from the final version sent to Bentonville.

Investigators were struck by Mr. Castro-Wright's response to the gestor audit. It had been shown to him immediately, Wal-Mart de Mexico's chief auditor had told them. Yet rather than expressing alarm, he had appeared worried about becoming too dependent on too few gestores. In an e-mail, Mr. Rodriguezmacedo told Mr. Cicero to write up a plan to "diversify" the gestores used to "facilitate" permits.

"Eduardo Castro wants us to implement this plan as soon as possible," he wrote.

Mr. Cicero did as directed. The plan, which authorized paying gestores up to $280,000 to "facilitate" a single permit, was approved with a minor change. Mr. Rodriguezmacedo did not want the plan to mention "gestores." He wanted them called "external service providers."

Mr. Halter's team made one last discovery—a finding that suggested the corruption might be far more extensive than even Mr. Cicero had described.

In going through Wal-Mart de Mexico's database of payments, investigators noticed the company was making hefty "contributions" and "donations" directly to governments all over Mexico—nearly $16 million in all since 2003.

"Some of the payments descriptions indicate that the donation is being made for the issuance of a license," Mr. Ainley wrote in one report back to Bentonville.

They also found a document in which a Wal-Mart de Mexico real estate executive had openly acknowledged that "these payments were performed to facilitate obtaining the licenses or permits" for new stores. Sometimes, Mr. Cicero told *The Times*, donations were used hand-in-hand with gestor payments to get permits.

Deflecting Blame

When Mr. Halter's team was ready to interview executives at Wal-Mart de Mexico, the first target was Mr. Rodriguezmacedo.

Before joining Wal-Mart de Mexico in January 2004, Mr. Rodriguezmacedo had been a lawyer for Citigroup in Mexico. Urbane and smooth, with impeccable English, he quickly won fans in Bentonville. When Wal-Mart invited executives from its foreign subsidiaries for several days of discussion about the fine points of the Foreign Corrupt Practices Act, Mr. Rodriguezmacedo was asked to lead one of the sessions.

It was called "Overcoming Challenges in Government Dealings."

Yet Mr. Cicero had identified him as a participant in the bribery scheme. In his debriefings, Mr. Cicero described how Mr. Rodriguezmacedo had passed along specific payoff instructions from Mr. Castro-Wright. In an interview with *The Times*, Mr. Cicero said he and Mr. Rodriguezmacedo had discussed the use of gestores shortly after Mr. Rodriguezmacedo was hired. "He said, 'Don't worry. Keep it on its way.'"

Mr. Rodriguezmacedo declined to comment; on Friday Wal-Mart disclosed that he had been reassigned and is no longer Wal-Mart de Mexico's general counsel.

Mr. Halter's team hoped Mr. Rodriguezmacedo would shed light on how two outside lawyers came to be paid $8.5 million to "facilitate" permits. Mr. Rodriguezmacedo responded with evasive hostility, records and interviews show. When investigators asked him for the gestores' billing records, he said he did not have time to track them down. They got similar receptions from other executives.

Only after investigators complained to higher authorities were the executives more forthcoming. Led by Mr. Rodriguezmacedo, they responded with an attack on Mr. Cicero's credibility.

The gestor audit, they told investigators, had raised doubts about Mr. Cicero, since he had approved most of the payments. They began to suspect he was somehow benefiting, so they asked Kroll to investigate. It was then, they asserted, that Kroll discovered Mr. Cicero's wife was a law partner of one of the gestores.

Mr. Cicero was fired, they said, because he had failed to disclose that fact. They produced a copy of a "preliminary" report from Kroll and e-mails showing the undisclosed conflict had been reported to Bentonville.

Based on this behavior, Mr. Rodriguezmacedo argued, the gestor payments were in all likelihood a "ruse" by Mr. Cicero to defraud Wal-Mart de Mexico. Mr. Cicero and the gestores, he contended, probably kept every last peso of the "facilitating payments."

Simply put, bribes could not have been paid if the money was stolen first.

It was an argument that gave Wal-Mart ample justification to end the inquiry. But investigators were skeptical, records, and interviews show.

Even if Mr. Rodriguezmacedo's account were true, it did not explain why Wal-Mart de Mexico's executives had authorized gestor payments in the first place, or why they made "donations" to get permits, or why they rewrote audits to keep Bentonville in the dark.

Investigators also wondered why a trained lawyer who had gotten away with stealing a small fortune from Wal-Mart would now deliberately draw the company's full attention by implicating himself in a series of fictional bribes. And if Wal-Mart de Mexico's executives truly believed they had been victimized, why hadn't they taken legal action against Mr. Cicero, much less reported the "theft" to Bentonville?

There was another problem: Documents contradicted most of the executives' assertions about Mr. Cicero.

Records showed Mr. Cicero had not been fired, but had resigned with severance benefits and a $25,000 bonus. In fact, in a 2004 e-mail to Ms. Munich, Mr. Rodriguezmacedo himself described how he had "negotiated" Mr. Cicero's "departure." The same e-mail said Mr. Cicero had not even been confronted about the supposed undisclosed conflict involving his wife. (Mr. Cicero flatly denied that his wife had ever worked with either gestor.) The e-mail also assured Ms. Munich there was no hint of financial wrongdoing. "We see it merely as an undisclosed conflict of interest," Mr. Rodriguezmacedo wrote.

There were other discrepancies.

Mr. Rodriguezmacedo said the company had stopped using gestores after Mr. Cicero's departure. Yet even as Mr. Cicero was being debriefed in October 2005, Wal-Mart de Mexico real estate executives made a request to pay a gestor $14,000 to get a construction permit, records showed.

The persistent questions and document requests from Mr. Halter's team provoked a backlash from Wal-Mart de Mexico's executives. After a week of work, records and interviews show, Mr. Halter and other members of the team were summoned by Eduardo F. Solorzano Morales, then chief executive of Wal-Mart de Mexico.

Mr. Solorzano angrily chastised the investigators for being too secretive and accusatory. He took offense that his executives were being told at the start of interviews that they had the right not to answer questions—as if they were being read their rights.

"It was like, 'You shut up. I'm going to talk,'" a person said of Mr. Solorzano. "It was, 'This is my home, my backyard. You are out of here.'"

Mr. Lewis viewed the complaints as an effort to sidetrack his investigators. "I find this ludicrous and a copout for the larger concerns about what has been going on," he wrote.

Nevertheless, Mr. Herkert, the chief executive for Latin America, was notified about the complaints. Three days later, he and his boss, Mr. Duke, flew to Mexico City. The trip had been long-planned—Mr. Duke toured several stores—but they also reassured Wal-Mart de Mexico's unhappy executives.

They arrived just as the investigators wrapped up their work and left.

A Push to Dig Deeper

Wal-Mart's leaders had agreed to consider a full investigation if the preliminary inquiry found Mr. Cicero's allegations credible.

Back in Bentonville, Mr. Halter and Mr. Ainley wrote confidential reports to Wal-Mart's top executives in December 2005 laying out all the evidence that corroborated Mr. Cicero—the hundreds of gestor payments, the mystery codes, the rewritten audits, the evasive responses from Wal-Mart de Mexico executives, the donations for permits, the evidence gestores were still being used.

"There is reasonable suspicion," Mr. Halter concluded, "to believe that Mexican and USA laws have been violated." There was simply "no defendable explanation" for the millions of dollars in gestor payments, he wrote.

Mr. Halter submitted an "action plan" for a deeper investigation that would plumb the depths of corruption and culpability at Wal-Mart de Mexico.

Among other things, he urged "that all efforts be concentrated on the reconstruction of Cicero's computer history."

Mr. Cicero, meanwhile, was still offering help. In November, when Mr. Halter's team was in Mexico, Mr. Cicero offered his services as a paid consultant. In December, he wrote to Ms. Munich. He volunteered to share specifics on still more stores, and he promised to show her documents. "I hope you visit again," he wrote.

Mr. Halter proposed a thorough investigation of the two main gestores. He had not tried to interview them in Mexico for fear of his safety. ("I do not want to expose myself on what I consider to be an unrealistic attempt to get Mexican lawyers to admit to criminal activity," he had explained to his bosses.) Now Mr. Halter wanted Wal-Mart to hire private investigators to interview and monitor both gestores.

He also envisioned a round of adversarial interviews with Wal-Mart de Mexico's senior executives. He and his investigators argued that it was time to take the politically sensitive step of questioning Mr. Castro-Wright about his role in the gestor payments.

By January 2006, the case had reached a critical juncture. Wal-Mart's leaders were again weighing whether to approve a full investigation that would inevitably focus on a star executive already being publicly discussed as a potential successor to Mr. Scott.

Wal-Mart's ethics policy offered clear direction. "Never cover up or ignore an ethics problem," the policy states. And some who were involved in the investigation argued that it was time to take a stand against signs of rising corruption in Wal-Mart's global operations. Each year the company received hundreds of internal reports of bribery and fraud, records showed. In Asia alone, there had been 90 reports of bribery just in the previous 18 months.

The situation was bad enough that Wal-Mart's top procurement executives were summoned to Bentonville that winter for a dressing down. Mr. Menzer, Wal-Mart's vice chairman, warned them that corruption was creating an unacceptable risk, particularly given the government's stepped-up enforcement of the Foreign Corrupt Practices Act. "Times have changed," he said.

As if to underscore the problem, Wal-Mart's leaders were confronted with new corruption allegations at Wal-Mart de Mexico even as they pondered Mr. Halter's action plan. In January, Mr. Scott, Mr. Duke, and Wal-Mart's chairman, S. Robson Walton, received an anonymous e-mail saying Wal-Mart de Mexico's top real estate executives were receiving kickbacks from construction companies. "Please you must do something," the e-mail implored.

Yet at the same time, records and interviews show, there were misgivings about the budding reach and power of Corporate Investigations.

In less than a year, Mr. Lewis's beefed-up team had doubled its caseload, to roughly 400 cases a year. Some executives grumbled that Mr. Lewis acted as if he still worked for the F.B.I., where he had once supervised major investigations. They accused him and his investigators of being overbearing, disruptive and naive about the moral ambiguities of doing business abroad. They argued that Corporate Investigations should focus more on quietly "neutralizing" problems than on turning corrupt employees over to law enforcement.

Wal-Mart's leaders had just witnessed the downside of that approach: in early 2005, the company went to the F.B.I. with evidence that the disgraced former vice chairman, Mr. Coughlin, had embezzled hundreds of thousands of dollars. The decision produced months of embarrassing publicity, especially when Mr. Coughlin claimed he had used the money to pay off union spies for Wal-Mart.

Meanwhile, Wal-Mart de Mexico executives were continuing to complain to Bentonville about the investigation. The protests "just never let up," a person involved in the case said.

Another person familiar with the thinking of those overseeing the investigation said Wal-Mart would have reacted "like a chicken on a June bug" had the allegations concerned the United States. But some executives saw Mexico as a country where bribery was embedded in the business culture. It simply did not merit the same response.

"It's a Mexican issue; it's better to let it be a Mexican response," the person said, describing the thinking of Wal-Mart executives.

In the midst of this debate, Ms. Munich submitted her resignation, effective Feb. 1, 2006. In one of her final acts, she drafted a memo that argued for expanding the Mexico investigation and giving equal respect to Mexican and United States laws.

"The bribery of government officials," she noted dryly, "is a criminal offense in Mexico."

She also warned against allowing implicated executives to interfere with the investigation. Wal-Mart de Mexico's executives had already tried to insert themselves in the case. Just before Christmas, records show, Mr. Solorzano, the Wal-Mart de Mexico chief executive, held a video conference with Mr. Mars, Mr. Senser, and Mr. Stucky to discuss his team's "hypothesis" that Mr. Cicero had stolen gestor payments.

"Given the serious nature of the allegations, and the need to preserve the integrity of the investigation," Ms. Munich wrote, "it would seem more prudent to develop a follow-up plan of action, independent of Walmex management participation."

The Chief Weighs In

Mr. Scott called a meeting for Feb. 3, 2006, to discuss revamping Wal-Mart's internal investigations and to resolve the question of what to do about Mr. Cicero's allegations.

In the days before the meeting, records show, Mr. Senser ordered his staff to compile data showing the effectiveness of Corporate Investigations. He assembled statistics showing that the unit had referred relatively few cases to law enforcement agencies. He circulated copies of an e-mail in which Mr. Rodriguezmacedo said he had been treated "very respectfully and cordially" by Mr. Senser's investigators.

Along with Mr. Scott, the meeting included Mr. Hyde, Mr. Mars, and Mr. Stucky, records show. The meeting brought the grievances against Corporate Investigations into the open. Mr. Senser described the complaints in Mr. Lewis's performance evaluation, completed shortly after the meeting. Wal-Mart's leaders viewed Mr. Lewis's investigators as "overly aggressive," he wrote. They did not care for Mr. Lewis's "law enforcement approach," and the fact that Mr. Scott convened a

meeting to express these concerns only underscored "the importance placed on these topics by senior executives."

By meeting's end, Mr. Senser had been ordered to work with Mr. Mars and others to develop a "modified protocol" for internal investigations.

Mr. Scott said he wanted it done fast, and within 24 hours Mr. Senser produced a new protocol, a highly bureaucratic process that gave senior Wal-Mart executives—including executives at the business units being investigated—more control over internal investigations. The policy included multiple "case reviews." It also required senior executives to conduct a "cost-benefit analysis" before signing off on a full-blown investigation.

Under the new protocol, Mr. Lewis and his team would only investigate "significant" allegations, like those involving potential crimes or top executives. Lesser allegations would be left to the affected business unit to investigate.

"This captures it, I think," Mr. Hyde wrote when Mr. Senser sent him the new protocol.

Four days after Mr. Scott's meeting, with the new protocol drafted, Wal-Mart's leaders began to transfer control of the bribery investigation to one of its earliest targets, Mr. Rodriguezmacedo.

Mr. Mars first sent Mr. Halter's report to Mr. Rodriguezmacedo. Then he arranged to ship Mr. Halter's investigative files to him as well. In an e-mail, he sought Mr. Senser's advice on how to send the files in "a secure manner."

Mr. Senser recommended FedEx. "There is very good control on those shipments, and while governments do compromise them if they are looking for something in particular, there is no reason for them to think that this shipment is out of the ordinary," he wrote.

"The key," he added, "is being careful about how you communicate the details of the shipment to Jose Luis." He advised Mr. Mars to use encrypted e-mail.

Wal-Mart's spokesman, Mr. Tovar, said the company could not discuss Mr. Scott's meeting or the decision to transfer the case to Mr. Rodriguezmacedo. "At this point," he said, "we don't have a full explanation of what happened. Unfortunately, we realize that until the investigation is concluded, there will be some unanswered questions."

Wal-Mart's leaders, however, had clear guidance about the propriety of letting a target of an investigation run it.

On the same day Mr. Senser was putting the finishing touches on the new investigations protocol, Wal-Mart's ethics office sent him a booklet of "best practices" for internal investigations. It had been put together by lawyers and executives who supervised investigations at Fortune 500 companies.

"Investigations should be conducted by individuals who do not have any vested interest in the potential outcomes of the investigation," it said.

The transfer appeared to violate even the "modified protocol" for investigations. Under the new protocol, Corporate Investigations was still supposed to handle "significant" allegations—including those involving potential crimes and senior executives. When Mr. Senser asked his deputies to list all investigations that met this threshold, they came up with 31 cases.

At the top of the list: Mexico.

After the meeting with Mr. Scott, Mr. Senser had told Mr. Lewis in his performance evaluation that his "highest priority" should be to eliminate "the perceptions that investigators are being too aggressive." He wanted Mr. Lewis to "earn the trust of" his "clients"—Wal-Mart's leaders. He wanted him to head off "adversarial interactions."

Mr. Senser now applied the same advice to himself.

Even as Mr. Halter's files were being shipped to Mr. Rodriguezmacedo, Mr. Stucky made plans to fly to Mexico with other executives involved in the bribery investigation. The trip, he wrote, was "for the purpose of re-establishing activities related to the certain compliance matters we've been discussing." Mr. Stucky invited Mr. Senser along.

"It is better if we do not make this trip to Mexico City," Mr. Senser replied. His investigators, he wrote, would simply be "a resource" if needed.

Ten days after Mr. Stucky flew to Mexico, an article about Wal-Mart appeared in *The Times*. It focused on "the increasingly important role of one man: Eduardo Castro-Wright." The article said Mr. Castro-Wright was a "popular figure" inside Wal-Mart because he made Wal-Mart de Mexico one of the company's "most profitable units."

Wall Street analysts, it said, viewed him as a "very strong candidate" to succeed Mr. Scott.

Case Closed

For those who had investigated Mr. Cicero's allegations, the preliminary inquiry had been just that—preliminary. In memos and meetings, they had argued that their findings clearly justified a full-blown investigation. Mr. Castro-Wright's precise role had yet to be determined. Mr. Halter had never been permitted to question him, nor had Mr. Castro-Wright's computer files been examined, records, and interviews show.

At the very least, a complete investigation would take months.

Mr. Rodriguezmacedo, the man now in charge, saw it differently. He wrapped up the case in a few weeks, with little additional investigation.

"There is no evidence or clear indication," his report concluded, "of bribes paid to Mexican government authorities with the purpose of wrongfully securing any licenses or permits."

That conclusion, his report explained, was largely based on the denials of his fellow executives. Not one "mentioned having ordered or given bribes to government authorities," he wrote.

His report, six pages long, neglected to note that he had been implicated in the same criminal conduct.

That was not the only omission. While his report conceded that Wal-Mart de Mexico executives had authorized years of payments to gestores, it never explained what these executives expected the gestores to do with the millions of dollars they received to "facilitate" permits.

He was also silent on the evidence that Wal-Mart de Mexico had doled out donations to get permits. Nor did he address evidence that he and other executives had suppressed or rewritten audits that would have alerted Bentonville to improper payments.

Instead, the bulk of Mr. Rodriguezmacedo's report attacked the integrity of his accuser.

Mr. Cicero, he wrote, made Wal-Mart de Mexico's executives think they would "run the risk of having permits denied if the gestores were not used." But this was merely a ruse: In all likelihood, he argued, Wal-Mart de Mexico paid millions for "services never rendered." The gestores simply pocketed the money, he suggested, and Mr. Cicero "may have benefited," too.

But he offered no direct proof. Indeed, as his report made clear, it was less an allegation than a hypothesis built on two highly circumstantial pillars.

First, he said he had consulted with Jesus Zamora-Pierce, a "prestigious independent counsel" who had written books on fraud. Mr. Zamora, he wrote, "feels the conduct displayed by Sergio Cicero is typical of someone engaging in fraud. It is not uncommon in Mexico for lawyers to recommend the use of gestores to facilitate permit obtainment, when in reality it is nothing more than a means of engaging in fraud."

Second, he said he had done a statistical analysis that found Wal-Mart de Mexico won permits even faster after Mr. Cicero left. The validity of his analysis was impossible to assess; he did not include his statistics in the report.

In building a case against Mr. Cicero, Mr. Rodriguezmacedo's report included several false statements. He described Mr. Cicero's "dismissal" when records showed he had resigned. He also wrote that Kroll's investigation of Mr. Cicero concluded that he "had a considerable increase in his standard of living during the time in which payments were made to the gestores." Kroll's report made no such assertion, people involved in the investigation said.

His report promised a series of corrective steps aimed at putting the entire matter to rest. Wal-Mart de Mexico would no longer use gestores. There would be a renewed commitment to Wal-Mart's anticorruption policy. He did not recommend any disciplinary action against his colleagues.

There was, however, one person he hoped to punish. Wal-Mart de Mexico, he wrote, would scour Mr. Cicero's records and determine "if any legal action may be taken against him."

Mr. Rodriguezmacedo submitted a draft of his report to Bentonville. In an e-mail, Mr. Lewis told his superiors that he found the report "lacking." It was not clear what evidence supported the report's conclusions, he wrote. "More importantly," he wrote, "if one agrees that Sergio defrauded the company and I am one of them, the question becomes, how was he able to get away with almost $10 million and why was nothing done after it was discovered?"

Mr. Rodriguezmacedo responded by adding a paragraph to the end of his report: They had decided not to pursue "criminal actions" against Mr. Cicero because "we did not have strong case."

"At the risk of being cynical," Mr. Lewis wrote in response, "that report is exactly the same as the previous which I indicated was truly lacking."

But it was enough for Wal-Mart. Mr. Rodriguezmacedo was told by executives in Bentonville on May 10, 2006, to put his report "into final form, thus concluding this investigation."

No one told Mr. Cicero. All he knew was that after months of e-mails, phone calls, and meetings, Wal-Mart's interest seemed to suddenly fade. His phone calls and e-mails went unanswered.

"I thought nobody cares about this," he said. "So I left it behind."

Critical Thinking

1. What is your overall impression about the allegations of bribery being faced by Wal-Mart?

2. Having read the article carefully, preparing talking points for class discussion about the efficacy of Wal-Mart's response to the allegation. Contrast the initial response to a time later when "the Chief (i.e., Mr. Scott) weighs in."

3. If you were an outside consultant advising Mr. Scott on ethical issues involved in the situation of the alleged bribery, what would be your advice?

4. What might Wal-Mart's management have done differently in the aftermath of the bribery allegations?

5. Prepare comments for class discussion on the "case closed" section of the article.

6. What are the lessons to be learned from the allegations of bribery and Wal-Mart's handling of the allegations?

Create Central

www.mhhe.com/createcentral

Internet References

Bloomberg
http://www.bloomberg.com/news/2014-03-26/wal-mart-says-bribery-probe-cost-439-million-in-past-two-years.html

Business Insider
http://www.businessinsider.com/new-details-in-walmart-bribery-scandal-2012-12

New York Times
http://www.nytimes.com/2012/11/16/business/wal-mart-expands-foreign-bribery-investigation.html?pagewanted=all

American Apparel and the Ethics of a Sexually Charged Workplace by Gael O'Brien   **149**

Article   Prepared by: Eric Teoro, *Lincoln Christian University*

American Apparel and the Ethics of a Sexually Charged Workplace

GAEL O'BRIEN

Learning Outcomes

After reading this article, you will be able to:

- Describe the nature of sexual harassment and a hostile work environment.

- Understand the need for congruent values within a work environment.

- Understand the role of organizational culture on employee behavior.

American Apparel finds itself once again in a familiar place—sued again for sexual harassment and creating a hostile work environment, because of the vulnerability its CEO's philosophy of sexual freedom in the workplace creates for the publicly held company.

In discussing a 2006 sexual harassment suit, founder, chairman, and CEO Dov Charney expressed the belief that consensual sexual relationships in the workplace were appropriate: "I think it's a First Amendment right to pursue one's affection for another human being."

Recently, Irene Morales, 20, sued Charney, 42, American Apparel, and its directors for about $250 million, alleging Charney forced her into sex acts when she was 18 and an employee. The company has accused Morales of extortion. A lawyer for the company dismissed the allegations, saying when Morales left the company and accepted severance, she signed a statement saying she had no claims against the company and agreed that any future claims would be addressed by confidential arbitration. A judge has halted Morales' suit until March 25, pending a decision on whether it should go to arbitration or trial.

Notwithstanding the distinction of being dubbed "American Apparel's chief lawsuit officer," Charney is a complex figure.

His website, filled with photos of him and provocative shots he took of the company's young models, tells the story of his immigrant family, religion, creating the company as a teenager, philosophy on sexual freedom, and politics. Passionate about immigration reform, proud his clothing is "made in America," he pays his 10,000 workers well above garment industry rate.

Charney owns 51.8 percent of the company and the board has thus far apparently gone along with his philosophy of sexual freedom. However, the company is no longer on solid financial footing. Blame the recession or other factors, but it appears that sexy marketing isn't selling American Apparel the way it did several years ago; stock prices have been dropping.

Among the questions Dov Charney's philosophy raises is whether there really can be consensual sex in a workplace if both parties aren't equal in status, salary, and intention?

Is the term a delusion if one of the parties is the CEO? For example, how can both parties freely accept responsibility for the consequences of a relationship when one party has power over the other's salary, promotion, or keeping the job?

If tone at the top encourages workplace sexual expression, what are the constraints to protect employees? American Apparels' ethics policy talks about "promoting ethical conduct, including the handling of actual or apparent conflicts of interest between personal and professional relationships."

So who decides if a conflict of interest has occurred between personal and professional relationships and if harm was done in a fleeting or more sustained expression of sexual interest? What about harm to bystanders who just want to do their job and are made uncomfortable by sexual innuendo and graphic language?

If you were doing a cost/benefit analysis of sexual drama (which is an inevitable byproduct of a sexually charged workplace), would the benefits come out ahead if everyone affected got to weigh in?

In interviews, Charney has tied the importance of sexual energy to creative energy on which he says the fashion industry depends. No argument about the value of released endorphins.

Interesting to note that many leaders have championed endorphin highs to stimulate creativity. Among dozens of examples, they set aside areas for ping pong, volleyball, or fitness equipment, or hold events recognizing employee achievements—few, if any of which, have resulted in litigation and loss of company and CEO reputation.

Every leader gets to figure out if what she or he is doing is working and what to change (before a board answers that question for them). Charney enjoyed the reputation as a wunderkind. Now the company is in a different phase facing financial and strategic challenges, as well as another lawsuit about its culture.

The irony of sexual freedom in the workplace is that it is about power, not romance. It often ends up exploiting those most vulnerable—the way, for example, immigrants have often been treated in some workplaces; it also gives ammunition to those who, seeing where a company has made itself most vulnerable, move in for their own kill.

Update–March 28, 2011: Justice Bernadette Bayne held a hearing March 25, 2011 with counsel from both sides in the sexual harassment suit, Morales v. American Apparel. Judge Bayne initially indicated the case should go to arbitration and later said she'd review the additional documents. She gave no indication when she'd rule if the case can go to trial. On March 23, Apparel chairman and CEO Dov Charney was hit with the second sexual harassment suit this month. Kimbra Lo, 19, a former sales associate, alleges she was sexually assaulted when she went to Charney's LA home seeking to be rehired as a model and photographer. Both Lo and Morales went on the Today Show to talk about their lawsuits. The company contends the relationships were consensual.

Critical Thinking

1. What is meant by the allegations of a sexually charged workplace and a hostile work environment?

2. How are the allegations related to ethics and ethical behavior?

3. What lessons for management might be drawn from the article?

4. Identify one lesson for management and defend its importance.

Create Central

www.mhhe.com/createcentral

Internet References

Bloomberg Businessweek
   http://www.businessweek.com/stories/2005-06-26/living-on-the-edge-at-american-apparel
Business Ethics: The Magazine of Corporate Responsibility
   http://business-ethics.com/2010/08/07/4535-mark-hurds-leadership-failure/
Los Angeles Times
   http://articles.latimes.com/2011/mar/10/business/la-fi-charney-lawsuit-20110310

GAEL O'BRIEN is a Business Ethics Magazine columnist. Gael is a thought leader on building leadership, trust, and reputation and writes The Week in Ethics, a weekly column where this article was first published.

Article   Prepared by: Eric Teoro, *Lincoln Christian University*

Intel Wants a Less White, Less Male Staff. Good Luck

Recruiting and retaining minority employees in a large company takes years, not months.

A KANE O TANI

Learning Outcomes

After reading this article, you will be able to:

- Describe the steps Intel is taking to increase workplace diversity.

- Describe the challenges with increasing workplace diversity.

Intel wants to be less male and white. Chief Executive Officer Brian Krzanich pledged on Tuesday to spend $300 million to boost the diversity of the workforce at Intel, which, like many other technology companies, has been criticized for employing woefully few women, blacks, and Hispanics. By 2020, Intel hopes, women and underrepresented minorities will be fully represented in its workforce.

Intel's ambitions are admirable. The company may well be the first tech giant to publicly set aside this much money to tackle workplace diversity, even as others—including Facebook and Microsoft—have paid lip service to the topic in recent months. Yet it would be premature to consider the battle anywhere near won. Making a large company more diverse is harder than most people think.

"Diversity isn't something you can buy quickly. It has to be an investment, and it has to take time," says Marilyn Nagel, CEO of Watermark, a nonprofit working to increase the representation of female leaders in companies.

The first problem is one of mathematics. Intel, according to its 2013 EEO-1 (Equal Employment Opportunity) report, has more than 57,000 employees in the U.S., 57 percent of whom

are white and 29 percent of whom are Asian. Just 8 percent of its employees are Hispanic; 4 percent black; 1 percent multiracial; 0.5 percent American Indian; and 0.2 percent native Hawaiian or Pacific Islander. Women are outnumbered 3 to 1 by men. The racial and gender disparities are even more stark at the top of the company, where white men hold 133 of 187 executive and senior management positions and white women hold an additional 23.

Intel hopes to attract more women and minorities to its ranks by funding engineering scholarships and working more closely with computer science departments at historically black colleges and other schools. But realistically, Intel will have to recruit and hire thousands of qualified software engineers and developers before it makes a dent in its percentage of minority and female employees—a venture that will take years, not months, to carry out.

It's Lonely at the Top
Number of Intel executives and senior managers representing each race

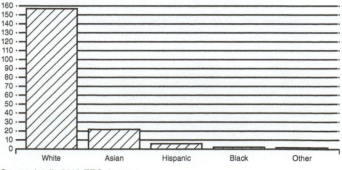

Source: Intel's 2013 EEO-1 report

Making things more difficult, it's not just a matter of getting more employees of different races and genders into the building. Diversity has to stick. Hiring may spike, but if minority employees don't feel like they're welcome, they'll leave. And there's plenty of evidence showing large swaths of minorities and women have felt isolated by peers in the tech industry—whether they've been told not to ask for pay raises; mistaken as a security guard or administrative assistant as a black employee; or assumed, as a female developer attending an industry event, to be the girlfriend of a man.

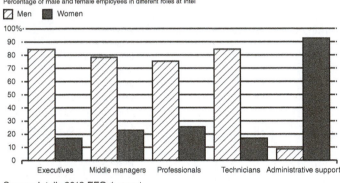

Where Are the Women in the Tech Industry?
Percentage of male and female employees in different roles at Intel

Source: Intel's 2013 EEO-1 report

"People who are being recruited have to be able to say they know Intel is a company that will support people like them at the highest level," Watermark's Nagel says. That takes seeking out diverse candidates for senior roles and "educating the entire organization to make sure there aren't unconscious biases, or even conscious biases, that are keeping the playing field from being level," she says. It requires making sure employees have advocates who can stand up for them in the workplace.

Companies have failed to take diversity seriously for years. Why? Often, employees say, they don't see their workplace putting enough skin in the game. In a *Forbes* survey of 321 executives working at large multinationals, 46 percent said they felt budget issues were holding them back. Another 46 percent said middle managers weren't carrying out diversity initiatives adequately, and 42 percent said people were more concerned with surviving the economy than improving diversity.

Abercrombie & Fitch offers a cautionary tale: After settling a $40 million lawsuit over allegedly putting minority employees in back-of-store jobs, the clothing retailer agreed in 2004 to conduct diversity training for hiring managers and to tie progress on diversity initiatives into managers' compensation. Since then, Abercrombie has been accused of telling an employee her hijab violated the company's dress code, wrongfully dismissing an employee with a prosthetic limb, and discriminating against plus-size consumers.

Making a company more diverse in a meaningful, lasting way requires more than a new policy here, a few polite words there. Intel should keep that in mind as it starts to transform this laudable commitment into a tangible reality.

Because of the company's size and reach, Nagel says, substantial change will be a challenge. "It's going to take a major cultural shift over time."

Critical Thinking

1. Is workplace diversity an ethical issue? Why or why not?
2. How can workplace diversity impact workplace ethics? Defend your position.
3. Should companies look for employees who have diverse ethical viewpoints? Why or why not?

Internet References

Houston Chronicle: Small Business
  http://smallbusiness.chron.com/cultural-diversity-business-ethics-26116.html
Sage Journals
  http://sgo.sagepub.com/content/2/2/2158244012444615
Texas Tech University
  http://sdh.ba.ttu.edu/OrgDyn07%20Ethics.pdf

Article

Prepared by: Eric Teoro, *Lincoln Christian University*

The Ethics of Not Hiring Smokers

HARALD SCHMIDT, KRISTIN VOIGT, AND EZEKIEL J. EMANUEL

Learning Outcomes

After reading this article, you will be able to:

- Describe ethical issues surrounding hiring decisions based on lifestyle choices.

- Appreciate the complexities involved in ethical deliberations regarding employer–employee relationships.

Finding employment is becoming increasingly difficult for smokers. Twenty-nine U.S. states have passed legislation prohibiting employers from refusing to hire job candidates because they smoke, but 21 states have no such restrictions. Many health care organizations, such as the Cleveland Clinic and Baylor Health Care System, and some large non–health care employers, including Scotts Miracle-Gro, Union Pacific Railroad, and Alaska Airlines, now have a policy of not hiring smokers—a practice opposed by 65 percent of Americans, according to a 2012 poll by Harris International. We agree with those polled, believing that categorically refusing to hire smokers is unethical: it results in a failure to care for people, places an additional burden on already-disadvantaged populations, and preempts interventions that more effectively promote smoking cessation.

One justification for not employing smokers, used primarily by health care organizations, is symbolic. When the World Health Organization introduced a "nonsmoker-only" hiring policy in 2008, it cited its commitment to tobacco control and the importance of "denormalizing" tobacco use. Health care organizations with similar policies have argued that their employees must serve as role models for patients and that only nonsmokers can do so.

A second, more general, argument is that employees must take personal responsibility for actions that impose financial or other burdens on employers or fellow employees. Accordingly, smokers should be responsible for the consequences of their smoking, such as higher costs for health insurance claims, higher rates of absenteeism, and lower productivity. These costs amount to an estimated additional $4,000 annually for each smoking employee.

Yet it seems paradoxical for health care organizations that exist to care for the sick to refuse to employ smokers. Many patients are treated for illnesses to which their behavior has contributed, including chronic obstructive pulmonary disease, heart failure, diabetes, and infections spread through unprotected sex or other voluntary activities. It is callous—and contradictory—for health care institutions devoted to caring for patients regardless of the causes of their illness to refuse to employ smokers. Just as they should treat people regardless of their degree of responsibility for their own ill health, they should not discriminate against qualified job candidates on the basis of health-related behavior.

The broader claim that it is fair to exclude smokers because they are responsible for raising health care costs is too simplistic. It ignores the fact that smoking is addictive and therefore not completely voluntary. Among adult daily smokers, 88 percent began smoking by the time they were 18,[1] before society would consider them fully responsible for their actions. Much of this early smoking is subtly and not so subtly encouraged by cigarette companies. As many as 69 percent of smokers want to quit,[2] but the addictive properties of tobacco make that exceedingly difficult: only 3 to 5 percent of unaided cessation attempts succeed.[3] It is therefore wrong to treat smoking as something fully under an individual's control.

In addition, all other diseases—and many healthful behaviors—also result in additional health care costs. People with cancer burden their fellow workers through higher health care costs and absenteeism. People who engage in risky sports may have accidents or experience trauma routinely and burden coworkers with additional costs. Having babies increases premiums for fellow employees who have none. Many of these costs result from seemingly innocent, everyday lifestyle choices; some choices, such as those regarding diet and exercise, may affect cancer incidence as well as rates of diabetes and heart disease.

We as a society have rejected the notion that individuals should be fully responsible for their own health care costs. In instituting health insurance, we acknowledge the fragility of health and the costliness of restoring it, and we minimize catastrophic consequences. The United States has chosen to pool risk predominantly through employers rather than the government. Consequently, U.S. law requires firms with more than 50 employees to provide risk-pooled insurance.

Finally, although less than one fifth of Americans currently smoke, rates of tobacco use vary markedly among sociodemographic groups, with higher rates in poorer and less-educated populations. Some 42 percent of American Indian or Alaska Native adults smoke, but only 8 percent of Asian women do. Among adults with less than a high school education, 32 percent are smokers; among college graduates, smoking rates are just over 13 percent. More than 36 percent of Americans living below the federal poverty line are smokers, as compared with 22.5 percent of those with incomes above that level. Crucially, policies against hiring smokers result in a "double whammy" for many unemployed people, among whom smoking rates are nearly 45 percent (as compared with 28 percent among Americans with full-time employment).[4] These policies therefore disproportionately and unfairly affect groups that are already burdened by high unemployment rates, poor job prospects, and job insecurity.

So what should employers do? We believe that offering support for healthful behaviors is the best approach. Central in this regard is assisting employees by providing evidence-based smoking-cessation programs, removing cost barriers, facilitating access, and providing necessary psychological counseling and other support. For example, many employers, such as Walgreens, provide free nicotine-replacement therapy and smoking-cessation counseling to employees.

Recent research also indicates that financial incentives can effectively promote smoking cessation. For example, a randomized, controlled trial involving employees of General Electric showed that a combination of incentives amounting to $750 led to cessation rates three times those achieved through information-only approaches (14.7 percent vs. 5.0 percent).[5]

But General Electric's experience also reflects the political challenges of instituting policies regarding smokers. When the company decided to provide the program to all employees, nonsmokers objected to losing out on what would effectively be lower insurance premiums for their smoker colleagues. In response, the company replaced the $750 reduction with a $625 surcharge for smokers.[5]

Just like policies of not hiring smokers, penalties imposed on smokers raise serious ethical and policy concerns. The Department of Labor is considering whether to permit employers to penalize smokers with a surcharge of up to 50 percent of the cost of their health insurance coverage (typically more than $2,000 per employee per year). Yet even rewards for quitting are hard to sell to nonsmokers, who might also object to free smoking-cessation programs that they subsidize indirectly through their insurance premiums. Underlying such opposition is a distorted notion of personal responsibility and deservedness, according to which refraining from smoking results from willpower and active choice alone. Although some employees may be nonsmokers through such efforts, most should have the humility to recognize that "there but for the grace of God go they."

Given nonsmokers' resistance, it would be helpful if employers providing smoking-cessation support engaged in early outreach emphasizing that helping smokers to quit adheres to the principle of risk pooling underlying health insurance. Successful cessation programs could lead to higher productivity and lower insurance contributions for nonsmokers, thereby benefiting all employees.

The goal of reducing smoking rates is important. Although smoking rates among U.S. adults have decreased from 42 percent in 1965 to 19 percent today,[5] more remains to be done, particularly for low-income and unemployed populations. Promoting public health is a shared responsibility, and employers have a social obligation to contribute to the public health mission outlined by the Institute of Medicine: "fulfill[ing] society's interest in assuring conditions in which people can be healthy." By cherry-picking "low-risk" employees and denying employment to smokers, employers neglect this obligation, risk hurting vulnerable groups, and behave unethically. The same goes for imposing high penalties on smokers under the guise of providing wellness incentives.

We believe that employers should consider more constructive approaches than punishing smokers. In hiring decisions, they should focus on whether candidates meet the job requirements; then they should provide genuine support to employees who wish to quit smoking. And health care organizations in particular should show compassion for their workers. This approach may even be a win–win economic solution, since employees who feel supported will probably be more productive than will those who live in fear of penalties.

Critical Thinking

1. Should employers have the right to make employment related decisions based on lifestyle choices? Defend your position.

2. Are all lifestyle choices equal regarding employment decisions?

3. What are employer' rights regarding employee lifestyle choices? Employee' rights?

Internet References

Albany Gov't Law Review

https://aglr.wordpress.com/2014/05/14/allowing-employers-to-make-tangible-employment-decisions-based-on-an-employees-use-of-tobacco/

Berkeley Journal of Employment & Labor Law

http://scholarship.law.berkeley.edu/cgi/viewcontent.cgi?article=1329&context=bjell

Lorman

http://www.lorman.com/resources/penalizing-applicants-and-employees-for-smoking-a-potential-smoking-gun-15586

San Francisco Chronicle

http://www.sfchronicle.com/business/networth/article/Can-your-boss-stop-you-from-smoking-medical-6067585.php

Notes

1. Preventing tobacco use among youth and young adults: a report of the Surgeon General, 2012. Atlanta: Office on Smoking and Health, 2012 (http://www.surgeongeneral.gov/library/reports/preventing-youth-tobacco-use/index.html).

2. Smoking and tobacco use: fast facts. Atlanta: Centers for Disease Control and Prevention (http://www.cdc.gov/tobacco/data_statistics/fact_sheets/fast_facts)

3. Novotny T, Cohen J, Yurekli A, Sweanor D, de Beyer J. Smoking cessation and nicotine-replacement therapies. In: Jha P, Chaloupka FJ, eds. Tobacco control in developing countries. Oxford, United Kingdom: Oxford University Press, 2000:287-307.

4. Garrett BE, Dube SR, Trosclair A, Caraballo RS, Pechacek TF. Cigarette smoking -- United States, 1965-2008. MMWR Surveill Summ 2011;60:109-113 (http://www.ncbi.nlm.nih.gov/pubmed/21430635?dopt=Abstract)

5. Volpp KG, Asch DA, Galvin R, Loewenstein G. Redesigning employee health incentives -- lessons from behavioral economics. N Engl J Med 2011;365:388-390 (http://www.nejm.org/doi/full/10.1056/NEJMp1105966)

Article

Prepared by: Eric Teoro, *Lincoln Christian University*

Gap's Inconsistent Corporate Ethics

The retailer should join an accord to protect Bangladeshi garment workers.

GREG RANDOLPH

Learning Outcomes

After reading this article, you will be able to:

- Understand how actions can lead to perceptions of inconsistency.

- Think more deeply about an organization's responsibility toward employees.

- Think more critically about what inclusion entails.

The liberal social media bloc was abuzz recently with praise for Gap, the ubiquitous apparel company known for its khaki, clean-cut sense of style and—most recently—an advertisement that featured a visibly Sikh male model, sporting a pagdi (turban), and a full beard. The ad achieved nationwide fame when the company produced a swift and emphatic response to racist graffiti scribbled over it in a New York subway station.

But another of Gap's recent decisions—its refusal to join a groundbreaking accord to protect Bangladeshi garment workers—calls into question whether the corporate ethic of inclusion extends beyond marketing campaigns.

By selecting Waris Ahluwalia to model in its "Make Love" campaign, and immediately denouncing the act of an intolerant graffiti artist who changed that slogan to "Make Bombs," Gap sent an important message of inclusion to 280,000 Sikhs living in the United States, telling them that Gap believes their faces and lived experiences are part of the American story.

Socially minded consumers might find it surprising then, that on another issue of justice and inclusion, Gap's response has been anemic. After the death of nearly 1,200 apparel workers in the horrific collapse of Rana Plaza—a dilapidated building housing several garment factories on the outskirts of Dhaka—retailers around the world sought channels for improving working conditions in the country. A landmark agreement emerged, aimed at strengthening worker protections in Bangladesh's massive apparel industry, but Gap has refused to sign on.

The Accord on Fire and Building Safety in Bangladesh goes beyond traditional corporate social responsibility. First of all, a broad coalition of corporations, trade unions and workers' rights organizations negotiated jointly and endorse the agreement. Second, its signatories are legally obligated to fund independent inspection of facilities, plus structural repairs and renovations of existing factories. Over 100 international brands—including Gap competitors like Abercrombie & Fitch, American Eagle Outfitters and H&M—have already signed on.

The accord is about basic human rights. Bangladeshi workers possess the right to safe working conditions, the right to fair wages and the right to life.

It's also about inclusion. Mirroring the globalization story in many countries, economic growth in Bangladesh has been rapid, but its rewards have not been shared broadly. Rather than creating an economic culture of shared prosperity, Bangladesh has engaged in a "race to the bottom"—maintaining substandard wages and working conditions in order to make production costs attractively, and artificially, low. The accord is a first step toward transforming those marginalized by globalization into its beneficiaries.

If it joined the accord, Gap would send another powerful message of inclusion to 4 million Bangladeshi garment workers: your economic opportunity, your ability to obtain a just job, and your right to share in the fruits of economic growth, matter to us. Further, it could demonstrate to its new Tweeting extollers that the company's progressive attitudes inform its supply chain management, not only its advertising.

Arsalan Iftikhar, the social commentator and online personality who made the Gap ad famous, wrote last month: "I want to live in an America where a fashion model can be a handsome, bearded brown dude in a turban who is considered as beautiful as a busty blonde-haired white girl in see-through lingerie."

That America does sound nice. But a fashion industry committed to diversity and inclusion stands on hollow ground if the products it markets are founded in economic exclusion. With the power of its brand and the size of its supply chain, Gap can and should do more to create just jobs in the apparel sector. Signing the accord is a necessary step.

Critical Thinking

1. Debate with a fellow student/colleague Gap's decision to not sign the Bangladesh accord, one defending Gap and one accusing Gap of an ethical lapse.

2. Do you think that Gap's unwillingness to sign the Bangladesh accord is conclusive evidence of a lack of concern toward employees? Why or why not?

3. Do you think Gap behaved unethically in not signing the Bangladesh accord? Why or why not?

Create Central

www.mhhe.com/createcentral

Internet References

CBC News
   http://www.cbc.ca/news/business/bangladeshi-garment-workers-protest-66-a-month-offer-1.2422470

Gap Inc.
   http://gapinc.com/content/gapinc/html/media/pressrelease/2014/med_pr_Most_Ethical_Companies.html

Rabble.CA
   http://rabble.ca/news/2013/11/how-gap-and-wal-mart-are-dodging-worker-safety-bangladesh

---

GREG RANDOLPH is the manager of strategy and outreach at JustJobs Network.

Article

Prepared by: Eric Teoro, *Lincoln Christian University*

Commentary: Markets Will Best Guard Environment

JOHN STOSSEL

Learning Outcomes

After reading this article, you will be able to:

- Describe how private property rights and the market system offer an alternative to governmental oversight regarding environmental protection.
- Understand potential problems of commonly held resources.

Last week I said the Environmental Protection Agency has become a monster that does more harm than good. But logical people say, "What else we got?" It's natural to assume greedy capitalists will run amok and destroy the Earth unless stopped by regulation.

These critics don't understand the real power of private ownership, says Terry Anderson of the Property and Environment Research Center.

"Long before the EPA was a glint in anyone's eye," said Anderson on my TV show, "property rights were dealing with pollution issues."

The worst pollution often happens on land owned by "the people"—by government. Since no one person derives direct benefit from this property, it's often treated carelessly. Some of the worst environmental damage happens on military bases and government research facilities, such as the nuclear research site in Hanford, Washington.

Worse things may happen when government indifference combines with the greed of unrestrained businesspeople, like when the U.S. Forest Service lets logging companies cut trees on public land. Private forest owners are careful to replant and take steps to prevent forest fires. Government-owned forests are not as well managed. They are much more likely to burn.

When it's government land—or any commonly held resource—the incentive is to get in and take what you can, while you can. It's called the "tragedy of the commons."

"No one washes a rental car," says Anderson, but "when people own things, they take care of them. And when they have private property rights that they can enforce, other people can't dump gunk onto the property."

That's why, contrary to what environmentalists often assume, it's really property rights that encourage good stewardship. If you pollute, it's your neighbors who are most likely to complain, not lazy bureaucrats at the EPA.

"Here in Montana, for example, the Anaconda Mining Company, a copper and mining company, ruled the state," says Anderson.

"And yet when it was discovered that their tailings piles (the heaps left over after removing the valuable material by mining) had caused pollution on ranches that neighbored them, local property owners took them to court. (Anaconda Mining) had to cease and desist and pay for damages. . . . They quickly took care of that problem." They also restored some of the land they had mined.

Property rights and a simple, honest court system—institutions that can exist without big government—solve problems that would be fought about for years by politicians, environmental bureaucrats and the corporations who lobby them.

In fact, it's harder to assess the benefits and damages in environmental disputes when these decisions are taken out of the marketplace and made by bureaucracies that have few objective ways to measure costs.

Markets even solve environmental problems in places where environmentalists assume they cannot, such as oceans and other property that can't be carved up into private parcels.

Environmental bureaucrats usually say, to make sure fishermen don't overfish and destroy the stock of fish, we will set a quota for every season. That command-and-control approach has been the standard policy.

So bureaucrats regulate the fishing season. They limit the number of boats, their size, and how long they may fish. The result: fishing is now America's most dangerous job. Fishermen race out in all kinds of weather to get as many fish as they can in the narrow time window allowed by regulators. They try to game the system to make more money. Sometimes they still deplete the fish stock.

But Anderson points out that there is an alternative. "In places like New Zealand and Iceland . . . we've created individual fishing quotas, which are tradable, which are bankable, which give people an incentive to invest in their fisheries."

Because the fisherman "owns" his fishing quota, he is careful to preserve it. He doesn't overfish because he wants "his" fish to be there next year.

The moral of the story: when possible, let markets and property protect nature. That avoids the tragedy of the commons.

Critical Thinking

1. Do you think the author's argument holds merit? Why or why not?
2. Do you think people are poor stewards of commonly held resources?
3. Debate with a colleague or fellow student how best to protect the environment.

Create Central

www.mhhe.com/createcentral

Internet References

Economist
http://www.economist.com/node/9136122

Ludwig von Mises Institute
http://mises.org/daily/5978/The-Libertarian-Manifesto-on-Pollution

The Atlantic
http://www.theatlantic.com/business/archive/2012/05/how-property-rights-could-help-save-the-environment/257756/

From *The Daily Record,* September 8, 2014, Copyright © 2014 by Dix Communications. Reprinted by permission.

Article

Prepared by: Eric Teoro, *Lincoln Christian University*

Even after Snowden, Quota System on Background Checks May Be Imperiling U.S. Secrets

CHRISTIAN DAVENPORT

Learning Outcomes

After reading this article, you will be able to:

- Describe ethical issues regarding the use of quotas for work performance.

- Describe the external and internal pressures faced by individuals pressed to meet quotas in security related industries.

For years, investigators charged with vetting the backgrounds of those who handle the nation's secrets have said they were pressured to churn through cases as quickly as possible. The faster they turned them in, the faster their company got paid—even if the investigations were rushed and incomplete.

The company, USIS (United States Information Service.), lost the contract to conduct background checks used in granting security clearances after an employee blew the whistle in a lawsuit, eventually joined by the Justice Department. In the wake of a scandal so fierce that members of Congress accused USIS of defrauding the government and prioritizing profit over the nation's security, federal officials vowed to prevent such abuses from ever happening again.

But a similar quota system used by USIS to drive its investigators continues at the companies that now perform the bulk of the investigations—and in some cases is even more demanding, according to internal company documents and interviews with current and former investigators.

The field workers at KeyPoint Government Solutions and CACI are required to meet pre-determined numbers that dictate how many people they have to interview per day. With their compensation tied to quotas—failure to meet them could lead to a cut in pay—field investigators say the focus on quantity over quality that was so pervasive at USIS persists. And the pressure to meet the goals often doesn't allow them the freedom to follow important leads to determine who should be granted access to classified material, they say.

Despite the congressional outcry, the contracts' payment system is still structured so that the faster the contractors turn over the cases to the federal government, the quicker they get paid. And the federal government imposes a financial penalty if the companies miss their deadline.

The constant pressure to move through cases quickly may be coming at a dangerous price, said Carolyn Martin, president of the American Federal Contract Investigators Association, a professional group.

The system is "just producing shoddy investigations," she said. "They are out there getting the points. Checking the blocks. They are not conducting investigations."

One investigator, who worked at both USIS and KeyPoint, said he left both companies because of the emphasis on speed over thoroughness.

"It was just too rushed," the former investigator said, speaking on the condition of anonymity for fear of reprisal. "I couldn't in good conscience continue. I refused to cut corners, and it made me look like I couldn't perform to their unreasonable expectations."

In a brief statement, KeyPoint said: "All security clearance investigations are subject to strict internal and external thresholds measuring quality, thoroughness and accuracy. Falsifying any element of a federal security clearance investigation is a felony."

On its website, KeyPoint says that its "commitment to time-liness and quality is unwavering." And that "because we know the work we do directly contributes to national security, we will never sacrifice quality for speed."

CACI's site says that it "fosters a culture based on integrity, strong ethics, quality, and professionalism." And that its investigators "contribute to the safety and security of our nation in the company of colleagues who value trust and integrity above all else."

The companies also evaluate their investigators based on the quality of their reports, they say, often sending files back for additional work so that they meet thoroughness standards.

Both KeyPoint and CACI said they were prohibited from responding to multiple requests for comment by the terms of their agreements with the Office of Personnel Management (OPM), the agency that oversees background investigations for most of the federal government.

In an interview, Merton Miller, the associate director for OPM's Federal Investigative Services, defended the investigative system, saying that he "absolutely" had full confidence in it.

There are "very strict quality standards for our field work contractors as well as our feds, so that when they do the work, they do it right," he said.

Miller said he was aware that the companies use productivity metrics but did not know that they have a tiered system that ties investigators' compensation to their productivity.

"Candidly, that has not been brought to my attention," he said.

OPM has recently developed, for the first time, quality-review standards used to judge whether the investigations are complete. That, Miller said, is a marked improvement from the previous system, which left determinations of quality to "the eye of beholder."

The agency, which said last week that it was the victim of a major cyberattack that included its security clearance database, has also created government-wide standards for training investigators. And last year, the agency, which oversees the investigative process for the Pentagon and the majority of the federal government, stopped awarding separate contracts for quality reviews of its cases, saying it was a conflict of interest.

Still, the companies are facing a daunting challenge. They had to pick up USIS's massive workload—which averaged 21,000 cases per month—when OPM suddenly did not renew USIS's contract last fall.

With millions of dollars at stake, CACI and KeyPoint leapt at the chance and went on hiring sprees to show they could handle the additional work. Yet they still had to meet strict congressionally mandated timelines that dictate how quickly clearances have to be granted. OPM has touted the drastic reductions in

the time it takes to process initial clearances, from 145 days in 2005 to fewer than 40 last year.

It has been a lucrative business. KeyPoint's revenue under the contract jumped from $117 million in 2013 to $214 million last year. And it is on pace to receive nearly $240 million this year, according to a *Washington Post* analysis of federal contracting data. CACI's revenue also spiked, growing from $47.5 million in 2013 to more than $93 million last year. This year it is on pace to hit more than $175 million.

U.S. Sen. Rob Portman (R-Ohio), who has been critical of the pressure placed on investigators, said the government "has long struggled to balance workload and quality."

"The issue has not gone away," he said in a statement to *The Post,* "and is just as apparent as OPM tries to make do after removing their largest contractor from the investigation process last year. . . . We have too many examples of background investigators and their supervisors taking shortcuts to meet deadlines."

"I Have to Pay My Bills"

The pressure to move through cases quickly can lead to short-cuts, investigators said.

Another former KeyPoint investigator, who now works at CACI, said that while he tried not to cut corners, the pressure from his bosses sometimes forced him into uncomfortable territory. In one instance while he was at KeyPoint, he was investigating a foreign national who had marked on his paperwork that he had not maintained contact with anyone from his home country.

The investigator was skeptical of this: "You're telling me that a kid who's been in a foreign country for five months and he doesn't talk to anyone in [his home] country? I find that hard to believe. He didn't have any friends there or anything?"

And so the investigator asked about it in the interview.

"I said, 'Are you sure?'"

The interviewee said he was.

"I just moved on to the next question because I was in a hurry," said the investigator, who spoke on the condition of anonymity for fear of reprisal. "I have to pay my bills, and clearly my company doesn't care. They want me to do it faster."

It's not just the numbers system but also the demands to meet deadlines, investigators said.

As a contract investigator for KeyPoint, Mary Cullings is paid by the leads she tracks down. Interviewing a reference listed by a security clearance applicant could yield $50, she said, as long as she makes her deadline. If she misses it, her pay is docked by as much as $15, she said.

There have been many times when she's been unable to track down the reference, only to have the person call right before her deadline. When that happens, Cullings blows her deadline, accepts the financial penalty and meets with the reference because "in all good conscience, I can't write that off."

But others could say they made the required efforts to interview the source but were unable to, and then they would still get paid the full amount.

"That happens all the time," said Cullings, a former special agent with the federal Defense Security Service who now contracts with several companies as an investigator. "What they are interested in is the bottom line."

An anonymous message board on ClearanceJobs.com, a placement firm for cleared workers, is full of posts by investigators complaining about the demands of their work.

"I worked for USIS for over 10 years and switched over to KGS and it's the same crap different day! KGS is so number driven it's sick!" read one post from last year. "Who cares about how complicated and long the case is it's all about your numbers."

Investigators say they should be granted the freedom to follow leads without worrying about meeting a quota.

"Each investigation is different. Each subject is different," one investigator said. "Then you go to your manager and say you need more time, and there's no flexibility. . . . There's too much of a conflict between the integrity of the process and the bottom line of these companies."

The consequences of this kind of system could be dire, said Greg Rinckey, the founding partner at Tully Rinckey, a Washington law firm that represents people with security clearances.

"We're not processing widgets here; we're talking about the people who are going to have access to our nation's secrets," he said. "This isn't a numbers game. We're dealing with national security."

Clear Financial Incentives

USIS, which performed the background checks on Edward Snowden, who leaked some of the NSA's secrets, and Aaron Alexis, the Navy Yard shooter, lost the contract after Blake Percival, a former field work services director, filed a whistleblower lawsuit. In it, he alleged that the company had submitted 665,000 cases that were incomplete, saying it was interested in clearing "out the shelves in order to hit revenue."

While it had the OPM contract, USIS used a mathematical formula used to rate the productivity of its investigators. An interview with the subject of a clearance was worth four points; a neighbor or co-worker was worth one; and a document, such as a police report, was worth half a point.

The company's quota system ranged from 17.5 points a week to 25 a week, depending on the pay grade; the higher

investigators scored, the more they got paid, according to investigators and internal documents obtained by *The Washington Post.*

KeyPoint uses a six-level program for its investigators that can be even more demanding, according to company documents. CACI uses a three-level system that also ties productivity to compensation, according to three investigators.

At KeyPoint, company officials make it clear that the faster workers process cases, the more they are rewarded. Those who perform at a higher level for six months "are eligible to be promoted to that level," the company says on its website which also says: "High performers can earn generous bonuses."

OPM's investigators, by contrast, are measured in "man hours," not by the number of people they interview per day, said Miller, the OPM associate director. The agency has studied how long each kind of case should take on average and measures workers' performance accordingly.

The agency has been pushing its contractors to adopt the man-hour approach over their current point system, he said, so that it can directly compare the federal investigators' output to the contractors'. OPM is also aware "that some cases take much longer," he said, and investigators are "required" to exhaust all leads.

Hitting tight deadlines and the high-level quotas set by the companies can be difficult, if not impossible, industry officials say. The overwhelming majority of the interviews have to be done in person. Neighbors and co-workers can be difficult to locate, reluctant to talk and sometimes don't show for an appointment, costing investigators crucial time in a race to meet their targets in a 40-hour workweek.

To meet their quota, investigators say they often have to work overtime, sometimes off the clock, working for free rather than face getting demoted to a lower level and a pay cut. But working off the books is prohibited under federal contracts. And KeyPoint executives recently sent an e-mail that was obtained by *The Post* to its employees, saying that "failing to record all time worked is timecard fraud."

Employees who worked overtime without previously recording it should come forward and they will be paid, the e-mail said.

But it also warned that any employees putting in for the extra pay would also face consequences: "Their employment will be terminated immediately."

Critical Thinking

1. Is the use of a quota system ethical? Why or why not? Does it depend upon the industry? Defend your answer.

2. How should an employee respond if he or she feels pressured to cut corners to meet a given quota? Why should he or she respond that way?

3. What are the ethical issues surrounding the use of quotas in hiring decisions? Are you supportive of such quotas? Why or why not?

Internet References

Baylor Business (Baylor University)
http://www.baylor.edu/business/kellercenter/news.php?action=story&story=135797

Ethics and Compliance Matters
http://blog.navexglobal.com/2015/01/16/2015-trends-6-gender-diversity-are-quotas-answer

Officer.com
http://www.officer.com/article/10697266/bounties-for-traffic-stops-and-brasss-hidden-quotas

---

CHRISTIAN DAVENPORT covers federal contracting for *The Post's* Financial desk. He joined *The Post* in 2000 and has served as an editor on the Metro desk and as a reporter covering military affairs. He is the author of "As You Were: To War and Back with the Black Hawk Battalion of the Virginia National Guard."

Alice Crites, Jennifer Jenkins and Steven Rich contributed to this report.

Article Prepared by: Eric Teoro, *Lincoln Christian University*

The Ethics of Hacking 101

ELLEN NAKASHIMA AND ASHKAN SOLTANI

Learning Outcomes

After reading this article, you will be able to:

- Describe ethical issues regarding teaching students skills that could hurt others.
- Describe ethical issues related to cyber-security.

At the University of Tulsa, professor Sujeet Shenoi is teaching students how to hack into oil pipelines and electric power plants.

At Carnegie Mellon University in Pittsburgh, professor David Brumley is instructing students on how to write software to break into computer networks.

And George Hotz, a largely self-taught hacker who became a millionaire in part by finding flaws in Apple and other computer systems, is now back in school, where he's one of the stars on Carnegie Mellon's competitive hacking team.

Shenoi, Brumley and Hotz are players in a controversial area of technology: the teaching and practice of what is loosely called "cyberoffense." In a world in which businesses, the military and governments rely on computer systems that are potentially vulnerable, having the ability to break into those systems provides a strategic advantage.

Unsurprisingly, ethics is a big issue in this field. Both professors say they build an ethics component into their curriculum; Shenoi won't even accept students who don't promise to work, if hired, for the National Security Agency, the Energy Department or another U.S. government agency.

But some experts say the academic community is not taking ethics seriously enough, and professors are not accepting responsibility for the potentially dangerous skills they are teaching.

The very nature of hacking means that a lot of its skills and standards evolve outside academia. (Hotz, known in tech circles by the handle "geohot," says he learned most of what he knows on the Internet "and from playing with things.") This leads advocates of teaching cyberoffense to say that the "good guys" have to keep up—which in turn raises more questions about whether such education is morally right.

"There's a very large stigma around saying we do anything offense-related," said Tyler Nighswander, 23, a computer science graduate student at Carnegie Mellon. "It's certainly understandable that you don't want to say your school teaches offense—'Oh, you mean you teach kids how to break into computers and steal stuff?'"

Some academics note that it may be too late to stop the worldwide expansion of offensive cyber tools and techniques.

"There is an escalating arms race in cyberspace as governments, companies and malicious actors are all going on the offensive, most of it under a shroud of secrecy and absent any meaningful political oversight," said Ron Deibert, director of the University of Toronto's Citizen Lab.

Seeking "Vulnerabilities"

No more than a handful of professors have the knowledge and resources to teach cyberattack skills at the level of Brumley or Shenoi, whose students are heavily recruited for government and industry positions.

At Tulsa, Shenoi, 54, obtains permission from energy companies for his students to attempt to hack into them, infiltrating the systems that run gas pipelines or power grids and gaining access to critical U.S. infrastructure. They also do penetration testing for other companies, finding "vulnerabilities," or flaws, that enemy hackers could exploit.

"We have a class where we teach people how to write things like Stuxnet," Shenoi said, referring to a computer worm, reportedly developed by U.S. and Israeli scientists, that was found in 2010 and damaged about 1,000 centrifuges in an Iranian uranium-enrichment plant, delaying the country's nuclear program. Stuxnet, whose deployment is often considered the first true use of a cyberweapon, was built around an unprecedented four "zero-day exploits"—that is, attack tools based on previously unknown software flaws.

Shenoi began teaching courses on offensive computer techniques in 1999, he said, and by 2008, Tulsa was offering an entire program. Now, he said, there are "four courses in reverse engineering, two in cyber operations, two in offensive SCADA (supervisory control and data acquisition), and one on malware analysis and creation."

Shenoi said that the potential power of offensive cyber techniques is so great that he accepts only students who intend to work for the government and who have records that would qualify them for government security clearances. He interviews all the applicants as well as their parents. He sends 15 to 20 students a year, he said, to work at the NSA or the CIA.

"In order for me to teach these real-world attack skills, these students have to be trusted," he said. "They cannot go to work for the private sector."

"There's no reason to teach private-sector people how to use Stinger missiles," he continued. Similarly, he said, you don't teach them to use cyber weapons.

Brumley, 39, has taught offensive cyber skills since 2009. A self-described "patriot," he says he discusses ethics in his classes at Carnegie Mellon—an introductory computer security course as well as more advanced vulnerability analysis, in which students learn techniques for breaking through computer defenses. Some of Brumley's students work for the government, but most go to start-ups, big companies such as Google or defense contractors.

To develop their skills, Brumley encourages his students to compete in hacking contests. In August, a recreational team he advises called PPP, made up of about 20 current and former Carnegie Mellon students, won the ultimate U.S. showcase of hacking skills at the DefCon hacking conference in Las Vegas—a "capture-the-flag" competition in which 20 teams tried to break into one another's computers.

PPP's top gun is Hotz, who gained fame in 2007 for "jail-breaking" the previously impenetrable iPhone. He left Carnegie Mellon as a 23-year-old sophomore to work on his own, and is now back as a junior at 25. Hotz is so skilled that he has won some contests solo—as in July, when he beat nine teams to win $30,000 at the SecuInside competition in Seoul. He earned $200,000 in April for finding bugs in Google's Chromebook computer and the Firefox browser. Brumley calls him "a machine." Hotz boasts that he is "maybe the best hacker in the world."

A Question of Profit

Obviously, these students are developing valuable skills. Shenoi says his students never make money off the vulnerabilities they discover or exploits they develop. They give the information for free to the companies whose systems they are testing, or to the government. Intelligence agency officials fly every so often to Tulsa to be briefed on the flaws the students have found.

Brumley agrees that it is dangerous to share vulnerabilities or exploits with anyone but the software vendor or the U.S. government.

"If you're selling exploits in a free market," he said, "then you're potentially selling them to the adversary."

Nighswander, a former student of Brumley's, said that he has never sold a vulnerability to a software vendor, but that he thinks it's ethical to do so, saying, "When you think that finding a vulnerability can take weeks and months, you can understand that the person wants to get compensated."

Hotz declined to say whether he has sold an exploit (although he was caught last year on a surreptitiously recorded conversation appearing to broker a $350,000 deal to sell exploits to jail-break the iPhone to a Chinese company).

"I have never worked with any country aside from the U.S.," he said. He says he doesn't dwell on issues of morality, saying, "I'm not big on ethics."

Brian Pak, 25, who created the PPP hacking team while studying under Brumley and now works for a start-up he cofounded, said that sometimes, noodling around on his own, he finds bugs in software and discloses them to the software vendor. He said he has never sold information about flaws, although some vendors offer "bounties" of up to several thousand dollars. He holds onto some vulnerabilities for use in research—a practice common among security researchers, he said.

"I also don't think it's unethical to provide vulnerabilities or exploits to the U.S. government," Pak said. "I trust the U.S. government. The government protects me. As long as it's not used against our own people, I see less of an issue."

But some experts disapprove of providing previously unknown or "zero day" vulnerabilities to the government—whether for free or for profit. They worry that, rather than disclosing these zero days to vendors, the government is stockpiling them for use against adversaries. Doing so would leave the software vendors ignorant of dangerous flaws in their products, making the Internet less secure, they say. They also charge that the government is using these tools with far too little public debate, for example, in the controversial area of domestic law enforcement.

Christopher Soghoian, chief technologist for the American Civil Liberties Union, said the government should have a policy of promptly disclosing any bugs it discovers so that software companies such as Microsoft can fix them before they cause damage. Not doing so can undermine network security, he said.

But Brumley said such a blanket policy would be unwise.

"The obvious example is Stuxnet," which destroyed Iranian centrifuges, he said. That, he said, was "an opportunity to use an exploit for good."

"Twenty years earlier, that would be the thing that we flew in bombers and bombed factories for, and people would die," he said.

Dual-Use Tools

Selling exploits and vulnerabilities is not illegal, per se, but selling them with the intent that they'll be used to hack someone else's computer is a crime. Software is a classic "dual use" product. It can be used to do something as innocuous as unlock an iPhone to allow consumers to switch providers or as destructive as causing an adversary's nuclear centrifuges to spin out of control.

Some academics say the teaching of hacking techniques should remain limited.

"I'm personally against the widespread or wholesale teaching of offensive cyber," said Arthur Conklin, associate professor of information and logistics technology at the University of Houston. For one thing, he said, vetting students for trustworthiness, as Shenoi does, would be impractical on a mass scale.

Giovanni Vigna, a computer science professor at the University of California at Santa Barbara, warned that not teaching offensive skills is "not a very smart option because the bad guys are going to develop them anyway." He added, "The key is to make the students understand what are the lines that cannot be crossed." So he integrates into his courses on offensive cyber "a very substantial chapter on ethical issues."

Some experts argue that the government should regulate the sale and use of offensive cyber technology—but others, including Shenoi, say regulation will only drive the market for such products deeper underground. At this point, the U.S. government is in the process of placing export controls on some hacking and surveillance tools. It already has forbidden the sale of such technologies to countries with particularly egregious human rights records, such as Sudan and Iran.

Meanwhile, interest in offensive cyber skills is growing. Experts estimate that several thousand personnel in private industry work at finding bugs and building exploits. More companies are training employees in offensive skills, and more people are competing in hacking competitions.

In this context, Soghoian of the ACLU fears that universities are teaching students high-end skills without a solid ethical foundation.

"The academic computer security community has not yet realized the role they are playing in cyberwar," he said.

Shenoi said that, above all, he wants to impress upon his students the responsibilities that come with their technological prowess.

"They have great power to do harm. They have power to intimidate. They have power to accrue money illegally," he said. "What I tell them is, 'You may be learning some potentially deadly skills. But use them gently and wisely, and use them for the good of society.'"

Critical Thinking

1. Is it ethical to teach hacking skills? Why or why not?
2. Create a set of ethical guidelines to be used when teaching hacking skills. Defend your guidelines.
3. What responsibility do teachers in these programs have for unethical behavior by their students? By their graduates?

Internet References

Bank Info Security
   http://www.bankinfosecurity.com/blogs/where-are-ethics-in-hacking-p-954

Forbes
   http://www.forbes.com/sites/parmyolson/2012/07/31/exploding-the-myth-of-the-ethical-hacker/

Markkula Center for Applied Ethics
   http://www.scu.edu/ethics/practicing/focusareas/technology/hacking.html

---

ELLEN NAKASHIMA is a national security reporter for *The Washington Post*. She focuses on issues relating to intelligence, technology and civil liberties.

Article

Prepared by: Eric Teoro, *Lincoln Christian University*

Marketing to Children: Accepting Responsibility

GAEL O'BRIEN

Learning Outcomes

After reading this article, you will be able to:

- Describe the debate between McDonald's and industry watchdogs regarding McDonald's marketing practices to children.

- Understand the potential impact of marketing to children.

- Discuss who is primarily responsible for the marketing messages children receive—parents or companies.

For all the significant achievements companies are making as corporate citizens, the issue of their real impact on society—and what as a result society may actually need back from them—raises the question of whether we are adequately defining what is expected by being socially responsible.

The issue of marketing to children really brings that into focus; with food marketing a timely lens, the issue of **obesity** a hot health care crisis, and McDonald's handling of responsibility, as one of the world's largest fast food chains, a case in point.

As background, McDonald's Happy Meals for children with toys has come under attack. San Francisco is one of the cities that has voted to **ban selling toys with fast food** for children that exceed certain levels of salt, fat, calories and sugar. McDonald's was accused of **deceptive marketing practices to children** over the lure of toys as an inducement to buy Happy Meals. Healthy alternatives are available, apple slices in place of fries and milk instead of soda—if kids are willing to eat them. But, there is still the issue of **high sodium content in burgers**.

At McDonald's May 17, 2011 shareholder meeting, activists focused attention on McDonald's marketing to children. In February 2011, in anticipation of McDonald's shareholder meeting, **Corporate Accountability International** launched a campaign to fire Ronald McDonald, the clown mascot for the last nearly 50 years, and encourage headquarters to stop marketing to children by delivering petitions to individual restaurants. They also asked the chain to address directly the relationship of fast food to obesity. Beginning the campaign in a **Portland, Oregon suburb**, by May they had gathered 20,000 parents' and community residents' signatures on petitions which they delivered to the shareholder meeting.

In Oregon, McDonald's threw down the gauntlet, and **affirmed Ronald's job security**, saying he is "the heart and soul of Ronald McDonald House Charities, which lends a helping hand to families in their time of need." The response demonstrated how McDonald's infuses the emotional and the marketing: Ronald, the symbol to families dealing with sick and dying children, is also the brand, signifying the food and fun atmosphere to eat it in.

A letter signed by 600 health professionals and organizations, critical of the link between fast food and obesity, was read at the shareholder meeting. It had run as full page ads in newspapers across the country. In addition, **shareholder Proposal 11**, by the Sisters of St. Francis of Philadelphia, requested McDonald's undertake a report on its "policy responses to public concerns about the linkage of fast food to childhood obesity, diet-related diseases and other impacts on children's health." The proposal was soundly defeated.

In **his remarks at the meeting**, CEO Jim Skinner asserted the company's right to advertise freely, to offer its menu and lifestyle selections, and leave to parent's the right to chose what their children eat, saying it is up to personal responsibility. McDonald's **Corporate Social Responsibility (CSR) information indicates** the company serves "a balanced array of quality food products and provides the information to make individual choices."

Marketing to children, whether the subject is food, toys, clothes or anything else raises enormous concerns for Susan Linn, director and cofounder of a national coalition of health care professionals, educators, parents, and others called the **Campaign for a Commercial-Free Childhood**.

"There is no ethical, moral, social, or spiritual justification for targeting children in advertising and marketing, said Linn recently at a **Conscious Capitalism Conference**. Linn, who also teaches psychiatry at Harvard Medical School, cited obesity and a number of other issues impacting children and society that stem from targeting kids, including youth violence, sexualization, underage drinking and smoking, excessive materialism, and the erosion of creativity.

"Kids are inundated with advertising in a way never before, she said in an interview. "I don't believe in any advertising to children."

The food industry has been effective in limiting the Federal Trade Commission's ability to regulate marketing to children, and unless Congress changes the rules, companies self-regulate. I asked Linn what protection the **Children's Food and Beverage Initiative** provides. Linn indicated it didn't provide any because it has no actual authority and the standards are voluntary.

The Coalition advocates that children be able to develop a healthy relationship to food, but McDonald's, Linn says, entices kids not because of the food but because of the toys and the message of happiness that is part of their advertising.

Marketing to children is inherently deceptive because kids take things literally and media characters play a big role in their lives, Linn says. They don't understand persuasive intent until they are 8 years old; and the brain's capacity for judgment isn't developed until their 20s which makes them very vulnerable as marketing targets.

Of course parents are accountable for educating their children about responsible choices and healthy foods. And, they have the choice not to take their kids to McDonald's. Except . . . if you serve **more than 64 million people in 117 countries each day** and many of your restaurants are open 24/7, the chain has created a compelling draw.

Add to that, a **recent report** by Yale University's Rudd Center for Food Policy and Obesity that more fast food marketing dollars for toys are being spent (to get kids in the door) while marketing efforts to promote healthy meals haven't really increased.

I asked Cheryl Kiser, the former managing director of Boston College's Center for Corporate Citizenship for her take on marketing to kids. "CSR has had an enormous influence helping companies reduce their global footprint by addressing human rights and other issues," said Kiser, now the managing director of **Babson College's Lewis Institute**. But "companies are socializing kids and the imprint on those kids is not necessarily creating common good outcomes."

"Having a young over-sexualized population of kids who have no awareness of the implications or consequences of their choices is unhealthy," she adds. "Foods appealing to kids because they are tasty, high fat and zero nutrition is also unhealthy. When we start to imprint early in behaviors and consumer choices things that don't lead to personal and common good, and that need to be corrected in teen years by good CSR programs, is CSR doing its job?"

Critical Thinking

1. What limits, if any, should be imposed on businesses regarding marketing to children? Explain your rationale.
2. To what degree are parents responsible for the marketing messages to which their children are exposed? Why are they thusly responsible?
3. Debate with a colleague or fellow student on the permissibility of marketing to children.

Create Central

www.mhhe.com/createcentral

Internet References

Association for Consumer Research
http://www.acrwebsite.org/search/view-conference-proceedings.aspx?Id=11328

Campaign for a Commercial-Free Childhood
http://www.commercialfreechildhood.org/

Wall Street Journal
http://online.wsj.com/news/articles/SB10001424052748703509104576329610340358394?mod=dist_smartbrief&mg=reno64-wsj&url=http%3A%2F%2Fonline.wsj.com%2Farticle%2FSB10001424052748703509104576329610340358394.html%3Fmod%3Ddist_smartbrief

GAEL O'BRIEN is a *Business Ethics Magazine* columnist. Gael is a thought leader on building leadership, trust, and reputation and writes **The Week in Ethics.**

Article

Prepared by: Eric Teoro, *Lincoln Christian University*

How Marketers Are Plotting to Use Neuroscience to Control What You Buy

Isha Aran

Learning Outcomes

After reading this article, you will be able to:

- Describe how the brain interacts with marketing messages.

- Describe how marketers could use the knowledge derived from neuroscience to influence consumer behavior.

Ever felt exceedingly pleased with yourself after splurging on a luxury good?

Blame marketers, who are becoming increasingly sophisticated and increasingly Orwellian. Case in point: A recent study published in the *Journal of Marketing Research* used brain imaging tech to test how the amount of grey matter a person has affects how he or she makes decisions about products.

Previous studies have shown that people are more likely to enjoy consuming a product that is labeled as more expensive, whether or not the product is actually of a higher quality. Termed the "marketing placebo effect" the perceived value of something can affect the actual experience of it—even the price of painkillers can affect how people experience pain.

We've known this for a while, but the researchers at the INSEAD business school in Fontainebleau, France wanted to see the effect in action—in the brain—while people were actually consuming stuff.

The researchers claim that the volume of grey matter in certain structures of the brain affects how susceptible a person is to marketing placebo effects, and that this varies by individual. Cool, got it. Then they creepily conclude that, in the future,

they could brainwash us and take advantage of this neuroscience to influence what we buy.

Before we get into how and whether this could actually happen, let's take a quick look at the study.

Placebos Don't Cost a Thing

The researchers performed three different types of studies.

For the first, they re-analyzed the results of previous research they conducted in 2008. In that study, 90 participants were told they would be consuming wines from five different price ranges between $5 and $90, when really they were only sipping two types of wine that were either $5 or $90. This study showed the placebo effect was alive and well. They liked the more expensive wines better.

Because participants' brains were being scanned by functional MRI machines while they judged the wine, the researchers were able to go back and analyze that same data for "grey matter volume." Then they took the grey matter data and plugged it into a database that looked for links between volume and cognitive functions. This time they found:

- Those who have a higher grey matter volume in the striatum, the part of the brain involved in processing rewards, responded more easily to the marketing placebo effect. The researchers took that to mean these poor suckers were more responsive to (perceived) rewards. If that wine says it's expensive, then it must be good!

- Those who have a higher grey matter volume in their prefrontal cortex, which is involved in making decision, social behavior, and personality, are also pretty susceptible to the placebo effect. Again, that wine's expensive and therefore must be good.

- Those who have more grey matter in the posterior part of the insula, a brain region involved in sensory processing, aren't quite as easily influenced—they know when they taste good wine and can't easily be tricked by a price tag.

In the second study, the researchers doubled back, testing whether these differences in grey matter correlated with different personality types, like being more responsive to rewards and paying more attention to your gut feeling rather than marketing. They essentially replicated the wine experiment, but also had subjects take a personality survey testing for reward processing, responding to statements like: "When I get something I want, I feel excited and energized." From this the researchers say they were able to confirm the grey matter/personality connection.

And in the third study, they tested to see if the placebo effect could be applied to aesthetic consumption—if someone told you a piece of abstract art was actually painted by Russian expressionist artist Wassily Kandinsky, would that change your perception of the piece's value? According to the researchers, the effect works for aesthetic consumption as well.

Fifty Shades of Grey Matter

Normally marketers identify and segment the population using various demographics, like age, race, or geography. But these researchers are aiming to use differences in brain anatomy to categorize you. Commence daydream about a dystopian future in which we are all indoctrinated by an Evil Board of Mad Men using our brains to further oppress us in a capitalist society driven by Funzos.

Before you freak out too much, however, it's important to keep things in perspective. First off, this study is quite small. And while the researchers say they are able to pinpoint individual differences in our brain function, what those differences mean is murky. After all, our understanding of the human brain is still not much better than Apple Maps' understanding of . . . geography. Without granular knowledge of how the brain's billions of neurons connect and give rise to individual behaviors, it's not possible to predict behavior, let alone whole personality types.

Also, our gray matter volume changes with age. So, if marketers really wanted to target you over your lifetime, they'd

have to have a very nuanced understanding of how brains respond to the things they're trying to sell you over time. And that's just not possible right now.

Brave New World?

When it comes to real-world application, Hilke Plassman, the first author of the study, reassured Fusion that she's not suggesting we collect biological data, but "sample customers personalities based on questionnaires that I could link to the brain data in my work." Right.

She also speculates that the marketing placebo effect may be more dominant in industries dealing with luxury goods. So if we're shopping at IKEA or drinking boxed wine, we'll probably be safe.

What can we as consumers do to combat the impending onslaught of hyper-personalized marketing? Well, for starters, try not to take certain data mining quizzes and exercise your self-control. Even if marketers can't do what Plassman describes now, it means they're thinking about ever more devious ways to play to your biases and vulnerabilities.

Oh, and whatever you do, don't eat the soma!

Critical Thinking

1. When do marketing tools and techniques become unethical? Defend your answer.
2. What are the ethical implications of using neuroscience to influence consumer behavior?
3. Are consumers fully responsible for their purchasing behavior? Are they ever victims? Explain.

Internet References

Academia
http://www.academia.edu/8281206/Ethical_Issues_in_Neuromarketing_I_Consume_Therefore_I_am_

Markkula Center for Applied Ethics
http://www.scu.edu/ethics/publications/submitted/greely/neuroscience_ethics_law.html

Neuroscience Marketing
http://www.neurosciencemarketing.com/blog/topics/neuromarketing/neuroethics

State of Digital
http://www.stateofdigital.com/crossroads-ethics-of-neuromarketing/

Article   Prepared by: Eric Teoro, *Lincoln Christian University*

A Donation-with-Purchase Might Not Be the Best Way to Support a Charity: Should You Buy a Toy and Save the Whales?

CONSUMER REPORTS

Learning Outcomes

After reading this article, you will be able to:

- Understand the nature of cause-related marketing.

- Understand ethical issues related to cause-related marketing.

- More critically engage in cause-related marketing as a sponsor or consumer.

The end of the year—which accounts for, on average, 41 percent of Americans' charitable giving—is often a prime time for cause-related marketing: when companies push items with the promise that part of the purchase price will go to a nonprofit. Also known as cause marketing, this phenomenon has grown into a $1.78 billion, year-round way for companies to support charities using your dollars.

You've likely seen some of the pitches:

- "A portion of proceeds" of adorable wild pony Christmas ornaments by Roost go to Return to Freedom, a wild horse sanctuary.

- "A percentage of the proceeds" of sales of the Cellairis Swag collection of cell-phone cases benefits Pencils of Promise.

- "One hundred percent of profits" of a special Smock card supports the Pesticide Action Network.

But is it really the best way for you to support your favorite cause?

Cause marketing has been around since at least 1983, when American Express offered to donate a portion of a particular credit card's revenues to the renovation of the Statue of Liberty. Today, countless other companies link up with charities. Nonprofits "are always short of cash," says Renee Irvin, director of the Nonprofit Management Program at the University of Oregon. "The need is always outstripping their resources."

The highly regarded Breast Cancer Research Foundation (BCRF) has been particularly good at using cause marketing to raise funds. It works with more than 100 companies, including Ann Inc. (includes Ann Taylor and Loft), Bloomingdale's, Estée Lauder, and Delta Airlines; 40 to 50 percent of BCRF's revenue—$27 million in 2014—comes from those partnerships.

"BCRF is a nonprofit and not a marketing organization," Christina Rose, its Chief Partnerships Officer, said. "We invest 91 cents of every dollar we spend in our core mission, which is breast cancer research and awareness. In working with national and global brands, we're able to extend the reach of our message more than we'd be able to do on our own."

The fight against breast cancer has widely benefited from those campaigns. "It's highly universal," Rose said. "It's hard to find someone who hasn't been impacted personally, or through family or friends." Other well-known health-related charities such as the Make-A-Wish foundation and St. Jude Children's Research Hospital are also popular for partnerships.

But as the number of cause-related campaigns has risen, so too has consumer skepticism. "The message of 'think before you pink,' has gotten out," Sandra Miniutti, VP of Marketing and CFO of Charity Navigator, which assesses charities, said.

After all, companies don't do cause marketing solely to give, but also to get more of your business. Surveys show that almost 90 percent of consumers say that given similar price and quality, they're likely to switch to a brand associated with a good cause. (Case studies suggest that is actually what happens in stores.) And businesses get to bask in the warm glow of good PR. "Nonprofits are lending their good name to the business, and consumers are well aware of that," Irvin said.

That's why consumers get upset when campaigns are not quite as generous as they seem at first glance. One source of dismay is the common practice of a company capping its total donation, no matter how many products are sold. "They'll say, we'll donate $10 per item up to $5,000," Miniutti said. "If you're the 501st purchase, nothing from your purchase is getting to the charity." And you might object to your $10 ending up in the company's coffers instead. (Conversely, some companies agree to a minimum donation, regardless of how many products are sold.)

Charities are subject to laws that forbid false or misleading advertising. And the Better Business Bureau includes, among its 20 standards for charities, one that addresses cause marketing. It requires disclosure at the point of appeal that identifies the amount of the purchase price going to the charity, if applicable, the duration of the campaign, and any maximum or minimum that will be donated. "The purchaser should know how much he or she is helping the charity by buying this product," Bennett Weiner, chief operating officer of BBB Wise Giving Alliance, which reports on charities, said. "The concern is, if there is no disclosure, the consumer will believe there is much more going than is usually the case." Charities violating BBB standards don't receive their charity accreditations.

> ## "Are you buying a $30 T-shirt from which $2 will go to the charity?"
>
> —Aradna Krishna, marketing professor, University of Michigan

According to the Wise Giving Alliance, the three charities at the beginning of this article fail to meet the BBB's standards because each doesn't specify the actual portion of the purchase price going to the organization. Others violate the BBB's guidelines by sending consumers to a website where it is difficult to find the disclosure or use vague language such as "net proceeds" or "some of our profits." "How is the consumer supposed to know what 'net proceeds' means?" Weiner said.

The Best Way to Give

Even if the donation-with-purchase charity is doing everything right, you still might want to reconsider that buy—especially because all of that in-store giving might actually cut into the amount that we, as individuals, allocate to our pet causes.

A 2011 study by Aradna Krishna, a marketing professor at the University of Michigan Ross School of Business, found that people gave less money in direct donations to charities when they made cause-marketing purchases. "People may mentally assign their cause-marketing expenditure as their charitable giving," Krishna said. She also found that cause-buying had a tendency to decrease happiness, probably because we realize that buying, say, a $40 necklace, is more self-serving than donating $40 directly.

Think before using a product as a go-between, Krishna says. "Are you buying a $30 T-shirt from which $2 will go to the charity?" she said. "Or could you give $30 to the charity and do without the T-shirt?"

Another advantage to giving straight to the charity: A donation is tax-deductible, unlike a cause-marketing purchase, for which the company selling the product gets the tax deduction for charitable giving. "I have a philosophical problem with that," Irvin said. "You're essentially getting your customer to do your donations for you."

"I'd encourage consumers to be passionate about their philanthropy and to keep it personal," Irvin said. Though well-known charities often bring in lots of cause-marketing dollars, thousands of other, lesser-known causes—that will never see their name on a yogurt container—also need your support.

Remember, too, that all of those well-positioned yogurt containers still aren't a charity's bread and butter. "Despite the hyperbole, corporate giving to nonprofits is a very small portion of overall giving to nonprofits in the U.S.," Irvin said.

So what should you do when you're faced with a cause-marketing item at the store? "All other things being equal, buy the product that helps a cause," Irwin said. "But all other things are not usually equal."

Critical Thinking

1. Do you think cause-related marketing is ethical or unethical? Why?

2. Find a cause-related marketing campaign you think is (un)ethical. Describe why you think the given campaign is (un)ethical.

3. Write a set of ethical guidelines for a product or service company wanting to engage in cause-related marketing. Write a set of ethical guidelines for a not-for-profit that wants to partner with a product or service company in cause-related marketing.

Internet References

About.com

http://nonprofit.about.com/od/fundraising/a/causemarketing.htm

Cause and Effect

http://www.ceffect.com/tools-for-change/articles/cause-related-marketing/

Cause Marketing Forum

http://www.causemarketingforum.com/site/apps/nlnet/content2.aspx?c=b kLUKcOTLkK4E&b=6415417&ct=8971401

GrantSpace

http://grantspace.org/tools/knowledge-base/Funding-Resources/Corporations/ cause-related-marketing

Article   Prepared by: Eric Teoro, *Lincoln Christian University*

Unethical Behaviors in the Workplace

Abuse of Social Media in the Workplace on the Rise

Steven Mintz

Learning Outcomes

After reading this article, you will be able to:

- Describe five types of unethical behavior in the workplace.
- Describe ethical issues related to violating company Internet policies.

I recently read a piece about the five most unethical behaviors in the workplace. Arthur Schwartz points out that each day roughly 120 million people walk into a workplace somewhere in the U.S. Within the past year, almost half of these workers personally witnessed some form of ethical misconduct, according to a recent survey conducted by the Washington, D.C.-based Ethics Resource Center (ERC).

Schwartz points out that the issue is not workers being privy to the CFO committing fraud. More likely, it's someone who lied to a supervisor or handed in a false expense report. Listed below, according to the ERC study, are the five most frequently observed unethical behaviors in the U.S. workplace.

1. **Misusing company time**

   Whether it is covering for someone who shows up late or altering a time sheet, misusing company time tops the list. This category includes knowing that one of your co-workers is conducting personal business on company time. By "personal business" the survey recognizes the difference between making cold calls to advance your freelance business and calling your spouse to find out how your sick child is doing.

2. **Abusive behavior**

   Too many workplaces are filled with managers and supervisors who use their position and power to mistreat or disrespect others. Unfortunately, unless the situation you're in involves race, gender or ethnic origin, there is often no legal protection against abusive behavior in the workplace.

3. **Employee theft**

   According to a recent study by Jack L. Hayes International, one out of every 40 employees in 2012 was caught stealing from their employer. Even more startling is that these employees steal on average 5.5 times more than shoplifters ($715 vs $129). Employee fraud is also on the uptick, whether its check tampering, not recording sales in order to skim, or manipulating expense reimbursements. The FBI recently reported that employee theft is the fastest growing crime in the U.S. today.

4. **Lying to employees**

   The fastest way to lose the trust of your employees is to lie to them, yet employers do it all the time. One out of every five employees report that their manager or supervisor has lied to them within the past year.

5. **Violating company Internet policies**

   Cyberslackers. Cyberloafers. These are terms used to identify people who surf the Web when they should be working. It's a huge, multi-billion-dollar problem for companies. A survey conducted recently by Salary.com found that every day at least 64 percent of employees visit websites that have nothing to do with their work.

The ERC study points out that most American workers and employers do the right thing. The survey reveals that most follow the company's ethical standards of behavior, and are willing to report wrongdoing when it occurs, except if it relates to the company's Internet use policy.

These results are retrospective and do not reflect the increasing trend of employees' use of social media at work for personal purposes. According to a *Forbes study,* 64 percent of employees visit non-work related websites daily, and wasted the most time on these social sharing sites (in descending order):

Tumblr–57 percent
Facebook–52 percent
Twitter–17 percent
Instagram–11 percent
SnapChat–4 percent

The question is how much control an employer should have over its employees' use of social media. This is an emerging issue and one where the rules and ethical guidelines have not caught up with technology. One of the most difficult things for employers to monitor is what an employee is looking at on his/her computer screen. Short of walking around frequently and checking it out, as a possible deterrent to improper use, an employer has to trust that employees will use good judgment when it comes to the use of social media in the workplace.

Part of the problem with defining social media abuse is how common Internet use is in our daily personal and professional lives. In an age when employers expect workers to respond to client emails immediately and social networking sites reload with new information every minute, it's often hard to define the limits between normal and abusive. Businesses need to be proactive in the workplace with establishing these limits, creating a clear and comprehensive acceptable use policy and communicating it to employees through presentation and workshops. Good communication can generate a workplace-wide consensus on the behavior that falls outside acceptable boundaries.

Most of all the Internet use policy should be tied to the general issue of ethics in the workplace. The use and abuse of social media in the workplace is an excellent way to give life to the provisions in a code of ethics.

Two of the five most unethical practices relate to the abuse of social media at work: violating company Internet policy and misusing company time. Those who excessively surf the Internet at work for personal reasons are stealing from their companies. They are being paid for work when they are not doing so. The ethics policy must be clear on this matter. In the end it is no different from coming in late; leaving early; or taking long lunch hours and being paid for that time.

Critical Thinking

1. In addition to the unethical behaviors outlined in the article, develop a list of unethical behaviors. Why are these behaviors unethical?

2. What types of unethical behaviors are you most prone to commit? Do you justify any of them? How can you safeguard against committing them?

3. What should you do when you witness a coworker violating one of the five unethical behaviors? Why?

Internet References

Academia
http://www.academia.edu/5164148/Positive_and_negative_deviant_workplace_behaviors_causes_impacts_and_solutions_Introduction_to_deviant_behavior

Ethics Alarm
http://ethicsalarms.com/2013/11/05/workplace-ethics-62-things-that-are-legal-but-22-of-them-are-unethical/

Houston Chronicle: Small Business
http://smallbusiness.chron.com/examples-unethical-behavior-workplace-10092.html

TU Jobs
http://www.tujobs.com/news/323116-the-10-most-common-examples-of-unethical-behavior

Article   Prepared by: Eric Teoro, *Lincoln Christian University*

Too Much Information?

The BMF's HR guru, Kate Russell examines the ethics of using social media profiles in the recruitment process.

KATE RUSSEL

Learning Outcomes

After reading this article, you will be able to:

- Describe ethical issues related to using social media research in hiring decisions.

- Describe the risks of using social media research in hiring decisions.

While most employers continue to use traditional methods to recruit new employees, there is a growing trend to utilise social media sites as part of the recruitment process. On-line job portals are already overtaking printed job ads in popularity with job seekers, and with many young people far more likely to view their Facebook and Twitter feeds than to read a newspaper on a regular basis, social media can only become even more important to recruiters over the next few years.

This raises two important questions. Is it ethical for business owners to access the personal social media profiles of prospective employees during the recruitment process? If so, how can employers ensure that discrimination is avoided?

Let's start by considering why both recruiters and job seekers are using social media.

Spread the Word

The key attraction for recruiters is that social media can spread the word about an available position to a wide network of people, usually at little or no cost. Meanwhile, those looking for a new position can leverage their contacts and their time to best effect.

The business networking site, LinkedIn, is one of the most popular social platforms for both those offering and those seeking employment. It enables job seekers to network with their own contacts and with a far wider group of people linked to those contacts. It also allows them to follow their targeted employers and quickly learn of any jobs they post.

The benefit for employers is the wealth of information available about the qualifications and experience of job seekers, and the wide network that can be accessed to find potential candidates.

Facebook was created to facilitate personal communications but it is widely used by organisations to create a presence to reflect their brand and develop a community of "fans". Once a business has established a network, they may also view this as useful medium to post jobs and find potential candidates.

As a medium to advertise positions, this is all well and good. The risk occurs when the process moves from sourcing to screening applicants.

Accurate Decisions

All recruiting managers want to find out as much as they can about prospective applicants and the more relevant data you have, the better able you are to make an accurate decision. The potential problem arises when recruiters use irrelevant information gleaned from social media sites to screen or eliminate candidates from consideration. Too much general information may cause you to make judgements about an individual that is irrelevant to whether or not they are a good candidate for your position.

Despite—or perhaps due to—complex privacy settings, people add information to their social media pages without too much thought about who can see it. Facebook pages, for example, may include a great deal of information that reveals protected characteristics (age, gender, religion, sexual orientation, etc).

> **"The key attraction for recruiters is that social media can spread the word about an available position to a wide network of people, usually at little or no cost"**

These protected characteristics will rarely be relevant to an ability to do the job, but if for example, you assume a mum with three kids can't travel and do a field sales representative's role because of her domestic circumstances and you block the appointment because of that, you will have acted unlawfully.

Similarly, information about what individuals like to do in their spare time, their interests and any common links you may have through other friends and acquaintances may tell you whether you are likely to get on with them—or not–but it doesn't say anything about their ability to do the job you are recruiting for.

Feedback

A job applicant is entitled to ask why they were turned down for a job or not given an interview. You must be able to give an objective answer, or you will leave yourself open to a claim.

It's a sad fact that there are bounty hunters who will repeatedly exploit weak recruitment processes to claim against companies that don't hire them.

If you are going to use social media as part of the assessment process, it is important to keep to the facts and focus on what is relevant to the job.

This means ensuring that your job description and person specification are properly thought through and justifiable. Then

if you do collect data online, confine the basis of your decision to the objective requirements of the job description and person specification.

Critical Thinking

1. Develop a set of ethical guidelines for using social media research in hiring decisions? Defend your set of guidelines.
2. If individuals post information on the open web, do they have a right to privacy regarding that information? Why or why not?
3. Is there material you posted on the web that you regret? That you should regret? What can you do about it?

Internet References

Ethics Sage

http://www.ethicssage.com/2015/04/is-it-ethical-for-employers-to-use-social-media-in-hiring-and-employment-decisions.html

HRZone

http://www.hrzone.com/talent/acquisition/social-media-screening-is-it-ethical

Society for Human Resource Management

http://www.shrm.org/publications/hrmagazine/editorialcontent/2014/0914/pages/0914-social-media-hiring.aspx

Society for Human Resource Management

http://www.shrm.org/publications/hrmagazine/editorialcontent/2014/1114/pages/1114-social-media-screening.aspx

KATE RUSSELL heads the BMF Employment Plus service that delivers practical HR solutions to BMF members of all sizes.
Follow Kate on Twitter@ KateRussellHR or Facebook www.facebook.com/russell-hrconsultingltd
The BMF Employment Plus Service includes a detailed review and regular updates of your contracts of employment and employee handbook, expert briefings, and telephone advice. Russell HR Consulting can also offer on-site help if needed.

Article   Prepared by: Eric Teoro, *Lincoln Christian University*

Everything We Know about Facebook's Secret Mood Manipulation Experiment

It was probably legal. But was it ethical?

ROBINSON MEYER

Learning Outcomes

After reading this article, you will be able to:

• Describe the facts of the Facebook Secret Mood Manipulation Experiment.

• Describe ethical issues related to informed consent.

Facebook's News Feed—the main list of status updates, messages, and photos you see when you open Facebook on your computer or phone—is not a perfect mirror of the world.

But few users expect that Facebook would change their News Feed in order to manipulate their emotional state.

We now know that's exactly what happened two years ago. For one week in January 2012, data scientists skewed what almost 700,000 Facebook users saw when they logged into its service. Some people were shown content with a preponderance of happy and positive words; some were shown content analyzed as sadder than average. And when the week was over, these manipulated users were more likely to post either especially positive or negative words themselves.

This tinkering was just revealed as part of a new study, published in the prestigious *Proceedings of the National Academy of Sciences*. Many previous studies have used Facebook data to examine "emotional contagion," as this one did. This study is different because, while other studies have observed Facebook user data, this one set out to manipulate it.

The experiment is almost certainly legal. In the company's current terms of service, Facebook users relinquish the use of

their data for "data analysis, testing, [and] research." Is it ethical, though? Since news of the study first emerged, I've seen and heard both privacy advocates and casual users express surprise at the audacity of the experiment.

We're tracking the ethical, legal, and philosophical response to this Facebook experiment here. We've also asked the authors of the study for comment. Author Jamie Guillory replied and referred us to a Facebook spokesman. Early Sunday morning, a Facebook spokesman sent this comment in an email:

> This research was conducted for a single week in 2012 and none of the data used was associated with a specific person's Facebook account. We do research to improve our services and to make the content people see on Facebook as relevant and engaging as possible. A big part of this is understanding how people respond to different types of content, whether it's positive or negative in tone, news from friends, or information from pages they follow. We carefully consider what research we do and have a strong internal review process. There is no unnecessary collection of people's data in connection with these research initiatives and all data is stored securely.

And on Sunday afternoon, Adam D.I. Kramer, one of the study's authors and a Facebook employee, commented on the experiment in a public Facebook post. "And at the end of the day, the actual impact on people in the experiment was the minimal amount to statistically detect it," he writes. "Having written and designed this experiment myself, I can tell you that our goal was never to upset anyone. [. . .] In hindsight, the research benefits of the paper may not have justified all of this anxiety."

Kramer adds that Facebook's internal review practices have "come a long way" since 2012, when the experiment was run.

What Did the Paper Itself Find?

The study found that by manipulating the News Feeds displayed to 689,003 Facebook users, it could affect the content which those users posted to Facebook. More negative News Feeds led to more negative status messages, as more positive News Feeds led to positive statuses.

As far as the study was concerned, this meant that it had shown "that emotional states can be transferred to others via emotional contagion, leading people to experience the same emotions without their awareness." It touts that this emotional contagion can be achieved without "direct interaction between people" (because the unwitting subjects were only seeing each others' News Feeds).

The researchers add that never during the experiment could they read individual users' posts.

Two interesting things stuck out to me in the study.

The first? The effect the study documents is very small, as little as one-tenth of a percent of an observed change. That doesn't mean it's unimportant, though, as the authors add:

Given the massive scale of social networks such as Facebook, even small effects can have large aggregated consequences. [. . .] After all, an effect size of d = 0.001 at Facebook's scale is not negligible: In early 2013, this would have corresponded to **hundreds of thousands of emotion expressions in status updates per day.**

The second was this line:

Omitting emotional content reduced the amount of words the person subsequently produced, both when positivity was reduced (z = −4.78, P < 0.001) and when negativity was reduced (z = −7.219, P < 0.001).

In other words, when researchers reduced the appearance of *either* positive or negative sentiments in people's News Feeds—when the feeds just got generally less emotional—those people stopped writing so many words on Facebook.

Make people's feeds blander and they stop typing things into Facebook.

Was the Study Well Designed?

Perhaps not, says John Grohol, the founder of psychology website Psych Central. Grohol believes the study's methods are hampered by the misuse of tools: Software better matched to analyze novels and essays, he says, is being applied toward the much shorter texts on social networks.

Let's look at two hypothetical examples of why this is important. Here are two sample tweets (or status updates) that are not uncommon:

- "I am not happy."
- "I am not having a great day."

An independent rater or judge would rate these two tweets as negative—they're clearly expressing a negative emotion. That would be +2 on the negative scale, and 0 on the positive scale.

But the LIWC 2007 tool doesn't see it that way. Instead, it would rate these two tweets as scoring +2 for positive (because of the words "great" and "happy") and +2 for negative (because of the word "not" in both texts).

"What the Facebook researchers clearly show," writes Grohol, "is that they put too much faith in the tools they're using without understanding—and discussing—the tools' significant limitations."

Did an institutional review board (IRB)—an independent ethics committee that vets research that involves humans—approve the experiment?

According to a Cornell University press statement on Monday, the experiment was conducted before an IRB was consulted.* Cornell professor Jeffrey Hancock—an author of the study—began working on the results *after* Facebook had conducted the experiment. Hancock only had access to results, says the release, so "Cornell University's Institutional Review Board concluded that he was not directly engaged in human research and that no review by the Cornell Human Research Protection Program was required."

In other words, the experiment had already been run, so its human subjects were beyond protecting. Assuming the researchers did not see users' confidential data, the results of the experiment could be examined without further endangering any subjects.

Both Cornell and Facebook have been reluctant to provide details about the process beyond their respective prepared statements. One of the study's authors told *The Atlantic* on Monday that he's been advised by the university not to speak to reporters.

By the time the study reached Susan Fiske, the Princeton University psychology professor who edited the study for publication, Cornell's IRB members had already determined it outside of their purview.

Fiske had earlier conveyed to *The Atlantic* that the experiment was IRB-approved.

"I was concerned," Fiske told *The Atlantic* on Saturday, "until I queried the authors and they said their local institutional review board had approved it—and apparently on the grounds that Facebook apparently manipulates people's News Feeds all the time."

On Sunday, other reports raised questions about how an IRB was consulted. In a Facebook post on Sunday, study author Adam Kramer referenced only "internal review practices." And a Forbes report that day, citing an unnamed source, claimed that Facebook only used an internal review.

When *The Atlantic* asked Fiske to clarify Sunday, she said the researchers' "revision letter said they had Cornell IRB approval as a 'pre-existing dataset' presumably from FB, who seems to have reviewed it as well in some unspecified way . . . Under IRB regulations, [of] pre-existing dataset would have been approved previously and someone is just analyzing data already collected, often by someone else."

The mention of a "pre-existing dataset" here matters because, as Fiske explained in a follow-up email, "presumably the data already existed when they applied to Cornell IRB." (She also noted: "I am not second-guessing the decision.") Cornell's Monday statement confirms this presumption.

On Saturday, Fiske said that she didn't want "the originality of the research" to be lost, but called the experiment "an open ethical question."

"It's ethically okay from the regulations perspective, but ethics are kind of social decisions. There's not an absolute answer. And so the level of outrage that appears to be happening suggests that maybe it shouldn't have been done . . . I'm still thinking about it and I'm a little creeped out, too."

For more, check *Atlantic* editor Adrienne LaFrance's full interview with Prof. Fiske.

From what we know now, were the experiment's subjects able to provide *informed consent?*

In its ethical principles and code of conduct, the American Psychological Association (APA) defines *informed consent* like this:

> When psychologists conduct research or provide assessment, therapy, counseling, or consulting services in person or via electronic transmission or other forms of communication, they obtain the informed consent of the individual or individuals using language that is reasonably understandable to that person or persons except

when conducting such activities without consent is mandated by law or governmental regulation or as otherwise provided in this Ethics Code.

As mentioned above, the research seems to have been carried out under Facebook's extensive terms of service. The company's current data use policy, which governs exactly how it may use users' data, runs to more than 9,000 words and uses the word "research" twice. But as *Forbes* writer Kashmir Hill reported Monday night, the data use policy in effect when the experiment was conducted never mentioned "research" at all—the word wasn't inserted until May 2012.

Never mind whether the current data use policy constitutes "language that is reasonably understandable": Under the January 2012 terms of service, did Facebook secure even shaky consent?

The APA has further guidelines for so-called "deceptive research" like this, where the real purpose of the research can't be made available to participants during research. The last of these guidelines is:

> Psychologists explain any deception that is an integral feature of the design and conduct of an experiment to participants as early as is feasible, preferably at the conclusion of their participation, but no later than at the conclusion of the data collection, and permit participants to withdraw their data.

At the end of the experiment, did Facebook tell the user-subjects that their News Feeds had been altered for the sake of research? If so, the study never mentions it.

James Grimmelmann, a law professor at the University of Maryland, believes the study did not secure informed consent. And he adds that Facebook fails even its own standards, which are lower than that of the academy:

> A stronger reason is that even when Facebook manipulates our News Feeds to sell us things, it is supposed— legally and ethically—to meet certain minimal standards. Anything on Facebook that is actually an ad is labelled as such (even if not always clearly). This study failed even that test, and for a particularly unappealing research goal: *We wanted to see if we could make you feel bad without you noticing. We succeeded.*

Did the U.S. government sponsor the research?

Cornell has now updated their June 10 story to say that the research received no external funding. Originally, Cornell had identified the Army Research Office, an agency within the U.S.

Army that funds basic research in the military's interest, as one of the funders of their experiment.

Do these kind of News Feed tweaks happen at other times?

At any one time, Facebook said last year, there were on average 1,500 pieces of content that could show up in your News Feed. The company uses an algorithm to determine what to display and what to hide.

It talks about this algorithm very rarely, but we know it's very powerful. Last year, the company changed News Feed to surface more news stories. Websites like BuzzFeed and Upworthy proceeded to see record-busting numbers of visitors.

So we know it happens. Consider Fiske's explanation of the research ethics here—the study was approved "on the grounds that Facebook apparently manipulates people's News Feeds all the time." And consider also that *from this study alone* Facebook knows at least one knob to tweak to get users to post more words on Facebook.

Critical Thinking

1. Prepare a position paper on whether Facebook behaved ethically. Defend your position.
2. Did Facebook exercise good faith in informing users of being potential research subjects? Why or why not?
3. Did Facebook's project cause harm to users? Provide rationale for your answer.

Internet References

Icahn School of Medicine at Mount Sinai
https://icahn.mssm.edu/static_files/MSSM/Files/Research/Resources/Program%20for%20the%20Protection%20of%20Human%20Subjects/EthicalIssueswithInformedConsent.pdf

National Center for Biotechnology Information
http://www.ncbi.nlm.nih.gov/pmc/articles/PMC2840885/

Washington Post
https://www.washingtonpost.com/news/the-switch/wp/2014/10/02/facebook-changes-its-research-rules-after-mood-study-backlash/

ROBINSON MEYER is an associate editor at *The Atlantic*, where he covers technology.

* This post originally stated that an institutional review board, or IRB, was consulted before the experiment took place regarding certain aspects of data collection.

Adrienne LaFrance contributed writing and reporting.